Against All Odds

Rural Community in the Information Age

Rural Studies Series

Against All Odds

Rural Community in the Information Age

John C. Allen

University of Nebraska at Lincoln

Don A. Dillman

Washington State University

Westview Press

BOULDER·SAN FRANCISCO·OXFORD

Rural Studies Series

Published in 1994 in the United States of America by Westview Press, Inc., 5500 Central Avenue, Boulder, Colorado 80301-2877, and in the United Kingdom by Westview Press, 36 Lonsdale Road, Summertown, Oxford OX2 7EW

A CIP catalog record for this book is available from the Library of Congress.
ISBN 0-8133-8821-X
ISBN 0-8133-8842-2 (pbk.)

Printed and bound in the United States of America

 The paper used in this publication meets the requirements of the American National Standard for Permanence of Paper for Printed Library Materials Z39.48-1984.

10   9   8   7   6   5   4   3

To

Lee J. Haggerty, Portland State University,
Joe M. Bohlen (1917-1990), Iowa State University, and
George M. Beal, Iowa State University

for teaching us how to look for and understand community

and

Kenneth P. Wilkinson (1938-1993)
The Pennsylvania State University

for encouraging us to
appreciate and respect community

Contents

Illustrations

Preface

Can a meaningful sense of community exist within rural towns and villages of the United States as we approach the 21st century? The answer is a resounding yes for at least one rural community in the Pacific Northwest. And the factors that keep community alive in Bremer, Washington, have implications for other places whose citizens are concerned about maintaining community services, identity, and pride.

Bremer is a tiny dot on the official highway map of Washington State. Its 1,000 residents, 500 within the city limits and the remainder scattered across the adjacent countryside, make it too small to count for much in the eyes of casual observers.

Physically there is little to distinguish Bremer and its people from other nearby small farming communities. Yet these residents, and many of the residents of larger towns and cities in the region, recognize that Bremer is somehow different. In a sentence, it defies most of the rules of what a community of a mere thousand people, with virtually no industry other than agriculture and too far from a city to be a bedroom community, should be like. It has a doctor, drugstore, grocery, hardware store, insurance agencies, and other small businesses. The official town population is about the same as it was 50 years ago, in sharp contrast to the decline of many other small communities in the region.

Bremer is also different in ways less visible. It has turned down government grants in favor of solving its own problems. A community club formed subcommittees to do what government grants do for other communities. The town has an annual fair, in which most residents participate, but doesn't advertise it, even while merchants post advertisements for similar events in other communities. A community calendar hangs on a wall in nearly every household, listing birthdays and anniversaries for most residents. The city council accepted a citizen's offer to cut down some old trees, but only after figuring out who planted them and checking with an appropriate relative for "approval." Then it upped the ante by offering gas for the chain saw and use of the city truck to haul away the wood. The bank pays below market rates and people have to stand in line and ask for loans at the window, but people still do business there. The mayor and many others keep track of how much they spend at each of the town's grocery stores, in order to be fair. One of the grocery stores doesn't sell toothpaste, because that's sold in the drugstore.

Most of all Bremer has a community spirit, an identity defended publicly and privately, and with anger or tears when necessary. The residents, most of whom are descendants or relatives of the original settlers, gauge both their actions and reactions according to what other community members expect of them. Bremer is a tightly knit community of people whose daily actions, both economic and social, take into account a shared identity—that of being Bremerites.

Interest in the Bremer community may at first seem to be only a matter of idle curiosity, justified mostly by intrigue with the unusual. However, our interest is motivated by a deeper, more profound concern. On the one hand there is the success of this small town in maintaining an institutional base of businesses and services and in its ability to solve its own problems, success nearby communities have not achieved. On the other hand there is clear evidence of community pride and spirit that affects the lives of nearly every resident. Are the two connected, and if so, how?

Early in this century, community was considered a sociological concept of primary importance for understanding human behavior. People's lives were often confined mostly to a particular community, and community was an umbrella social group, without which the reasons for people's behavior could not be understood. In the face of technological developments, urbanization, and evolution toward a mass society, knowledgeable sociologists declared the death of community and looked to other sociological concepts for the explanation of human behavior.

In describing and analyzing Bremer, as the 20th century draws to a close, we will revisit the question of whether community really is dead, or whether its death has been overestimated. We will also take a look at the internal dynamics of this community in an effort to understand why it exists. It is a particularly opportune time for asking these questions, as the forces of the mass society recede in favor of the forces of an emerging information age.

Often, as one talks with people in rural communities of the U.S., a concern over the lack of community identity is heard. People sometimes ask what it would take to create a sense of community belonging. In this book we report one community's experience in creating community, and we also probe the provocative questions raised about the cost of the process and the desirability of its consequences.

John C. Allen
Don A. Dillman

Acknowledgments

The people of Bremer made this book possible. Individually and collectively they shared their experiences of what it means to live in Bremer. To them we offer our deepest thanks for sitting through long interviews, filling out questionnaires, and teaching us about life in Bremer.

When the senior author and his family moved into the Bremer community in 1984, it was the end of a search for a place to live. Only later, after his driveway had been voluntarily plowed by neighbors, a farmer had taught him how to drive a loaded grain truck down a steep hill by visualizing how a snowball would roll down it, and many other lessons of what it meant to be a resident of Bremer had been learned, did that move turn out to be the beginning of this book.

When the idea of writing the book became known in the Bremer community, people opened up their history, their current lives, and their hopes for the future. Their willingness to do that made this book possible.

A number of social scientists read and commented on early versions of this book: James H. Copp, Olaf F. Larson, Edward O. Moe, James A. Christenson, Kenneth P. Wilkinson, Robert E. Howell, John E. Carlson, Ed Michaelson, Viktor Gecas, John Wardwell, and Lewis Carter. At a critical time in the writing process, Sonja Salamon visited Bremer, participated in a seminar with us, and generously shared the insights of her own extensive research on community in helping us to comprehend the complexities of life in Bremer. Janet Fitchen also visited Bremer, read and reread the manuscript, and provided several years of encouragement and suggestions, more than any authors have a right to expect. Thanks to all of you.

We also appreciate the support provided by our employers. Robert Haskell at the University of New England and Sam Cordes at the Department of Agricultural Economics at the University of Nebraska--Lincoln provided strong support to the senior author throughout portions of the writing effort. The Department of Rural Sociology and the Social and Economic Sciences Research Center at Washington State University provided substantial support for data collection activities and for work by the junior author.

Kathy Allen, who lived the Bremer experience as wife, mother, and community member, provided insights into the workings of the

Bremer community that can be found on virtually every page of this book. She also made sure the book got finished, providing the emotional support essential to resolving the inevitable collisions of job hunting, career development, and family responsibilities that accompanied the writing and rewriting.

Tammy Small at Washington State University contributed much to this effort by keeping the writing activities organized and processing the final manuscript. Her attention to detail and marvelous computer and organizational skills have made our work much easier. Excellent editorial assistance from Jane Henicke is also appreciated. Our thanks also go to David Flaherty for the photographs and Kenneth Clark for the graphical illustrations that appear on the pages of this book.

A deliberate effort has been made to protect the identity of the community and the anonymity of people who shared many and sometimes intimate details of life in Bremer. In addition to changing the name of the community, we have sometimes changed dates, locations, and names and positions of people who supplied information, where anonymity seemed especially difficult to protect. Each change of this nature was individually decided. We have also omitted entirely certain items of information that support our eventual conclusions but that we could find no easy way of changing in a way that would protect anonymity while maintaining the integrity of the analysis. These decisions were often difficult and made through joint consideration of potential impact on the lives of individuals and the accuracy of the analysis. Although we frequently consulted with people mentioned above on these issues, we alone accept responsibility for the final decisions as well as any errors of interpretation.

J.C.A.
D.A.D.

1

Confronting the Inevitable

The Meeting

It is 6:55 p.m. on a gray Monday in March, well past the State Class B basketball tournament, but spring has yet to make a convincing arrival. In the school building near the edge of town, several of Bremer's six school board members are milling in the long narrow hallway, still wearing jackets. They converse on nothing in particular and stop even that as headlights flash in the window, indicating that yet another car has pulled into the parking lot.

The topic for tonight's special school board meeting is whether Bremer should consolidate its school district with that of Flemington, a town some 18 miles away. The meeting had been called a few days before, with the only announcement being informal phone calls to members. A small turnout is hoped for by the board members. Yet the steady stream of headlights flashing in the window is not unexpected. At 7:05 p.m., without fanfare, the board members wisely decide to move the meeting from the library to the much larger auditorium/gymnasium.

Ironically, attendees at tonight's special school board meeting pass by the obvious problem as they walk the length of the long, flat building that houses all 13 grades of the Bremer school system to enter the auditorium. Hanging on the hallway walls are the pictures of every Bremer high school graduate of the last 79 years. The picture for 1907 shows four graduates, two men standing dressed in high button collars with black coats, and two seated women with their hair piled high on their heads. The 1940 picture includes 31 students. The casualness of their dress contrasts markedly with most of the earlier pictures; women are standing as well as sitting. The picture of the 1960 graduates displays 63 students standing stiffly in straight rows. This class was the largest ever to graduate from the Bremer high school. The 1986 picture shows only 12 graduates standing side by side displaying their diplomas, the smallest class to graduate from Bremer High since 1923.

Next to the principal's office, near the main double doors to the school, sits a large trophy case overflowing with gold plated figurines of basketball players frozen in the act of shooting. Engraved into the bases of several are the words State B Champions. Large silver footballs sit atop pedestals with similar inscriptions indicating other championships for Bremer. Gold plates on hardwood plaques list the players on the winning teams for each of the championship years. The plaques from later years have the same names as earlier years, such as Snyder, Balkum, and Felder, the only difference being the "Jr." notation. Names on the older trophies are all male. Basketball and volleyball trophies topped by women figurines begin in the early 1980s.

For those not familiar with the winning and losing years for the local teams, the trophy case might appear to contain all of the trophies a small school could garner in over 70 years of competition. But most community residents, including the attendees at tonight's meeting, know that many have been moved to the top shelves in the library "to make room for the new ones." These trophies are not collecting dust but are kept shiny and reflective of the pride this small school takes in its "winners," who often remain in the forefront of community discussion throughout their lives.

By 7:15 p.m. the crowd has grown to over 100 people. Husbands in Bremer Grain Growers baseball caps accompanied by wives, most wearing blouses and slacks, are still entering the gym. The men nod and stop to talk in muffled tones with other men who have already found a seat. Some of the women are carrying manila folders, which they wave at other women in the crowd, who nod and smile approvingly in return. Except for a few nervous visitors near the door, everyone knows everyone else, not just by name but in most cases by life history.

As the wall clock ticks past 7:30 p.m., the chairman of the school board, a farmer in a plaid shirt, levi's and cowboy boots, the standard dress of most locals, calls the meeting to order. Known to most of those seated in the gym as Fred Miller's son who married Bill Davis's oldest daughter and lives on Miller Road and farms the Miller place, he begins by explaining that this is an information meeting only. No decisions will be made tonight. He welcomes the small cadre of nervous visitors from Flemington with whom the board has been discussing the possibility of consolidation and who sit together near the door. His introduction results in many of the Bremerites turning their heads to stare briefly at the "outsiders" with silence and expressions that seem to reflect distaste.

The chairman turns the floor over to another board member who explains what consolidation would mean to Bremer. He tells the citizens that consolidation or cooperation with another school district would increase the number of class offerings to Bremer students and would enable the school to retain its current number of teachers. He also notes that the school district is the largest employer in the community and abruptly ends his remarks. With that brief introduction the floor is opened for discussion.

The first member of the audience to speak is a farmer, whose picture hangs in the hallway and whose athletic trophies remain displayed in the trophy case near the principal's office. He is in his late 30s and dressed in the obligatory boots and jeans and a pullover dress shirt. His credentials of having been a star Bremer basketball player in a community that expects state champions adds credibility to his voice. His opinion is that neither consolidation nor cooperation is needed. Instead, he says, Bremer needs to lobby the state capitol to permit the raising of school-bond levy levels, a reference to a decade-old law that limits how much money schools can raise locally to supplement state funds. His presentation is applauded, providing momentary relief to the tenseness that permeates the room. The next few people to speak are parents of Bremer school children. Their concerns are pointed toward the other district and range from bad teachers to the "undesirable character" of Flemington residents. The applause gets louder with each speaker.

The next speaker, a woman, stands and opens a manila folder. Newspaper clippings fall to the floor. She nervously bends down and picks up the clippings as she begins to speak. She talks very rapidly and her voice cracks from the obvious stress. Flemington is described as a community full of trouble. She reads from one newspaper clipping about a local deputy sheriff who after having been called to serve a warrant on a Flemington resident said that the town has changed for the worse in the last few years. She goes on to read another brief article about a small school in a neighboring state where the students are ranked academically with the best in the nation. She concludes that Bremer doesn't want to be consolidated with Flemington and that the school board should listen to her because she speaks for a lot of her friends. Many women in the crowd nod their heads in agreement as she continues to speak.

The chairman next recognizes the residents from Flemington, who had met previously to select a spokesperson. They have chosen a schoolteacher who has come prepared with diagrams and data that show the ability of Flemington students to be as good as or better than Bremer students. The crowd interrupts in protest of his comparisons several times until the chairman of the school board stands and shouts his frustration that this is a public meeting and that the least Bremer residents can do is to be polite.

The Flemington teacher strongly counters the argument that the Flemington students are poorly educated and mostly migrants from outside the area. He shows SAT scores and notes where the graduates attend college. This year Flemington graduated one student, but in 1987 six seniors are expected to graduate. The current number of high school students is 21. The Flemington representative talks about the outstanding Flemington graduates, mentioning a congressman, an author, and the new valedictorian, who will be attending an Ivy League school. Bremerite hands begin to wave urgently for recognition and a turn to speak. However, the teacher goes on to explain that Flemington uses a satellite receiving dish to offer advanced college-preparatory classes that they could not otherwise offer, a technology not yet accepted by Bremer. He concludes by saying that his community welcomes the consolidation effort or another version of cooperation.

The crowd is disruptive and the chairman calls for a 15-minute recess for tempers to cool. Small crowds of five to six people stand around the gym talking and gesturing in animated ways. Voices are raised and the gym hums with sounds that override individual voices. When the meeting is called back to order, the faces of the board members express deep concern. Members of the crowd are waving their hands and even manila folders to get the attention of the chair. A young mother is recognized by the chair to speak next. She begins with the fact that she graduated from Bremer and wants her daughter to have the same advantages that she had. She declares her dislike for the Flemington kids and their parents who are "all from the city anyway." Her contention that Flemington residents are from the city is based on a community-wide belief that because of cheap housing, state residents on state or federal assistance programs have relocated to Flemington and changed it for the worse. She finishes with her voice rising and declares that she will not have her kids go to school with welfare kids from Flemington. Her voice breaks and tears flow down her cheeks as she sits down.

The speakers who follow carry on the theme of protest, repeating that Bremer could survive without the kids from the other community and so the board should vote against consolidation or cooperation. At 10:00 p.m. the atmosphere remains heated and the board reschedules another public meeting for two weeks from that night.

The Flemington members who are seated in a group by the door leave quickly and silently. Their cars are out of the parking lot before the first group of Bremerites reaches the outside doors. As the remaining Bremerites walk slowly down the corridor, the pictures above the lockers are once again ignored, as are the trophies and basketballs inscribed by players of winning teams in the enclosed glass case standing sentinel just outside the principal's office.

The Outcome

Only a week after the public meeting, the Bremer school board met with the school board from Flemington and a cooperation agreement between the two schools was signed. Those in attendance sat quietly as the midday light filtered through the school library window reflecting off the trophies standing above the rows of books. In contrast with the earlier meeting, the conversation was quiet and subdued, although one retired farmer dressed in faded work jeans and boots attempted to lighten the atmosphere with an off-color joke about Democratic politicians.

The cooperative agreement stipulated that each community would keep its elementary school. It was agreed that the junior high school would be situated in Flemington, with students from both Bremer and Flemington attending. A bus schedule was worked out whereby the Bremer junior high students would ride a Bremer school district bus to a point about seven miles on the Bremer side of Flemington and then would be moved to a Flemington bus to continue their journey to the school in Flemington. Both boards decided that it would be best if a teacher from Bremer rode both ways with the school children for the first month "to make the adjustment easier."

The high school, it was agreed, would be in Bremer. The students from Flemington would ride the bus to the exchange point and then would go the rest of the way on the Bremer bus. The high school teachers in Flemington would be given positions in the junior high in Flemington or at the Bremer high school, with some teachers splitting their teaching day between the two schools.

The importance of athletics to both communities was a topic of heated discussion. Both communities wanted to retain their name and mascot. In the end Bremer, because of its larger enrollment, won the right to retain the high school athletics and its original mascot.

A week after the signing, and two weeks following the emotional night meeting in the Bremer gym, the Bremer school board met again with the community members of Bremer. This meeting lacked the fervor of the previous public meeting. Several board members explained the new contract as an experiment. If it did not work, the schools would be returned to their past organizational structure. One Bremer school board member explained:

> We just didn't have a choice. If we didn't do something the state was going to make us get rid of one and a half teachers. We just didn't have the students to justify that many teachers. If we lost the teachers we were going to lose some classes and we really can't afford to get any further behind in our curriculum compared to bigger schools. So we did what we had to do.

The silence of those in attendance signified their resigned acceptance and the meeting was soon adjourned. Once again the audience ignored the pictures and trophies as they dispersed out the doors and into the night.

To an outside observer, the contrast between the trauma of the first meeting and the quiet acquiescence of the second may seem at best impossible. At worst, it might be seen as a sign of protest without commitment, psychological withdrawal, and powerlessness. Nothing could be further from reality.

The seven days in between provided a remarkable illustration of how decisions are made in Bremer. Community leaders, many of whom did not hold elected positions, spent hours in the coffee shop and cafe explaining the options if the school board did not consolidate. The Bremer community acted. During the intense two-week period between meetings, board members each received dozens of telephone calls, and made dozens of others. Community residents stopped their pickup trucks along fields and in farm driveways, where they talked first about the weather and the price of wheat, and then about the schools. The purchase of bags of groceries involved not only the exchange of money for groceries, but the exchange of ideas about the school, and the sharing of concerns. No formal "pro" group formed; no formal "con" group formed. People talked, and the same people listened. By whatever means, the community of Bremerites came to understand the issues and worked through what became defined as the only possible solution. That gray Monday night, on which such intense emotions were expressed and the community seemed on the verge of extended controversy, was well on its way to becoming only a memory.

What causes the expression of intense emotion on behalf of something that the participants themselves call their "community"? How does a school board meeting called a few days before with no general announcement become a forum for protest attended by more than one-tenth of the residents of this place called Bremer? Why does a proposed cooperative agreement between the schools of Bremer and Flemington, only 18 miles apart, and mostly indistinguishable by physical features, dominant occupation, and ethnic background, evoke such intense emotions? Perhaps most perplexing of all, how can an intense meeting of frustration be followed by a decision that runs counter to the theme of that protest, with the decision itself being followed only a few days later by a meeting of resigned acceptance? In the following chapters we will search for answers to these and other questions about this small rural community.

2

Locating Bremer: Influences of Space and Time

Like other inland communities of the Pacific Northwest, Bremer is oriented toward the west, the direction from which the first settlers came. Politics, markets, services from metropolitan areas, and even the weather flow from west to east. Thus, to understand Bremer it is useful to start from the west.

Retracing the nearly 400-mile path of the first Bremer settlers, from near Portland, Oregon, to the fertile Palouse hills of far-eastern Washington, reveals much about the Bremer community. A convenient vantage point from which to comprehend the enormous climatic and geological variations along the route is at the 20,000-foot altitude and 275-mile-per-hour speed of the many prop jet aircraft that serve inland cities of Washington and Oregon, taking passengers toward Spokane, some distance north of Bremer. Ironically, flights originating from the Portland airport begin within sight of the giant elevators where barges full of white soft wheat, the main source of Bremer's livelihood, are being transferred to ocean-going ships for export. These barges have just finished stair-stepping their way through the eight giant dams of the Snake-Columbia river system that facilitate ocean-bound barge shipments of what locals have tagged "Palouse Gold."

The early-spring scene that unfolds below is as dramatic as it is ever changing. Only minutes away from Portland, the Columbia River begins its bisection of the Cascade Mountain Range. Until early in this century, this near-sea-level valley was the only year-round passage to the Inland Northwest and thus the logical route for pioneers in the 1800s. The jagged, snow-covered peak of Mount Hood can be seen rising 11,245 feet on the Oregon side of the river. The more rounded, 12,307-foot Mt. Adams dominates the Washington side of the river. Mt. Adams, generally thought of as the bulky big brother to the nearby and more perfectly formed Mt. St. Helens (until the violent 1980 eruption, which turned its top 1,000 feet to ash), in tandem with Mt. Hood, are the dominant sentinels that overlook this route to the east.

From high above, one's progress through the heart of the Columbia Gorge is most easily measured by the location of the giant dams that extract hydroelectric power and whose locks allow passage of the wheat barges. The alternately wide and narrow ribbons of water connecting the reservoirs of one dam to those of the next exhibit a tranquillity that seems strikingly inconsistent with the Columbia's original free-flowing and wild state, which greeted the wagons of the first Bremer residents a mere 100 years ago.

Between Bonneville and The Dalles, the first and second of these giant concrete dams, one begins to see the contrast between the moist western and drier eastern mountain slopes. The western slopes are densely covered by Douglas fir and other dark green vegetation watered frequently and heavily by storms from the Pacific Ocean. The drier eastern slopes, made that way by the curtain of mountains that drain moisture from Pacific storms before allowing their winds to pass eastward, are more sparsely covered by lighter-colored ponderosa pine and other vegetation more tolerant of cold winters and dry summers. Continuing eastward, the patches of brown earth and rock show up with greater frequency among the trees and give evidence that spring in the Inland Northwest is about to make its annual appearance.

Past John Day, the third dam in this series, the transition is complete. It is here that one is forced to begin comprehending the vastness of the nearly flat drylands that cover much of central Oregon and Washington. Some 200 miles upriver from Portland, just past McNary Dam, the Columbia River turns directly north and enters Washington State. We are now over the nearly treeless northern desert, where rainfall comes mostly during the long gray winters, averaging in some places no more than seven inches per year, a fraction of the amount that gives the coastal region of the Pacific Northwest its year-round cloak of green. Just inside Washington and dominating the view from the air is the confluence of the Snake River with the larger Columbia. It is here that the Columbia turns back westward to the Cascade Mountains, which it will skirt for more than 100 miles before again turning eastward to surround on three sides the central Washington area known as the Columbia Basin.

The basin, once a formidable expanse of sagebrush and rocky terrain, is irrigated by the waters of the Columbia pulled from Roosevelt Lake, behind Grand Coulee, the largest dam of all, and far out of sight to the north. Irrigated fields are now the basin's most prominent feature. Even in this area of southern Washington, near the

Figure 2.1 The Region Where Bremer Is Located

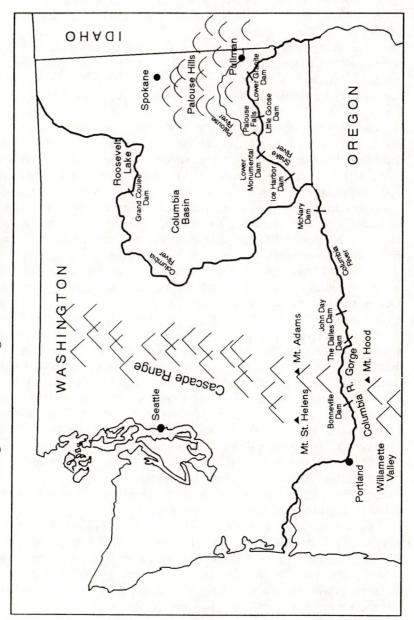

confluence of these two mighty rivers, one can see rectangles fed by canal irrigation and circles fed by water drawn from pivot wells. The water pulled from these wells is in a sense recycled, coming from an aquifer fed by three decades of excess flow from the canal irrigation. Our attention, however, instead of following the Columbia back westward, turns toward the east, where the Snake, true to its name, makes a wiggly half circle eastward toward the Idaho border in its several-hundred-mile journey that will end at the Grand Tetons of Wyoming.

The waters of the Snake alternately narrow and widen in relation to the four dams, closer together than their predecessors, that control the flow of water from the upper regions of the Snake, beyond the Palouse. First comes Ice Harbor, then Lower Monumental, Little Goose, and finally Lower Granite. The name of each dam gives an image of its historical location, if not its function. Their distinctive names withstanding, the dams are functionally redundant, each of them providing for flood control, discharge of water through turbines to make electricity, the passage of the wheat barges through giant locks on their way to Portland's grain terminals, the migration of adult salmon and oceangoing trout (known as steelhead) through surging fish ladders back to their Idaho spawning waters, and the creation of recreational reservoirs.

It is between Lower Monumental and Little Goose that one confronts the first evidence of the Palouse. The view is at first surprising, even shocking. The northern half of the reservoir for a stretch of several miles looks like a chocolate shake yet to be mixed with the sparkling blue and green water along the southern shore. The source of this muddy water, which appears to float like feathers as it mingles quietly with the peacock-colored water of the Lower Monumental Reservoir, is the Palouse River at the end of its 100-mile formative run through the agriculturally rich but erosive hills that comprise the Palouse hills. This early-spring runoff, fed by warm rains on still-frozen hillsides, gives an unmistakable indication of land that is different from the regions already traversed.

Looking northward beyond the 100-foot-high Palouse Falls, which add finality and a chocolate soda appearance to the river's terminus, the dividing line between the Columbia Basin and the Palouse hills becomes evident. The division is in some ways gradual and in others striking: gradual in the vegetative evidence of increased rainfall that will more than double between the area of the milky brown discharge and the Idaho border, striking in the rocky scablands that range from a mile to several miles wide and that sharply divide the flat, farmable drylands of the Columbia Basin from the distinctive hills of the

Palouse. These rocky, sagebrush-covered scablands are a legacy of the great Spokane floods of the Ice Age. Violent ruptures of ice dams that held back water in a giant lake over Montana, because of the volume and speed of the discharge, left deeply etched and permanent scars, visible even from circling NASA spacecraft, so it has been learned. From this altitude, and with the perspective of modern geology, these barren trenches are far more easily understood than they could have been by the Palouse pioneers who traversed these lands slowly and precariously by horse and wagon a brief 100 years ago.

The Palouse itself is less easily comprehended at first. To the pioneers the hills must have seemed a welcome relief from the apprehension created by the rocky, unfarmable scablands that preceded them. Originally covered by prairie grasses, the hills rise abruptly from the edge of the scablands, with immediate evidence of a deep soil that could be easily farmed, even on the hillsides, without fear of implements being damaged by hidden rocks. By contrast, even the steepness of the sidehills must not have seemed a great concern to the first Bremerites. Now, a century later, it is this aspect of the Palouse hills that delineates the sharp contrast with the clear reservoir waters below and exists as a substantial worry to area farmers.

The vantage point from above also helps to clarify the nature and origin of the hills. Shadows from the morning sun make the hills appear much like ripples along the lakeshore. The crest of each of these tightly compacted ripples exhibits a repetitive southeast-to-northwest gradient, organized at first, but given slight irregularity by thousands of years of climatic forces and a mere 100 years of intensive agriculture. The regularity of the ripples seems almost mystical and one wonders if the close-up views of the pioneers gave them an inkling of the repetitive pattern so visible from an aircraft. These hills, known to agronomists as loess deposits, were formed by windblown particles from floodplains of the prehistoric Columbia River deposited here in repetitive dunelike formations. Closer examination suggests gradual southwesterly slopes and more acute northeasterly slopes, which would be farmed with the same equipment to raise similar crops in similar ways, but with different erosive consequences.

Finally, directly above the first of the Palouse hills, another type of pattern begins to dominate one's view and our imagination. Divided-slope farming, an erosion-control practice that involves following contour lines to divide large fields into smaller ones so that different crops can be grown on upper and lower slopes, gives the hills a surreal quality. An imaginative mind can identify tops of interconnected hills that have become letters of the alphabet, birds, animals, or simply a

pretty design--each of which encloses 50, 100, or even 200 acres. Only
the occasional section lines, which are maintained as farm boundaries,
interfere with the artistic images wrought by the combination of nature
and human efforts to cope with the erosive consequences of farmers'
attempts to make a living. The juxtaposition of river barges, chocolate-
colored river water, and artistry of the hilltops does much to convey
the characteristics of life in the Palouse hills and the place called
Bremer, even before one arrives there.

The Palouse itself, which we can see stretching from the scablands
to the now-visible Bitterroot Mountains just across the Idaho border,
was named for the Appaloosa horse first domesticated by the Nez
Perce´ Indians who lived nearby. The hills themselves extend from the
Snake River in the south nearly to Spokane, 100 miles to the north, and
are some 90 miles in breadth. It is here that the clouds disrupted by
their passage over the Cascades begin to reform and a trajectory of
increasing rainfall becomes clear. Historic records show an annual
average rainfall of 14 inches on the western edge, and 26 inches along
the eastern edge. Few population centers are immediately evident.

For a person familiar with the checkerboard geometry of
midwestern agriculture, the pattern from the air seems at first
confusing. With few exceptions, roads follow the sometimes-narrow
valleys between hills, and towns tend to be located where tiny streams
come together to form the many small tributaries of the Palouse and
other small rivers. The largest of these towns is Pullman, location of
the state's land grant university. Originally named Three Forks
simply because three small streams came together to form the south
fork of the Palouse River, it lies within eight miles of the Idaho
border.

Some two dozen smaller communities dot the Palouse landscape,
appropriately distributed across the entire region to serve nearby
farmers. Bremer is one of these small towns. From the air there is little
to distinguish it from any other small community. No mountains,
plateaus, rivers, or other physical boundaries isolate it. Yet, as we
shall see, Bremer is more than a geographic spot on the map. It consists
of about 1,000 people within 12-15 miles of the Bremer town center, most
of whom identify themselves proudly, emotionally, and sometimes
defiantly as Bremerites. It is a voluntary, protected distinction that
separates them from all other residents of the Palouse hills.

". . . the hills rise abruptly from the edge of the scablands, with immediate evidence of a deep soil that could be easily farmed, even on hillsides, without fear of implements being damaged by hidden rocks."

The Beginning

The wagon trains of the late 1800s transported thousands of settlers from the Midwest and East to the Pacific Northwest. They traveled the difficult Oregon Trail to the Columbia River before moving on to Portland, Oregon, west of the Cascade Mountains. As the settlers reached Oregon's fertile Willamette Valley they found that the many trees and persistent rain were not particularly good for the traditional growing of small grains. It was then that the dissatisfied new settlers began investigating unsettled land available in the Palouse Plain, in far eastern Washington nearly 400 miles to the northeast.

Prior to 1880, the range-cattle industry had occupied the area, but the "bitter winter of 1880-81 resulted in the financial ruin of many cattlemen" (Scheurman and Trafzer, 1985, p. 137). Grain marketing had been stalled by lack of a railroad. However, the completion of the Northern Pacific Railroad in 1883 facilitated the transporting of grain to eastern markets. The new railroad connection plus the fact that many of the new immigrants' relatives were dissatisfied with their homes in the Midwest, where many had relocated from the Volga region in Russia, provided the impetus for the settling of the Palouse Plain. One prospective migrant to the Palouse describes their midwestern existence:

> Our houses consist of "Dug outs" and "Sod houses." Our people are all discouraged and homesick, but too far to go back to Russia, and we want to see . . . the Territory we have heard so much of its great yielding wheat fields and wonderful Fruit Country. (Scheurman and Trafzer, 1985, p. 134)

Finding a place to build their communities was a careful, deliberate action. The Oregon Improvement Company had previously been given over 150,000 acres of land to assist in the settling of the area. The new migrants sent out scouts to the Palouse, where the improvement company was selling land for $5 to $10 per acre on a six-year installment plan at 7 percent interest (Bryan, 1936, p. 144). They found that it was less expensive to homestead than to buy the land from the improvement company, although the land owned by the improvement company was carefully selected (alternate sections of 14 townships). The selection of sites by the improvement company influenced the settlement patterns in the Palouse region. The company staked out large tents for the newcomers in the new communities in the Palouse and sent fliers around the world encouraging settlers to relocate to the Palouse.

"For a person familiar with the checkerboard geometry of midwestern agriculture, the pattern from the air seems, at first, confusing."

In its 1883 guidebook the Northern Pacific described the Palouse country:

> One of the most fertile and extensive agricultural regions on the Pacific Coast. The Palouse country extends from the base of the Coeur d'Alene Mountains westward 60 miles, so is partly in Idaho and reaches northwardly from Snake River 75 to 100 miles. The railroad will push east to the mountains nearly 100 miles ... West of the Palouse there is very little arable land, but east of that stream is a fertile country of the best description. (Winser, 1883, pp. 219-20)

The Palouse that the new settlers found was a land of vast, rolling hills covered with bunch grasses. The original settlers to the area lived within the towns and farmed land adjacent to them. As farming techniques improved, new families began to move onto the approximately one million acres available for farming. They found that wheat, barley, and fruit grew well. During the early years the seeding was done by hand broadcasting either on foot or from horseback, but by 1884 mechanical broadcasters and self-rake reapers were introduced to the area. The problem associated with this technology was that it left the seed on the surface, where it sometimes lay for months without germinating. In 1890 the disc-drill was invented, which allowed the seed to be deposited in uniform rows below the surface, nearer to the moisture level.

The growing demand for wheat in the 1890s, in addition to the new technology, provided the impetus for the solidifying of the rural farm communities in the Palouse. It is the descendants from these early pioneers and the communities they founded that are the focus of this book. As a result of Bremer's late settlement, compared with that of most locations in the United States, Bremer residents are connected to their origins. Older residents knew many of the original settlers personally, and ownership of many farms remains within the families that settled them.

Bremer Today: Deceptively Serene

When viewed on a sunny spring morning from a Bremerite's typical vantage point, a vehicle maneuvering the basalt-gravel-covered roads, Bremer is deceptively serene. This is an ideal time of year for viewing Bremer. It is well after the last heavy frost has disappeared from the shaded northern slopes, and spring fieldwork is proceeding rapidly. In some fields winter wheat is several inches high, covering from view rills cut into the soil by the last of the winter runoff. Yet much of the

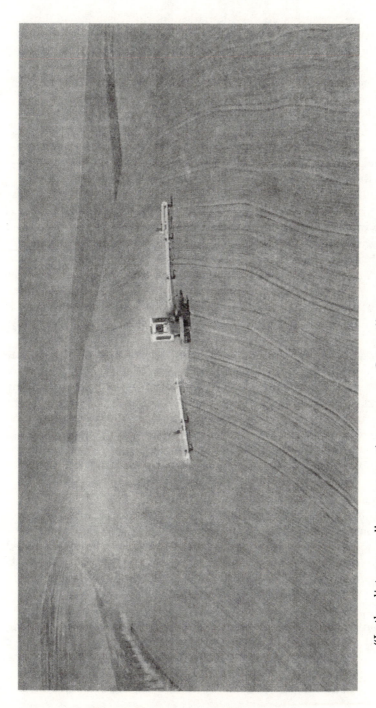

"In the distance, yellow, or sometimes orange, Caterpillar tractors can be seen as they move slowly around the steep Palouse hills, pulling harrows, seed drills, or sprayers with their 30-foot booms."

spring wheat remains to be planted. In the distance yellow, or sometimes orange, Caterpillar tractors can be seen as they move slowly around the steep Palouse hills pulling harrows, seed drills, or sprayers with their 30-foot booms. The individual dust clouds hovering above each of the distant machines identifies for knowledgeable locals who is working in these fields. Where once carefully tended fences separated farms, now only slim rows of dry weeds barely reveal where one farm ends and another begins.

The typical western breezes are absent this morning and yellow bi-winged planes, themselves survivors of an earlier era, speed low over the hills dumping herbicides on the seemingly endless fields of wheat, occasionally separated by plantings of barley, peas, or lentils. More than a few drivers experience, on this spring day, the shock of coming over the crest of a hill and without warning being face-to-face with these highly maneuverable planes. Locals recover quickly enough to guess which Bremerite is behind the goggles as they watch the planes pull up sharply at the weed dividers, bank, and disappear over the next hill. As quickly as it appeared, one of the pesky yellow machines, with its distinctive roar, is gone, leaving behind only the white paper streamer that slowly ripples to the green field after being thrown from the cockpit to mark the next run.

Driving down the winding, unfenced roads of Bremer, one can see isolated farmsteads with well-kept lawns that blend into the edges of the adjacent tilled fields. Satellite dishes dot the yards, bringing CNN and dozens of other TV channels to peoples' homes. Barns originally designed by German craftsmen to stable the workhorses used in earlier years now house the large International Gleaner combines with automatic four-way levelers that keep the cab vertical while the cutter and wheels adjust to fit the hill, apparatus essential for operation on the steep hillsides. Large farming implements are arranged in rows near the barn. Grain storage bins from 20 to 40 feet tall provide gleaming silver accents to the hilly backgrounds. It is not uncommon to see rows of implements standing alone on sights where the original homesteads were located or where the land is currently leased from someone who no longer farms. The leased land still retains its earlier name, such as Johnson's Forty or Calhoun's Flat, giving a continuity to the residents who first farmed it.

The windmills that previously marked the existence of a home now stand alone in the midst of wheat fields, with bent fan blades turning irregularly or not at all in the westerly wind that brings the Palouse's wet winters and dry summers off the distant Pacific Ocean. A few vacant homes stand sheltered in groves of trees where the great-grandson still mows the grass just "to keep the place up." While the

"Driving down the winding unfenced roads of Bremer, one can see isolated farmsteads with well-kept lawns that blend into the edges of the adjacent tilled fields."

farm population has declined, the value system of cleanliness still prevails, as does the strong tie to the past, which makes keeping up even vacant properties a community expectation.

Of the land that is farmed in Bremer, which is almost all the visible landscape, 41 percent is owned by the actual people that farm it. The rest of the land is leased by relatives from retired farmers who remain in the area or from their descendants. Over 80 percent of those currently farming had parents or other relatives who previously worked the same land. It is difficult to get an accurate picture of the average farm size in Bremer primarily because the response by those farming the land is often, "I own 600 acres, my sister owns 400, and then we lease another 200 from her husband's father." These different sections are farmed as one farm, but over 30 percent are incorporated, with the grain being identified as coming from different farms. When asked in our survey to identify specifically how many acres they farm, almost 30 percent of the farmers reported farming fewer than 800 acres, compared with 28 percent farming more than 2,000 acres.

The Town Proper

The town of Bremer is situated in the middle of this 30-to-35-mile-wide community of a thousand people. Its population of over 500 people in 1986 was less than a 1-percent increase from 1980 and only slightly below its peak population of nearly 600. The population of the countryside has obviously declined more, probably by half, as farms have increased in size and families have become smaller, consistent with the trend for the U.S. as a whole.

The average age of adults in the Bremer community is 53 years. The town, which traditionally held a blend of young and old, today is home for the majority of the elderly in the community: 78 percent of those over 60 live inside the town. The average household size is 2.4 people. Bremer has been undergoing some changes similar to those in small rural communities throughout the U.S. The population is aging while individual farm operations are increasing in size. Yet there is a difference in Bremer that may be a determining factor in Bremer's ability to maintain traditions. Though some authors write of the increased poverty in rural areas (Fitchen, 1981), Bremer, up to this point in time, has been able to maintain its fairly high standard of living. Its estimated 1986 per capita income ranked second in the state. This high income was an increase of more than 40 percent from 1979. Bremer is *not* a "poor" rural community. The historical reason for establishment of the town was, of course, to support agriculture. Bremer now persists as a service center for the agricultural producers in the area. Agriculture is still important to the community, as 42 percent of the adults in the community are involved in farming. The community boundaries, located with surprising precision by systematically driving the roads and asking dozens of residents to identify members of the community and then verifying that with those who were named as community members, reach out each way from Bremer for about 15 miles.

Bremer is situated at the edge of the daily commuter zone for the metropolitan city to the north and the state land grant university city to the south, an hour's drive each way. These substantial distances undoubtedly figure in the consideration of the boundaries as social facts and not simply as an artifact of an officially defined geographic area. As more Americans work outside of their homes, a change has also occurred in Bremer. In 1988 about 20 percent of the working population worked outside of the Bremer community. Of those who commuted out of Bremer to work, only 5.4 percent were women.

A casual, drive-through visitor to Bremer is likely to see no more than just "another small agricultural town." The housing is similar, the landscape is similar, people dress about the same and appear to earn their living in about the same way. Physically, there is no architecture that is distinctive, no apparent distinctive farming methods, no geological formations, and no other physical features that are particularly memorable.

The Bremer main street runs through the center of town for approximately three city blocks. Railroad tracks form the boundary of the city limits on the east. These tracks merge with a secondary rail line that runs the length of the small valley, east to west. All but two of the local businesses are situated within this short distance. To the north of Main Street stands the large silver grain elevators with Bremer Grain Growers painted in black. An American flag, illuminated at night, flies from a 60-foot pole next to the elevators. To the south of these elevators sit the homes of most of the "town" residents. Situated intermittently in the residential neighborhoods are its three small churches: simple structures with crosses and small signs that indicate which denominations the buildings represent. The four-story red brick school is at the southwestern corner of the residential area and is marked by a combination football field and running track. Wheat fields form the backdrop for the school and all other buildings on the outskirts of Bremer.

On another edge of town is a small building that houses the local gun club. The annual crab feed occurs here. More important, the community club regularly meets in this 20-by-40-foot building with trap bunkers leading into the fields, where pieces of broken orange clay pigeons can be seen littering the ground.

A few miles to the east sits the Grange hall. Originally located to meet the needs of the many farmers in the area, the Grange was historically a center of much activity. The weeds peeking up through the gravel parking lot indicate the minimal use of the building in the late 20th century.

On the western edge of the town are rows of farm machinery. One row is for used combines, often sitting at angles as tires have become deflated. The other row is for the new machinery, standing straight, with light glinting off the plastic covering of the never-before-sat-on hydraulic seats. Large fertilizer tanks, giving off a strong odor of ammonia, are the last evidence of a town as one moves west into the seemingly treeless countryside.

Bremer is located, as it has always been, far from the power centers of the state and region. Many, perhaps most, of the state's political leaders would need a map to find its exact location. Like other small towns in the Palouse, Bremer is described by outsiders as just another small eastern Washington town in the middle of a giant wheat field, near the edge of the effective political and economic region. It is not on a main highway that would bring distant visitors through its main street on a daily basis.

A more in-depth, second look produces the realization that some things are different. Other small agricultural towns of the region lack a nearly complete array of basic businesses, a doctor's office and drugstore, the many recreational facilities, and, in some cases, the neatness that seems to be "required" of both town and country homes. Yet, as we shall see, this is just the tip of the iceberg of what makes Bremer different.

3

Gaining Perspective:
A Framework for Analysis

Our earliest experience in Bremer suggested a throwback to earlier times. People on the town streets inevitably spoke to passersby and usually stopped to talk for at least a minute or two. Even strangers elicited a cheery hello, plus a comment about the weather or "How are you doing today?"

Community events seemed out of sync with a modern society. A baby shower had over 100 guests in attendance, but no invitations had been sent. An announcement of the time and place had been made only by word of mouth. More remarkably, most who had heard the announcement interpreted it as an invitation, even an expectation, to attend. One grocery store loaned a freezer to the competing grocery, "to help them out," when theirs had broken down. Well-kept fairgrounds, a golf course, and a swimming pool were built and maintained by volunteers. The city council refused state disaster funds for cleaning up ash from the Mt. St. Helens volcanic eruption—farmers came to town with their equipment, others used garden equipment, and it got done. No one could be found locally who thought this was the least bit strange or unusual. These and dozens of other events suggested a common community identity supported by a strong communication system, and willingness to commit time and other resources in support of it.

This commitment also had geographic boundaries. Traveling out the various roads leading away from Bremer and asking residents if they thought of themselves as part of the Bremer community elicited a clear sense of boundaries—about 15 miles out in each direction. Asking a number of people to describe where they felt the boundaries of the Bremer community were, if there were any that could be defined, inevitably drew a yes, and a marked consistency in their efforts. It also drew commentaries like "You can tell when you are in it, because people recognize your car and start waving, even if they can't tell who is driving."

The attempt to determine whether residents of Bremer saw themselves as "belonging" to a common community brought to mind the work of Charles Galpin, one of the nation's first rural sociologists who identified community boundaries by observing road turnings (Galpin, 1915). A common life continued outward from a community center until the indentations of wagons in the dirt roads no longer turned mostly in the direction of the trade center being studied, but toward a town in the opposite direction.

Looking for road turnings along the asphalt and basalt gravel roads of Bremer would be as outdated and dissatisfying as recognizing the possible existence of a geographically based group of people whose lives were heavily influenced by the perceived existence of something called community. It is a concept from an earlier time, which most sociologists appear to have abandoned as useful in describing or explaining people's behavior. Community was in essence declared dead in the face of the industrialization, urbanization, and suburbanization processes that dominated America during the 1950s. People's ties to work, unions, and other organizations; the separation of work from residence; frequent moves from one region of the country to another; and the pull of people's interests from locality to society by an ever-growing mass media—all these acted in concert to decrease the importance of local ties as an influence on people's attitudes and behavior.

Even rural sociologists found less and less utility in the concept of community. Community-oriented concepts and theories, it was argued by many, e.g., Newby (1983) and Friedland (1982), not only lacked usefulness but placed the discipline in a theoretical crisis. Increasingly rejected as not very useful was the idea that strong ties to locality, and meaningful social ties, created an "umbrella" group influencing behavior in most aspects of life, from work to education to recreation.

Many examples of life in Bremer supported the idea that community lacked overriding importance in people's lives. Satellite dishes dotted the countryside and farmers looked to CNN as a major source of news. State government precipitated the school crisis by forcing the local board to consider curriculum requirements that small schools would increasingly find difficult to meet. Most of all there was the soft white wheat, the same varieties of which were grown on most farms in about the same way, as well as government subsidy programs that supported its growth and export from the community. The economic life of Bremer was clearly outside its control.

Seemingly contradictory behaviors were the result. A farmer would think nothing of buying and selling future contracts by telephone through a commodities broker, yet the same farmer would not consider using no-till production methods because of the "kidding he would have to take" from other farmers. Another farmer would visit several out-of-town automobile dealers trying to get the "best deal" on a new car, but simply call up the local fertilizer dealer and ask for thousands of dollars worth of fertilizer to be delivered without asking the price. A grocery store would not sell toothpaste, because the druggist did that, but would use a computer to order and get delivered almost immediately a brand of beer favored by a railroad crew working in the area for a few days. Daily decisions in most people's lives reflected a juxtapositioning of societal and locality influences. Various perspectives on community life have been found useful by different authors but provided only limited help in resolving these contradictions and in determining the kinds of issues to focus on in seeking to understand the behavior of Bremerites.

Forces of a mass society, the emergent nature of which was detailed by Vidich and Bensman in the 1950s (1958) seemed to dominate some aspects of Bremer, namely, agriculture and selected business, but seemed strangely absent from other spheres, notably, politics and people's social lives. The existence of class distinctions identified in Springdale by Vidich and Bensman, or in Yankee City by Warner and his colleagues (1963), could be argued, perhaps, but in the social life of this fairly homogeneous rural community seemed at best minor axes for social organization.

Roland Warren, whose work contributed much to our understanding of communities in the 1960s, resolved the seeming contradictions between local and societal pulls on people's lives; he recognized the persistence of many local (or horizontal) ties but also a great increase in vertical ties of local organizations to parent or national organizations outside the control of the locality (1978). These vertical ties, which were consistent with the mass societal forces described by Vidich and Bensman, exist in the case of Bremer, but so do countervailing forces such as a community club that actively seeks to moderate its influence on the community. This model, which allows for the seeming contradictions observed in Bremer, did not seem sufficient for understanding the relatively greater strength of local ties and the overarching control by a community club in so many spheres of life.

Cultural ethnicity has been found to be an important factor influencing community cohesion in the Midwest. Salamon found that in German communities a top-priority family goal of each generation was producing a farmer to assume the family operation (1980). In these "yeoman" communities the church played an essential solidifying role, not evident in less-cohesive communities of "Yankee" farmers. At first glance this model seemed useful, but upon closer examination of Bremer, the lack of a single church, substantial church attendance, and strong expression of ethnicity became apparent. Ethnicity seemed not to be a strong variable for creating current community cohesion.

Neither did Bremer fit the cultural-and-demographic-decline model of community that seemed to account for changes observed in rural places of upstate New York, described by Fitchen (1991). Bremer's residents were not being replaced in significant numbers by immigrants with low incomes and marginal ties to the area. Although the number of farmers and size of families had declined significantly, the town proper had not declined, and a curious stability seemed to persist.

It was also apparent that Bremer was not immune to forces of the information age. Farms were becoming computerized, a modern telecommunications system was locally owned and provided up to date telephone service, farmers used homemade "cellular" telephones to maintain instant access to commodity brokers in distant cities, computer ordering was becoming the norm for local businesses, satellite dishes were common throughout the countryside, a cable system served the town, and a few entrepreneurs were experimenting with how computers could help them make a living.

A Framework for Understanding Community Change

The seeming inability of any single theoretical orientation toward community structure and action to account for the patterns of life being observed among Bremer's residents led us to develop and apply a general and somewhat eclectic model of community organization and change, one that helped us ask appropriate questions and analyze the resulting data in order to gain an understanding of how community considerations influenced the lives of Bremer residents.

In its simplest form, the model posits three distinct eras of social and economic organization—community-control, mass-society, and information eras—the relative strengths of which, over time, are shown in Figure 3.1 (Dillman and Beck, 1986; Dillman, Beck, and Allen, 1989). The community-control era represents a time in which numerous forces—technological, social, and economic—act in mutually supportive ways to strengthen internal ties within a community so that the community exerts a powerful influence over its residents. The mass-society era represents the development of forces that strengthen extra-local community or vertical ties, such as those described by Vidich and Bensman (1958) and Warren (1978). People's ties to the nation as a whole are dramatically strengthened, in large part at the expense of

Figure 3.1 Relative Strength of Three Eras of Social and
Economic Organization in U.S. Society

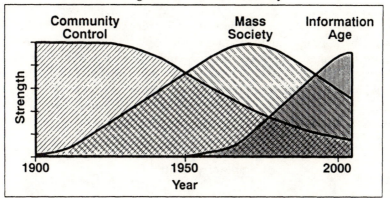

local community commitment. The information era, just now in its early stages, is the result of forces that destroy hierarchy and strengthen people's direct ties to the global economy, irrespective of national or community ties. The development of neither the mass-society nor the information era is simply an extension of forces responsible for the preceding era(s), but the result of new forces coming together in new ways.

We propose that the importance of local community in people's lives can be understood by examining the relative importance of each era's constituent forces in people's lives. In some communities, forces consistent with the community-control era may predominate; in others, forces consistent with the mass-society era may dominate; and in still others, forces of the information era may have major importance. Seemingly contradictory behaviors may be accounted for by people's efforts to adapt to the simultaneous and also contradictory expectations associated with each era. It seems reasonable to expect that in some communities residents may individually and/or collectively resist forces of one or more eras, or alternatively, actively embrace them. In either case, gaining some understanding of how communities may differ is a goal of this book.

In a societal sense, the U.S. is well past the community-control era. People often live in one community, work in another, shop in a third or fourth, and recreate in still another. People's lives need not be and in most cases are not confined to a single community. We are also past the mass-society era, with its emphasis on mass production of the same goods and services that were consumed by most people in most U.S. communities. Clearly, we are entering an information era with emphasis on a global economy and the targeting of goods and services to individual needs and preferences. Nonetheless, it is possible that specific geographic areas differ greatly in the extent to which their residents are influenced by the forces that have shaped each era—some communities may retain structures and processes that maintain local control as a powerful force in their lives, and others may not. By examining specific communities, in search of forces that encourage the existence of one or another era, we may gain some understanding of how and why geographic community influences people's lives. To do this, it is first necessary to examine in some detail exactly what forces encourage or discourage the existence of these postulated eras.

Community-Control Era

Hans Bahrdt once described a ruralite as one who when lost in a large city and compelled to ask directions of a stranger, also feels compelled to explain why he needs to get where he is going and why he became lost in the first place (Bahrdt, 1966). This need to communicate fully stems from living in an environment in which the private and public lives cannot be distinguished.

Similarly, Thomas Bender, a historian who studied small New England communities from the 17th to 19th centuries, found them "remarkably undifferentiated" where "it was difficult to draw a line between family and community, private and public" (Bender, 1978, p. 68). The settling of the United States produced thousands of homogeneous rural communities in which virtually everyone who lived there understood, and was dependent upon, agriculture for their well being. The Homestead Act and other government policies encouraged the ownership of agricultural land by the family who farmed it.

Prior to the development and widespread use of modern communications and transportation technologies, the lives of rural people were largely confined to the community in which they lived. "Community" was thought of by many as a place people could and typically did get all their daily-living needs met. A reflection of the limits of motorless transportation is that trade centers in farming areas were located only 8-10 miles apart. Counties in midwestern states, seldom larger than 24 x 24 miles, were established on the "team haul" concept, which was based on the maximum distance a team of horses could pull a wagon to the county seat (typically located near the center) and return the same day. Although the telephone was widely diffused through rural communities early in this century, its use by most people was mostly for internal community communication (Pool, 1983).

Under these technological constraints, the essence of the community-control era stemmed from four mutually supportive attributes—small size, homogeneity of interests and behavior, lack of population turnover (in particular, inmigration), and an overlapping institutional structure, the first three of which were discussed as defining rural characteristics by Louis Wirth in the 1930s (Wirth, 1938).

Small size (of, say, a few hundred or a thousand) makes it possible for everyone to know one another, at least by one's family and other local connections. Homogeneity, such as most people's being dependent upon one source of livelihood, encourages a recognition of community interests and concerns as being the same. Being tied to a community, as is the case in particular for farm owners, provides the potential for people to get to know one another in depth, both as personalities and with regard to their connections to ancestors and other residents.

In an overlapping institutional structure, people interact with the same people in different spheres of life, i.e., work, politics, education, religion, and recreation. The combined effect of these four factors is to encourage the development of consistency across all aspects of people's lives—for example, by preventing role conflicts. Community becomes an umbrella social group influencing people to do some things and not to do others, because that's what the "community" expects of them.

The community-control era was the predominant social form when small agricultural settlements were isolated from one another by the lack of rapid transportation and communication technology. Small communities were mostly self-sufficient and the goods and services that they produced were primarily consumed locally and regionally. The lack of highly mobile transportation and the inability to communicate over long distances without physically moving from place to place created an economic and social environment in which the residents of a community were constrained and interacted mostly with one another.

Labor in the community-control era was physical, that is, it focused on the physical strengths of the members to produce the buildings, food-stuffs, and other necessities for living. The economic orientations were local and regional, with businesses owned locally and designed to meet local and regional needs.

The dominant source of information in this era was local friends and neighbors and was dominated by verbal rather than written communication. Transportation forms made it difficult for individuals to move easily from their community and to have information about people outside their particular region. Members of the community were forced to rely upon one another for security. If a community member was injured and needed a physician, it was a local doctor or midwife who provided the medical help. The homogeneity of the community and the low population mobility led to increased reliance upon one another within the group.

The essence of rural community in the community-control era was that it existed as a concrete collectivity of people in a geographic location. It was a place where people could and in fact often did go about the rounds of their daily lives and have most of their needs met, physical as well as emotional.

Under these conditions certain kinds of behaviors, attitudes, and rules for governing interaction with other community members developed. Their nature has been described in some detail by Loomis and Beegle (1957) and Loomis (1962), and is based upon earlier work by Tonnies (1940) and Parsons (1950). To the extent that the community-control era us dominant in a locality, we expect to find the following conditions:

Statuses are ascribed. People are expected to accept leadership positions and/or perform certain community activities because their father or mother did it before them. Such statuses are also likely to be gender-specific.

Reliance on informal rules and expectations is evident. Rules are not written down or codified into law. However, most people know they exist and what the penalties are for ignoring them.

Particularism governs the making of decisions; i.e., people are selected for positions of responsibility because of who they are rather than how well they measure up to a set of criteria applied equally to everyone.

Role expectations are fit to the individual rather than the position. If a person is not sufficiently talented or qualified to carry out a task, others are called upon to help, or the expectations are adjusted.

Role expectations in different spheres of life are complimentary. Obligations in work, education, and politics are considered in light of other obligations, so that role conflicts are minimized. Community-wide norms exist that provide an umbrella of uniformity for what is expected of individuals, with the result, for example, that the assessment of how good a church member a person is could be affected by the perception of how good a farmer that person is. The structural basis for this uniformity is an overlapping institutional structure in which people who interact because of their jobs also interact in educational, religious, recreational, and other activities.

Goals and means of achieving those goals are blended together. A farmer's reputation for being a good farmer is based not just upon crop yields or income, but on how his fields look and whether community norms are followed in the planting and growing of crops. Certain desirable farming practices might not be pursued because the means of doing so are considered unacceptable.

Obligations toward other community members are not precisely specified or limited. An attitude exists of doing whatever is necessary to get important things accomplished. Much as a parent's obligation to children is not precisely specified and limited, but depends more upon what is needed, the expectation for community members is to do what is needed for the good of the community. What one will do for other members of the community is not written down and circumscribed in a role description.

Tradition, or how things were usually done in the past, is considered an appropriate guide for correct behavior, even though it might not have a basis that is strictly rational.

Relationships are mostly primary rather than secondary. When people interact with one another they tend to use informal rather than formal names and take the whole person into account. One person's action toward another community member in a particular instance is influenced by concerns about how other areas of that person's life are affected, how other people (for instance, parents or children) might be affected, and perceptions about what is good or bad for the other person. People are acquainted as whole persons, and emotional or affective considerations are accepted as an appropriate part of day-to-day interactions.

Informal sanctions are effective as a way of punishing inappropriate behavior. Because people's lives are mostly invested in one community, without alternatives, casual words of disapproval, or in the extreme, simply ignoring or avoiding someone, can be an effective deterrent to such behaviors.

Participation in community activities is often mandatory. It is not left up to individuals whether they want to participate in certain community activities, from work to celebration. Not participating will elicit disapproval and informal sanctions.

The United States, as a society, is well past the community-control era. Nationwide, conditions have diminished that would be expected to create the kinds of attitudes and behaviors outlined above (people's lives being constrained to one community by technology, for example). However, in some localities these community-control characteristics may persist, being held in place by deliberate efforts to keep them, as well as cultural lag—the frequently observed tendency for beliefs and attitudes to change more slowly than technology itself would allow.

Our observations in Bremer included attempts to discern the existence of ascribed statuses, informal rules and sanctions, complimentary role expectations, primary relationships, and other community-control characterizations. This does not mean that we were looking for the existence of only harmony and agreement. Wilkinson has observed that "community entails squabbles and fights as well as cooperation and affectionate touches" (1991, p. 17). It also involves competition. Our search involved looking for rules and expectations that governed competitive as well as cooperative processes. The critical question was, To what extent were community-control processes influencing life in Bremer? We also searched for the existence of a quite different set of attitudes and behavior that flowed from another era of social and economic organization, the mass society.

The Mass Society

The start of mass society can appropriately be traced to the beginning of mass production and the distribution of production which resulted in people in virtually every community of the United States being able to consume identical products and services. Henry Ford's development of assembly line production of cars in the 1920s marked its beginning. The assembly line production of tens of thousands of identical black cars, with each worker performing a specific production task, enabled the price of each car to be much lower than craft production had allowed. Over time, mass production marketing and distribution techniques were extended to virtually all products and services, from breakfast cereals (Cheerios and Wheaties) to the distribution of news (ABC, NBC, and CBS).

Mass production was predicated upon meeting the average needs of consumers in the U.S. market, i.e., producing products that would achieve maximum overall acceptance. This trend resulted in the development of large, multi-tiered organizations and affiliates that reached into communities throughout the country. Montgomery Ward, Gambles, A & W Root Beer, State Farm Insurance, General Electric, General Motors, Woolworth, Safeway, and many other organizations serves as examples.

At the same time, technologies that facilitated the building and operation of large organizations in multiple locations were being developed. They included automobile transportation, long-distance telephone, television, and air transportation. These technologies in conjunction with the growth of giant manufacturers and distributors resulted in people's lives becoming more closely connected to individual companies than to communities. Corporations offered retirement benefits and unprecedented salaries that rewarded people for being willing to give lifetime allegiance to a corporation. Such allegiance meant being willing to move from one location to another, and particularly to major cities where the largest manufacturing plants and corporate headquarters existed.

The effects on rural communities were dramatic. First, organizations within communities became oriented more to parent organizations or affiliates outside the community than to other organizations within the community. A clear sense of hierarchy existed, with local organizations reporting to regional ones, which in turn often reported to state organizations and eventually on to national ones. This trend was captured by Roland Warren, who described the building of vertical ties between community organizations and higher-level ones, which do not take into account community ties or norms (1978).

Second, the institutional bases of rural communities were weakened. People traveled outside of local communities to work and purchase consumer goods. The decline in patronage of local businesses and services weakened them, so that many could no longer exist. Their demise was hastened by general rural population declines as farms became more efficient and jobs more plentiful in cities.

The combined result of people's loyalties being increasingly directed toward corporate affiliations, stronger ties developing between of community-level organizations and higher-level organizations, and institutional bases weakening in rural communities was to diminish the influence of community over people's lives. Increasingly, community as a geographic place became a temporary place of residence where allegiances and identities were invested only tentatively, so that when it was necessary to move, such dislocations were less difficult. Even when people lived for a long time in one community, they might have worked in another location, gone shopping in yet another, and recreated in still another. These trends provided a basis for Stein's conclusion that community as an important social grouping had been eclipsed (1960). They also led to the view that non-geographic groups, e.g., professional and interest organizations where people developed strong identities with others, might more fittingly be called communities than could geographic places.

Still, localities had problems to be solved, from provision of water and garbage services to maintenance of law and order. For this reason the view of community as a concrete collectivity of people with high commitment and its own unique norms that governed the collectivity was abandoned in favor of an "interactional field" approach, which emphasized community as a place where different degrees of interaction took place among individuals and organizations, but which did not necessarily have a complete institutional base or an umbrella of norms governing people's lives (Wilkinson, 1991; Kaufman and Wilkinson, 1967). Thus, the community was viewed less as a social system and more as a field where social interaction took place.

Development of the mass society also tended to reverse the manner in which local and national norms were related. Rather than local norms being strong and influencing views of the national culture, the reverse happened. Wilkinson noted that:

> institutions and associations . . . are described as elements of the larger society represented on the local scene. There are values and rules of behavior, but these are rooted more in national culture or in individual and family experiences than in local structure. (1991, p. 34)

A major effect of the trend toward the mass society was the production of much uniformity in the values and norms of the nation as a whole, which in turn permeated communities. The kinds of norms and values that facilitated the working of a hierarchical society (with communities at the lower levels), in which much geographical mobility existed, and in which people's lives were often only temporarily and partially invested in localities were quite different than the kinds that prevailed in the community-control era. To the extent that attitudes and behaviors based in the mass society govern life in Bremer, we expect to find the following conditions:

Achieved statuses are dominate. The selection of people to fill jobs and leadership positions and/or perform community activities is based upon their personal achievements and how well they meet announced qualifications.

Reliance on formal rules and expectations is evident. Expected behaviors are expressed in writing, e.g., city ordinances and organizational rules, as are the penalties for not complying with them.

Universalism governs the making of decisions. People are selected for positions of responsibility on the basis of how well they meet written qualifications expected for anyone who fills the position.

Role expectations are fit to the position rather than the person. If a person is not sufficiently talented or qualified to carry out a task, he or she is likely to be dismissed from the position and another person sought as a replacement.

Role expectations in different spheres of life may conflict. Because the expectations for people in various areas of responsibility are developed more or less independently of one another, those expectations may (but do not necessarily) conflict with one another. As a result, pressure is placed on individuals to decide which expectations have priority. The lack of an overlapping institutional structure makes it difficult to establish or enforce complementary role expectations.

Goals and means of achieving goals are considered separately and goals are generally more important than the means. Goals are deliberately set, which people then attempt to achieve. In a complex world the achievement of desired goals (e.g., profitability) may require means (e.g., firing people) that are considered undesirable, yet necessary.

People's obligations toward one another are precisely specified and limited. People's obligations for work and other activities are considered contractual matters, and are often the subject of extensive negotiation prior to deciding to take on a responsibility. Such efforts contrast sharply with agreeing to do something while having only a vague idea of the amount of effort involved, or how much effort one is willing to commit to it.

Rational connections between goals and means are considered an appropriate guide for correct behavior, even though the process may ignore previous or traditional ways of doing things.

Relationships are more secondary than primary. People are less likely to know histories of individuals, to feel obligations that are diffusely oriented toward other people, and to know one another as personalities. Terms such as "Mr." or "Dr." are more likely to be used than are affectionate names or titles such as "Skip" or "Doc."

Emotional involvement in day-to-day interactions is very limited. People are known by one another in limited ways, and emotional or affective considerations are considered inappropriate in day-to-day interactions.

Formal sanctions are relied on for punishing inappropriate behavior. Because informal sanctions (such as ignoring people) cannot be counted on to produce feelings of remorse or regret, formal sanctions previously codified (such as fines, suspension, dismissal, or even jail, are more likely to be used to punish undesirable behavior.
tions.

Participation in community activities is voluntary. It is left up to individuals to decide whether they participate in most community activities. Lack of participating will not necessarily generate disapproval.

The kinds of norms and activities described above, which contrast with the ones described earlier for the community-control era, have been described generally by Tonnies as "Gessellschaft" (as opposed to "Gemeinschaft") in nature. Durkheim captured them as the difference between organic and mechanic solidarity (1947). For Hawley it was the difference between corporate and categoric community (1950). The orientations described here are the kinds of behaviors and attitudes expected to produce efficiency and effectiveness in hierarchical organizations where people must work with others whom they know relatively little about.

To the extent that the mass society heavily influences behavior in Bremer, we would expect many written rules, universalism in how decisions are made, an achievement orientation to govern decisions on who does what, etc. Our study of Bremer was aimed in part at determining the degree to which these kinds of orientations prevailed over the ones described earlier as stemming from the community-control era.

However, in our view it was not sufficient to limit our search to determining which of these orientations were most prevalent, and the reasons why. Another change in societal social organization, the shift towards an information era, is once again reshaping relationships in the larger society, and it too may hold implications for local community.

Information Era

Fundamentally, the information age results from the substitution of information for time, energy, labor, and other resources in the production of goods and services (Dillman, 1985; Dillman and Beck, 1988). This idea is deceptively simple. When a manager or innovator looks at how to save money, produce a product for less, or expand a market, he or she can focus on many distinct issues, for example:

- Warehouses can be mostly eliminated by insisting upon coordinated, just-in-time delivery.

- Equipment can be retooled very quickly by computers and software to provide many versions of a product, and production runs of dozens or even single-digit quantities become profitable. In the past the difficulty of retooling meant that only large numbers of a standard product could be produced efficiently.

- With the increased ability of computer software, precision tooling of equipment, and other automation, far fewer people are needed to produce virtually all products.

- Multiple pricing structures and purchase requirements can be used to sell a product cheaply to people who won't buy it otherwise (e.g., air travel) and to sell it at a higher price for people or businesses who cannot plan ahead.

- Being able to figure out exact stress points in products makes it possible to remove hundreds of pounds of metal from cars, and the development of new alloys and plastics make it possible to remove additional weight.

- Farmers can grow specific crops for targeted markets rather than a general commodity aimed for a general market.

- Knowledge of changes in market prices and condition, as well as the ability to act on that knowledge, is available as quickly to people in remote areas as to those who are centrally located.

- Equipment can be designed to recognize different languages and respond accordingly, reducing language barriers between countries.

In each of these instances, information is being substituted for other resources. The marriage of computers and high-speed, high-quantity transmission capabilities means that coordination, precision, and production capabilities unthinkable only a decade or so ago now are routine. This substitution is the driving force behind companies' being able to out-source the production of component parts that require tolerances to the thousandths of an inch, resulting in their fabrication in countries throughout the world. Without fiber optics, the low-cost long-distance communication it facilitates, and the bringing of computer capabilities to individual workers, the global economy could not develop.

The information age directly attacks the essence of the mass society—cheap production of goods and services through mass production. It is bringing about a mega-shift in jobs, structures, and just as inevitably, individual behaviors and attitudes. The exact nature of such changes in people's orientations, however, is not yet clear. The development of computer abilities to manipulate enormous quantities of information and to transmit those large quantities of information large distances quickly and at low cost is essential, and these interconnected dynamic forces shape the information age.

One of the most obvious and important changes being fostered by the information age is the change in labor force composition. Agricultural employment has declined from about 50 percent of the work force in 1980 to less than 2 percent today. Manufacturing employment has dropped from about 45 percent in 1920 to just over 20 percent today. In contrast, the segment of the U.S. labor force employed in "information knowledge and education" jobs has risen from about 15 percent in 1960 to nearly 55 percent today (Cleveland, 1985). The person who cannot operate a computer in his or her work and thus be able to manipulate information quickly has become an exception to the norm, much as a telephone operator in front of a switchboard became obsolete during our transition to a mass society.

To equate information jobs to personal-service jobs, as is sometimes done, misses the point of the transformation that is taking place: there is an increasing portion of the population that is handling information—absorbing it, reorganizing it, and adding to it in a creative way that enhances value. These jobs are important because information is being substituted for other resources in production processes. These figures don't mean that agriculture and manufacturing aren't important—they simply mean that we are substituting information for other components of production in large amounts, and it takes a lot fewer people to directly produce products.

The implications of these three eras for many social and economic activities are shown in Table 3.1, where the dominant forms of activities, shown at the left, are specified for the three eras, beginning with labor force trends already described (Dillman 1990, 1993).

We expect that the markets for local products change as a result of these developments, from local and regional in the community-control era to national during the peak of the mass society and now to worldwide. This change is central to why there has also been a dramatic shift in product orientation. At one time handcrafted products dominated the market, and then the mass production of thousands and thousands of identical products, from which the mass society draws its name, dominated. Now, through computer software and rapid communication, which shorten the time between ordering and delivery, products are produced in very small production runs of dozens or fewer—increasingly, it is possible to do production runs of one or two on an as-needed basis and deliver them to customers everywhere.

Whereas the dominant feedback for improving production was once received from friends and neighbors, in the mass society it came from the organizational hierarchy and was often a slow and tortuous process. Decisions had to be made about which of many alternative designs would best, on average, meet customer demand, and then, through marketing, that product was actively promoted to all consumers. In the information age, the emphasis is on individual consumer reactions, illustrated best perhaps by the "bar code." In the mass society, large manufacturers and distributors could often compel retailers to provide a certain amount of space on their shelves to carry their product line. In recent years retailers could bring printouts back to them showing the shelf turnover for each individual product as well as profit/loss. As a result it became necessary to negotiate for each individual product and to provide different products for different stores in a chain. To a considerable extent power shifted from the manufacturer to the consumer through the bar code check-off that gave regular reports of which products were selling how fast in which stores.

The time orientation to tasks has also changed. Whereas planning and implementation of ideas were once done in relation to the regularity of seasons and years, during the mass society the time orientation was shortened to correspond more closely to weeks and months. It did not take as long to plan and carry out new ventures. Now, in the emerging information era, the urgency of hours and minutes is often felt. The time required for carrying out projects tends to be budgeted in hours of people's time rather than the months it will take. Communication by fax, modem, and even two-way video, as well as the production of information by quick computer runs, makes it possible to start and complete projects in the time it used to take to make the decision to undertake a project. "It's in the mail," or "It'll take a couple of weeks to run this up to the top" (of the hierarchy) are no longer acceptable reasons for delay of decisions. Many of the changes toward fewer levels of management and development of lower-level quality circles that are empowered to review information and make decisions reflect this changing orientation toward time.

The most highly valued work skill for the average worker, when the U.S. was predominantly an agricultural nation, was physical strength in combination with a work ethic. It is hard to imagine farming and much of the early manufacturing being done efficiently without this combination of work skills. In the mass society the most important worker skills changed to assembly line dexterity and the discipline to work long hours on repetitive, often uninteresting tasks. In the information era, the important skills have changed to the ability to manipulate often abstract symbols and the self-motivation to perform such tasks.

Robert Reich, in *The Work of Nations*, has described three types of future jobs: routine work, in-person service workers, and symbolic analysts (1991). Routine work is going to go where wages are lower, and if it is to be kept in the United States, it will happen only with significantly lower wages. The second type of worker is the in-person service provider. There will be a lot of these types of people in the future. How well they are rewarded will depend in large part on the wealth of the people they directly serve. Symbolic analysts are information workers. Fundamentally, they create procedures for pro-

Table 3.1.   Dominant Characteristics of the Three Eras of Social and Economic Organization in U.S. society

Dominant Characteristics	Community-Control	Mass-Society	Information-Age
Occupation	Agriculture and manufacturing	Manufacturing, services	Services and information
Markets for local products	Local and regional	National	Worldwide
Product orientation	Handcraft, limited market	Mass production	Individual, targeted design mkt.
Most highly valued work skills	Craft, individual strength	Assembly, dexterity, following orders	Manipulate symbols (mind work), self-motivation
Most valued production resource	Land	Plant and equipment	Symbolic analyst worker
Form of work organization	Small independent businesses	Large vertically integrated assembly line production	Temporary networked affiliations
Feedback for improving prod.	Neighbors	Organizational hierarchy	The customer
Time orientation to tasks	Seasons and years	Weeks and months	Hours and minutes
Inexpensive tools	Hand tools (e.g., shovel)	Gasoline engine and electric motors	Computers and electric motors
Use of telephone	Local voice (e.g., party line)	Voice, long distance	Machine-to-machine; Distance— mostly irrelev.
Ecology of important relationships	Community, locality, focused	National, organizationally focused	Anywhere, network focused and individually controlled

ducing goods and services and are the creators of "value" in the information age.

An implication of this shift in worker skills is a shift in the most valued production resource.. In the community-control era, land was the most valued production resource—labor was inexpensive, and there was a heavy emphasis on extraction of natural resources as a means of creating wealth. In the mass society the emphasis was on huge production plants and their assembly lines. In the information age the wealth of companies will less and less be reflected in their buildings, equipment, and land; increasingly, wealth will be reflected in the quality of their symbolic analysts.

The most dominant form of work organization is also changing. In the community-control era small businesses predominated because that was about all that the available modes of communication and organization would allow—it was hard to run businesses from afar. The mass society saw the building of large, vertically organized corporations where companies expanded by trying to buy elements of the production chain, so that automobile companies manufactured many of their component parts and had interests in controlling raw-material sources as well. Now, we see a distinctly different kind of work form emerging whereby companies are smaller and develop temporary affiliations with others. Manufacturing, and perhaps more accurately, assembling, companies can depend upon manufacturers of component parts to meet very exacting specifications and deliver them on schedule—faxing and sending software instructions for programming production equipment are possible from virtually anywhere in the world to anywhere else.

The dominant types of inexpensive tools illustrate another aspect of change. Whereas the dominant tool of workers in the community-control era was the handtool, as might best be illustrated by the hand shovel, in the mass society it was mechanical power supplied by gasoline engines and electric motors. An important stage of development in the mass society was when such engines of power became dedicated to certain tasks, to be thrown away with the equipment to which it was a part when the equipment's useful life was over. The computer promises to become the dominant inexpensive throw-away tool of the information age. The largest investment in capital equipment since the early 1980s has been computers, and increasingly they are getting smaller and are embedded in other workplace equipment.

Changes in the dominant use of the telephone undergird these changes. In the first third of this century, the telephone helped farmers through the infamous party line. They could call one another and save enormous amounts of time needed for planning cooperative work efforts, finding out market prices, etc. In the middle third of this century, long-distance telephone, radio, and television contributed to development of the mass society by facilitating the coordination essential for developing large corporations, a development that brought rural America into the mainstream of American society. In particular, development of long-distance voice phone underpinned these new organizational and production methods.

The convergence of advanced computer and transmission capabilities and, in particular, machine-to-machine communication in the emerging information era provide a basis for new forms of effective organizations. Long distance outsourcing and coordination of production activities are predicated upon sending massive amounts of information very quickly between distant locations. Facsimile transmission and electronic mail are now commonplace, and we are approaching the point where about half of telephone communications consist of data rather than voice transmissions.

Finally, the ecology of important relationships has undergone a transformation. In the community-control era the important relationships one had to establish and maintain to be successful were largely locality focused. In the mass society relationships were focused on organizations and were national in scope. Whereas cottage industries were once very important in the United States, where high levels of craft skills resided, during the mass society work was moved away from people's homes to assembly lines in very large plants. A new work form is now emerging with similarities to cottage industries, but also dramatic differences—it is telecommuting, whereby people can work from their homes or small buildings on computers and integrate the product of their work with that of other workers located some distance away. Consequently, networks that involve people and groups that are located quite far apart geographically become important. An important aspect of these new networks is that they are often controlled by individuals and not attached to large organizations.

In this context, the fundamental linkage of rural towns to large cities may be changing. In the community-control era, many rural communities were fairly independent. During the mass society urban centers dominated rural towns. Ideas were developed there, and people in rural communities who were at the bottom of the mass society hierarchy mostly accepted them. The information age introduces the possibility of a somewhat different kind of interpenetration between residents and businesses of rural communities and those in other communities and countries, regardless of size. The information age has made it possible to bypass hierarchy.

The shift away from community-control and now to the information era does not just *make possible* individual shifts in the orientations described above. Instead, it makes them *mandatory* in order to achieve consistency. Thus, the information age implies a mega-shift in social and economic organizations that permeates nearly every facet of life.

Not yet addressed is the question of what attitudes and behaviors are expected to develop as a result of the information age, and how they might differ from either the community-control or mass-society eras. In a sentence, the information age has not yet developed to a degree that such individual orientations can be defined. However, clues exist, and it is to those clues that we now turn our attention.

John Naisbitt describes a result of the advancing information age as the "optional society" (1982). It encompasses the idea that people are no longer compelled to develop either uniform community orientations, as in the community-control era, or uniform national orientations, as in the mass society. Rather, a multiplicity of lifestyles and orientations can develop. People's behavior is constrained neither to a single set of shared community nor to national norms. Therefore, rigid, seemingly blind adherence to a set of consistent community norms or national norms may decrease.

In recent years a trend has developed whereby ethnic and racial groups in the United States reject the idea of assimilation into one national culture. Rather, the idea is promulgated that important aspects of heritage and culture that are different from those of the dominant white culture can persist, while cooperation and consensus can be reached on distinctly national goals and objectives. Development of connections among members of these groups, regardless of geographic locale, is made possible through high levels of frequent communication facilitated by information-age technologies.

Figure 3.2 depicts certain ways in which internal and external community relationships may differ across the three eras. In the community-control era, internal community ties were stronger than vertical ties to the society, and the opposite was true under conditions of the mass society. However, in the information age the possibility exists that national organizations no longer pull out of the community allegiances that occur at the expense of local ties. Indeed, national organizations may themselves be bypassed as local communities gain the capability to interact directly with both nearby and distant organizations they deem relevant. The bypass of national organizations to reach out directly to others offers two possibilities. One is that local organizations may lose their autonomy to these other organizations. The second possibility is that local communities may in

Figure 3.2   General Patterns for Strength and Direction of Linkages Between Local Community and Outside
Organizations in Three Eras

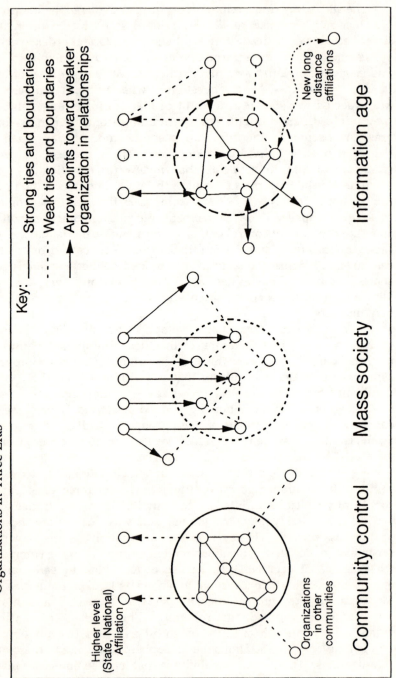

Key: —— Strong ties and boundaries
        ---- Weak ties and boundaries
        ——► Arrow points toward weaker
             organization in relationships

Community control   Mass society   Information age

fact gain control over when and how they relate to others in a way that was largely lost during the peak of the mass society.

The information age is in its early stages, and the implications for attitudes and behaviors are anything but clear. Inasmuch as change typically comes slower at community and, particularly, rural-community levels, we aimed our study of Bremer to focus on how and to what extent changes consistent with those outlined here are occurring in that community. We looked for evidence of

- Increased reliance of businesses and individuals on computers

- Increases in service jobs and decreases in agricultural employment

- Changes in agricultural production from mass production of commodities for general markets to production for targeted markets

- Increased use of telecommunication advances for rapid communication and decision making

- New business practices, groups, and individual behaviors that appeared to come about as a result of the application of information technologies

- Establishment of direct linkages that bypass state or national organizations in reaching out to extra-community groups and individuals

- Individual adherence to norms, the origins of which were neither local nor national, but more associated with individual connections to groups outside the community

We also sought to determine whether any changes in attitudes and behavior were occurring that could be traced to such structural changes. The time in which this study was conducted was the time when information technologies were rapidly penetrating U.S. society and the global economy was developing. Facsimile transmission was mostly nonexistent when we began the study, and nearly omnipresent in society when we finished it. By looking for evidence of information-age development in Bremer, we hope to identify precursors of change so that we might begin to understand how the information age is likely to impact rural America and rural communities in particular.

4

Agriculture: Reconciliation of Making a Living, Government, and a Way of Life

How Farming Used to Be

Even while driving up the long gravel lane that leads to the yellow farmhouse where a retired farmer sits waiting to tell how "it used to be," we observe that farming appears to have been good to him. Aluminum siding covers the structure of the 80-year-old remodeled farmhouse. A late-model pick-up truck sits in front of the well-kept home and a new Oldsmobile can be seen sticking out of the garage. A three-wheel all-terrain vehicle is parked near the front gate, next to which lies an overweight yellow Labrador retriever. The front door opens before we can knock and a large, smiling man in his early seventies wearing blue overalls reaches out with a tanned, calloused hand and says, "Come on in. I saw you coming up the road."

We enter the kitchen door; it is unlikely anyone has used the front door in 20 years. Just inside of the kitchen entrance is a room with a metal shower stall and several freezers and a refrigerator. The shower is a remnant of the past, when the farm hired 20 men during harvest. The men would shower before coming into the house for a late dinner. Today the shower holds a large tin of apples and a source of the yellow lab's plump look—a 50-pound bag of dog food.

In the kitchen a microwave oven is recessed into the cabinet above the range, and a small color television set is built into the wall over the kitchen counter. The television is on and tuned to CNN. It is controlled remotely from a device lying on the built-in kitchen table. The satellite dish in the yard is also remotely controlled.

Bill asks if we would like coffee. As he walks to the water faucet to get the water before placing it in the microwave, he explains that he is "batching it" because his wife took a trip to Seattle to visit her friends and won't be back for two days.

He tells about beginning farming just after he got out of the army following World War II.

> I actually was farming since I could walk. But Dad and his brother really ran the place so I say I started farming after the war. You know the war to end all wars, again. Anyway, I came back and got married and Dad helped us move into the little house down by the highway. Well, it's gone now but it was quite something when we got it all fixed up. You can still see the windmill sitting there but that's it.

Then, talking as he walks into the living room and stops in front of a large picture window, he points with his right hand down the lane to where a large windmill stands. There are no fences or remnants of the small house he talks about. Continuing on about change in agriculture, he turns and walks back into the kitchen.

> We farmed quite a bit different in those days. There weren't air-conditioned cabs on any of the tractors, or radios or TVs in combines in those days. We sat out on the tractors in the dust and it was hard work. Down in the flat we grew hay for the cattle. We ran about 80 head of cows and then we had about 40 sows [mature female pigs] over there next to the barn. We hadn't torn out the orchard yet so we had the orchard up on the hill there. During the bad years, and let me tell you there were a few, we would store the apples in holes in the ground and then feed them to the pigs. It was a lot of work but it got us through. We also had Dad's brother's sheep—he's gone now—but we would move them out in the stubble after harvest and they fertilized [laughs] the ground and then we'd bring them down in the flats and they'd eat there. Yes, you could say times have changed. We have always had a garden. We still do and it made a lot of difference. But now, everybody wants to be a manager. No one wants to farm. You can't even give the produce away. They want it frozen ready for the microwave. Yeah, things have changed.

Bill's description of the Bremer farms 40 years ago is characteristic of comments by other farmers who have retired in the area. The diversification of crops that was a part of Bremer agriculture is illustrated by the variety of stock animals that Bill, his father, and his uncle raised. The same farm at one time supported Bill and his wife and his father and mother, along with his uncle and his wife and children. It has now doubled in size to around 3,000 acres and today supports only Bill, his wife, his son and daughter-in-law, and their two children. The fences that at one time kept the sheep and cattle in their pastures have been torn down, "to let the large combines and machinery have a little room." Seldom in Bremer does one see cattle or hogs or more than four or five sheep on a farm. Those that one does see are generally kept for children so that they can belong to 4-H or FFA. The flour mill that once processed locally grown wheat has long since closed, and the breweries that turned barley into beer are an even more distant memory.

Upon leaving, we notice that the corral next to the large empty barn has been sprayed with nonselective herbicide to keep the weeds down. There isn't a horse in sight. The back of a large silver Gleaner combine can be seen through the open door of the large barn.

How Farming Is Today

Nearly 150 unfenced farms, averaging 1,200 acres, producing mostly wheat, with some barley, peas, and lentils, and a (very) few animals and hobby crops, comprise Bremer's agricultural community. To understand the business of farming on these 150 farms, it is useful to start 2,000 miles east of Bremer, in the other Washington, the nation's capital. Decisions that determine what Bremer's farmers grow and how they grow it are mostly made here.

The productive capability of Bremer's farmers, as well as wheat farmers throughout the rest of the nation, far exceeds the ability of the United States, and world market's ability to consume their product. Over many decades, a system of production controls has evolved whereby farmers hold a certain amount of land out of production each year in return for federal subsidies. The agricultural price supports provided by the federal government tie Bremer farmers to a system that is beyond their control.

Of the farm-related expenditures of the United States Department of Agriculture in 1987, $22 billion of the total of $25,492 billion were price supports (USDA Estimates, 1988). Examination of the average net farm income due to subsidies shows by one calculation that 63 percent of wheat farmers' average net farm income can be attributed to subsidies (USDA, Economic Research Service, 1988). The price-support system is administered by the Agriculture Stabilization Conservation Service, known locally as "the ASCS Office."

Requirements for participation in the price-support program are complicated and frequently change, but in the late 1980s they basically required that a farmer agree to plant only two-thirds of his average acreage of wheat, figured over the previous 10-year period. The farmer must also agree in writing to grow only the crops stipulated by the ASCS. These crops are wheat, barley, field peas, and lentils. Through following these basic regulations the farmer becomes eligible for price supports for his wheat. The first benefits the farmer receives is that he will be reimbursed for a deficiency payment that is the difference between the market price of wheat and a ceiling price set by the ASCS. The total reimbursement payment is limited to $50,000 per farm per year. As of 1989 the ceiling was $4.23 per bushel of soft white wheat. The 1987 wheat deficiency payment to Whitman County farmers was $1.28 per bushel. In 1987, 146 Bremer-area farmers produced approximately 4,077,500 bushels of soft white wheat, much of which was trucked to an elevator located along the bank of the Snake River and barged to Portland. The total money from federal subsidy programs in 1987 for the Bremer area was approximately $5,000,000. If this subsidy money had been divided among all residents of the Bremer community, every man, woman, and child would have each received about $5,000 in 1987 from the farm-subsidy program.

Philip Grant has approximately 1,700 acres of farmland. He is allowed 850 acres of planted wheat to be able to remain in the federal subsidy program. Philip's farm averages 59 bushels per acre of soft white wheat, based on the last ten years of production. His total deficiency payment could have been $64,192 in 1987, except for the fact that a $50,000 limit is placed on each farm. In 1987 he received the maximum payment of $50,000. His yield this year was up slightly to 63 bushels per acre. He was able to sell the 53,550 bushels of wheat he produced at the market price of $2.95, from which he realized $157,972.50. He was then paid the deficiency payment of $1.28 per bushel for each of the 59 bushels per acre in his production base.

Under the price-support program for wheat, if a farmer cannot find a buyer for his crop he may put it under loan to the government and receive his total payment of the ceiling price minus storage costs. The farmer then has the option to sell his crop later or just allow the government to keep the wheat. This option has been taken by a considerable number of farmers in the Palouse area in the last few years, as the large, tentlike structures filled with wheat sitting next to grain elevators indicate. These structures hold the excess grain that cannot be stored in the local grain elevators.

The carryover of unsold wheat increased from less than one billion bushels in 1980 to over two billion bushels in 1986 (Washington Agricultural Statistics, State of Washington, 1986-1987). The carryover was due to several factors, including the increased yields of the type of wheat grown in the Palouse. While the national average yield of wheat in 1985 was approximately 35 bushels per acre, in the Palouse the average was over 57 bushels per acre and increased to 65 bushels per acre in 1986; the national average increased only to 38 bushels per acre. This high yield is due to several conditions ranging from climate to better varieties developed specifically for use in the Palouse.

No family or aspect of life in Bremer is left untouched by wheat and the government program that supports its production. Understanding agriculture and the act of funding is critical to understanding life in Bremer. What at first seems beyond the control of the people of Bremer is also, in important ways, outside the control of people in the big stone USDA building on Independence Avenue in Washington, D.C.

The Act of Farming

Growing a crop of wheat typically begins in the fall just after the harvest is finished. The yellow stubble is tilled under or burned off and any land left fallow over the summer is harrowed. Large dark dust clouds covering the horizon indicate the lack of moisture in the topsoil after the typically dry summer. A big late-summer rain may bring three-tenths of an inch, if it rains at all. Dust clouds move the topsoil from place to place as the fall winds pick up the fine particles of soil and move them miles away. The rolling hills that in the spring looked green and smooth are now mostly a faded yellow, the wheat stubble covered by a fine gray dust.

Yellow Caterpillar tractors can be seen pulling large white tanks containing liquid fertilizer with 40-foot booms on them as the fields are prepared for the planting of winter wheat and winter barley. Occasionally one is confronted with the eerie sight of a huge dust cloud that moves methodically across a field and completely obscures the tractor and tillage complement that create it. The seed is dropped into the soil by drills pulled around and around the steep hills. Seeding is a highly skilled task done only by those who are very familiar with the drills and the terrain. A plugged drill can mean a loss of several hundred bushels of grain, not to mention a farmer's reputation, and once the fall rains begin it is impossible to go back into the fields to pick up those places missed in the seeding. They are left for every friend and neighbor to see, many of whom are not at all reluctant to remind the farmer of his error.

Fall rains are a necessity. Otherwise, the wheat will not sprout and begin to send down roots so critical for next spring's growth.

Farmers wait anxiously for the rains to come. When planting is past and the rains do come, farmers watch just as anxiously for seedlings to emerge and the field to take on a uniform green cast visible from the roadways, indicating no error in planting and the growth of vigorous seedlings that will survive the winter, ready to push down their roots and draw out the moisture needed to produce next year's crop. Seventeen to 20 inches of rain per year is enough to produce a bumper wheat crop, but leaves none to be wasted. Timing is critical.

Winter is a time for repairing machinery—virtually every farmer has a well-equipped shop—and worrying about the weather. Cold weather, with temperatures near zero and without a snow cover over the emergent seedlings, will kill the wheat. Too much snow, on the other hand, will smother it. A period of high temperatures will bring wheat out of dormancy; too much freezing and thawing followed by a sudden freeze will kill it. Then there is the concern with winter rain. Most rain comes in the winter, as storm after storm comes off the Pacific Ocean, dropping the majority of its moisture in the Cascade Mountains, but saving enough for Bremer and next year's Palouse wheat crop. Year in and year out this expectation of sufficient moisture is almost always met.

The way the rain comes, however, is a different concern. In a good year the storms are spaced throughout the fall and winter and produce snow in the winter months, which melts gradually in February, revealing a uniform carpet of green wheat. A bad winter will see no snow at all. Sometimes events converge to produce a disastrous winter. Fields that are saturated from heavy rains freeze and are covered by deep snow. When warm Chinooks blow from the west and the spring melt begins, it may happen all at once. Warm winter rainstorms push through the region one after another, resulting in overwhelming erosion. In the course of a few days the fields thaw, with both soil and water being pushed into tributaries of the Palouse River system. Sometimes the erosion appears mostly as rills, small ditches no more than a foot apart, as precious water and soil drain from the long slopes. Occasionally, departing water cuts through the deep loess soil, forming gullies several feet deep. Worst of all are the occasional soil slips whereby a very steep slope may become completely saturated with water and suddenly hundreds of tons of soil may slip dozens of yards down a hill. The severe erosion fills ditches along roads and requires regular cleanings by county road crews. The most visible consequence is when the normally quiet, clear waters of the Palouse tributaries turn to a chocolately brown and dump soil into the Snake River. The sight of this erosion has led some to observe that the Palouse ships its bounty to the river twice each year—first in spring as soil and later in summer as wheat. Eliminating the first and maintaining the second is a major worry for all those associated with Palouse agriculture, of which Bremer is one small part.

Soil erosion is a concern of farmers who, for the most part, feel they are doing all they can to control erosion—likewise for an agency of the federal government, the Soil Conservation Service (the SCS), whose employees feel that more can be done. Many techniques are tried; one of them, no-till agriculture, relies on very large drills that plant wheat directly into the untilled soil left from the previous year's crop. Use of no-till drills requires the largest tractors available to farmers in the Palouse and leaves weed control to the use of herbicides dropped from the yellow airplanes, which create their own problem when washed off the untilled ground and into the river system. Another technique, minimum-till, requires turning soil over only partly with plows in the fall, thus leaving stubble on top of the soil as a retardant against run-off. Other methods are frequently tried and farmers receive government payments for the use of good management practices. Perhaps the biggest barrier to erosion control is what brought the first settlers to the Palouse—its deep loess soil. Past erosion and many, many years of future erosion will not reveal the basalt rock that undergirds the Palouse hills. Also, increased fertilization and better wheat varieties and other management practices result in higher yields, even while soil is being transported to the rivers in enormous quantities. Further, all evidence of the winter erosion, and even gullies a few feet deep, can be erased from memory with one pass from a yellow Caterpillar and the large tillage implement it pulls. Out of sight, out of mind.

As the snow melts and the frost leaves the ground, the farmers are back working the fields. The winter wheat that had been covered by snow can now be seen as a brilliantly green carpet covering the rolling hills. While the weather warms, spraying is done to keep weeds out of the wheat and barley. Spring barley is planted now, and by mid-April all of the grain to be harvested in fall is in the ground.

In May and June, the aesthetic side of Palouse agriculture becomes evident. The few remaining pastures and fields of spring-planted crops turn green. Now, without the benefit of more than an occasional shower, farmers can be assured of a crop. It is the winter rains, the ones that produce the deep rills of erosion, that guarantee the summer crop.

Part of being a Bremerite is appreciating the consummate beauty involved in the making of the harvest. In June, the barley and wheat "head out" and the westerly winds produce ripples, much like waves in an ocean, that continue as they cross the grain-covered slopes. It is possible for an observer to stand and watch a single wave move a mile or more from one end of a field to another. Most remarkable of all is the realization that within a period of three to four weeks the dark green lightens, turns yellow, and finally becomes a dusty gold, leaving no one wondering about the meaning of the expression "Palouse Gold." Peas, barley, lentils, and the drying of pastures from lack of rain turn the entire Palouse into the brownish fallow fields, where the first of two years of moisture is being saved in some fields to grow next year's crop of winter wheat. In early August, one can stand on a high point and see from horizon to horizon an entire landscape that has changed in one short month from green to the color of harvest, the activity that for one long month will change the complexion of the Bremer community.

During the transition of colors, work has slowed down on most Bremer farms. The family-owned trucks have all been serviced in the family-owned machine shops where the fertilizer tanks are now removed and the tilt beds—with solid racks and the names of the owners written on their sides—are placed on the trucks. Names are painted on the beds so that as the trucks dump their load at the local elevators, the young men who weigh the trucks and calculate the weight of grain for the daily tally will know to whom to assign the credit. Combines are pulled out of the large barns and the headers and reels are removed. New sickles, the cutting teeth, are placed on the front of each combine and any maintenance not finished at the end of harvest last fall is done. By the end of July farmers work late as they prepare for the "mad rush" of harvest.

Harvest has a centralizing focus, the combine. Each farmer has at least one of these giant machines costing as much as $200,000 each. The larger farms will have two or three of them. Occasionally, when relatives or friends harvest together, they take pictures of these technological behemoths crossing fields in formation, and enlarged color portraits are hung in people's homes. Combines of the Palouse are similar to those used elsewhere in the United States, with one essential exception—the four-way levelers. An accommodation to the steep hills, these levelers make it possible for the combine header to hug the steep slopes, cutting each stock of wheat a few inches above the ground while the driver and grain-separation apparatus remain vertical. One of the most chilling reports one can hear is to learn that another farmer has "rolled" his combine. Even with levelers and other safety devices, the job of running a combine is never to be taken lightly and occasional tragedies still happen. Rubber tires being driven on 40 percent slopes create apprehension no matter how good the technology. Learning to master those slopes is not for the fainthearted.

The harvest itself begins slowly. When a farmer thinks that the grain is dry enough to store, a test load will be cut. A coffee can full of that grain is taken to the elevator, where it is tested for moisture. Often there are other farmers waiting to test their grain and they stand around the elevator waiting to see who will be first into their fields. The magical number is 12, the percentage of moisture below which the grain is dry enough to store. With that, harvest begins.

For the next 20 to 30 days, all normal community activity stops. Virtually every farmer will be working 16-hour days that start with weather reports and end with weather reports. Even though the typical forecast is for day after day of cloudless skies and humidity that matches the moisture in the grain and allows for late-night and early-morning harvest, everyone lives in fear of rain. Any hint of clouds on the horizon is watched anxiously. The fear of rain creates concern; a day of rain, even if a shower drops only a few tenths of an inch, produces stress, and two or three successive days of rain (rare as they might be) create terror at the thought of wheat seeds beginning to germinate on the stalks. Each harvest season starts with the hope of a few more bushels of wheat per acre than the previous year, where 70 bushels per acre is not uncommon.

The assignment of who does what job during harvest has long since been determined. Husbands drive the expensive combines; children and city cousins, when old enough, drive trucks; and wives, who often take their turn at driving trucks, become "parts runners" as well as the preparers and deliverers of meals. Grandmothers become babysitters, as do girls in their early teens. Everyone is expected to pitch in and they do, from 5:00 a.m. until 10:00 p.m. or later if mechanical work must be performed. Machinery dealers and their mechanics are on call late at night and, like everyone else, work seven-day weeks. It is unthinkable that anyone in Bremer would take an August vacation.

For these few critical weeks phone conversations are shorter, visits to Bremer fewer, and conversations on the street abrupt, focused on harvest, and quickly terminated. People act as if their livelihood is dependent upon the dusty golden grain from combine spouts, and no one doubts for a minute that it is.

Riding atop his combine in an air-conditioned cab, circling a hundred-acre field, an operator's mind focuses alternately on one problem in particular—cutting wheat at just the right level so that the combine has to handle no more straw then necessary—and everything in general: How many acres will I get done today? Will the truck be able to keep up with me? Will the fuel I ordered last night get delivered? How is this field yielding compared to what it did two years ago? What time is it? When will Sally be here with sandwiches? Sixteen-hour days spent mostly in isolation give operators a lot of time to contemplate important as well as minor details of life. Calculating the minutes it takes to go around a field and the spot where the next dump will have to take place are among them. Much of the operation of the combine becomes a reflex action geared to the sound of the motor, a hum that should not be there, or the uneasy feeling that this area of the field had some fairly deep rills from the winter rains, which need to be avoided. The periodic stops to dump bins full of grain into the truck provide the only breaks in these long and grueling days.

Even during these breaks, the communication above the noise of the combine is mostly by hand signals. When the combine's bin is empty, the truck will be waved away with the expectation of getting it to and from the Bremer elevators as quickly as possible.

Knowing they are expected to hurry, drivers frequently start too fast over the rough terrain only to look in the rearview mirror and see thin sheets of wheat kernels spilling over the sides of the truck. The trucks themselves are noisy, as the sound of the exhaust pipes, which rise above the fenders of the truck as a precaution against field fires, reminds the driver that the responsibility of driving a heavily loaded truck is not to be taken lightly.

Learning how to drive the grain truck off the steep and uneven Palouse hills is a task that is taught at a very early age. Young children sit in the cabs of the large combines with their fathers, older brothers, or grandfathers, and are taught to look at how the hills are formed. One farmer explained to a novice driver:

> To drive a truck off this hill you need to envision how a snowball would roll. You make a snowball in your mind, lay it on the ground and watch the trail it makes as it rolls to the bottom. That is the same line you drive when you are carrying a load of grain off here.

The drive to the elevator is marked by light whiffs of grain sprinkled along the roadway, where flocks of blackbirds have congregated to clean it up. As loaded trucks pass empty trucks, the drivers honk. Not to do so, besides being rude, would convey that the harvest may not be going well at that person's farm. At the least, it conveys that unloading went slowly in Bremer and the driver expects to be greeted with a scowling face of a combine driver waiting impatiently for that truck.

The elevator is where most communication among rural Bremerites occurs during harvest, for there is a perpetual line of trucks waiting their turn to dump their 100-bushel loads and hurry back to the field. The trucks line up at the elevator, where teenage boys supervise the weighing, dumping, and crucial ticketing. Exchanges among the drivers involve a not-always-truthful exchange about how the harvest is going. The question about how much a field is yielding, easily known to the combine driver by the digital readout in the combine, even as the grain is being harvested, produces answers about the prospects of hitting 80 or 90 (it is unnecessary to mention "bushels per acre") when they get to the "good part of the field." Like catching the biggest fish, that will occur on the "next trip." The pink slips held in a magnetic clip attached to the dashboard of the truck, which show the true amount being delivered by each farmer, are never referred to in these exchanges.

As a farmer's truck, with his farm name stenciled on the door or racks, approaches the elevator, the first stop is the scales. There, one of the high school students presses the weight button that records the amount onto that farmer's daily tally sheet. Many farmers have several tally sheets, depending upon how much of their land is rented and owned and whether they operate under more than one family corporation. Once the grain is weighed, the scale person waves the driver to proceed into the elevator. In this dark and noisy cavern several employees, wearing white masks to minimize the dust that they breathe, are simultaneously cleaning up from the previous dump and preparing for the next one. One of the white-masked employees motions the driver forward or backward in order to center the truck's dump gate over the grills in the floor that house the augers that take the grain and move it to the storage areas. When the truck is centered the elevator operator motions with a thumbs-up so that the driver can engage the power hoist to raise the bed and allow the grain to slide into the dark hole below. Once the truck bed is nearly empty an elevator operator takes a wide broom with a long handle and reaches into the truck bed to sweep out the last vestige of this trip's cargo. That completed, the elevator operator motions with a thumbs-down so that the hoist can be lowered and the truck can leave.

The process of dumping wheat reveals one of the games played between the elevator and combine operators. When the truck's dump gate is open, a sample is taken in order to test for foreign matter such as dirt, weed seeds, and other material that is picked up, especially when the combine grain head is run to the ground to pick up wheat flattened by wind, rain, or simply its own weight. This test sample is anticipated by most farmers, who avoid letting wheat contaminated by dirt or weeds be dumped into the rear of the grain trucks. The elevator workers are amply aware of the technique and often try to out-guess the combine operator by testing another portion of the truck.

No aspect of agriculture better illustrates its mass-society orientation than the dump at the elevator. Here every farmer's wheat loses its unique identity as it is combined with wheat from other farms.

No matter how much care might have been used in raising the wheat, here it becomes blended with everyone else's crop, and the pink ticket given to the driver as a record of the dump absolves the farmer of all additional responsibility for the wheat he has produced.

It is also here that it makes no difference how much fertilizer was used to grow crops, what herbicides and pesticides were used and in what quantities, or how much soil was eroded to produce them. Nor does it make any difference how many extra trips around the field a farmer made to control the few weeds in the summer fallow or to keep the field looking clean. The customer in a foreign country who uses the Palouse grain is far from the mind of either the farmer, the truck driver, or the elevator operator. The important competition among farmers is the highly coveted bushels per acre. If they have done well, word will get around. When winter comes, harvest is complete and the books are balanced. Privately, farmers total the monetary value of their year's work. The community knows relatively little about individual fertilizer bill, which, for a 2,000-acre farm, might reach over $30,000 per year; nor does it know how much a farmer delivers to the elevator, where total bushels are divided by number of acres harvested to derive a single indicator of "my yield this year was 62.8 bushels per acre," thus providing a basis of comparison with other Bremer farmers. And each farmer knows that this yield per acre—and not his profit—is the one indicator that makes a difference on the all-important yield base on which government price-support payments are based.

There is not enough room in Bremer's elevator for all of the wheat produced by Bremer farmers: some goes to nearby elevators. In a good year, when elevators are full, grain is dumped on the ground, and again both farmers and elevator operators hope that fall rains will not come before trucks have hauled it to the river, where its trip through the dams of the Snake and Columbia rivers and its oversees trip will begin.

Farmers move quickly from harvest to plowing their fields in preparation for planting next year's wheat crop. There is more time now to stop for coffee in Bremer, discuss prospects for the local football team, and talk about the need for rain, the ultimate contrast to the hope of last month for dry harvest weather.

The harvested grain is handled by a local grain cooperative of which each farmer owns a part. Each farmer has an option to sell his grain personally or to have the manager of the co-op handle the transaction for him. The farmer is charged for storage of the grain not sold and for shipping to the Portland, Oregon, docks about 300 miles down river. Most farmers watch the price of grain on the open market and sell around October or November. The reason they sell during this period is not because grain has reached its peak in price (which it generally does around the first of the year or later) but because their fertilizer and other farming bills are due in the early winter. These bills range from $15,000 for a small farm of about 800 acres up to $100,000 for a large farm of over 5,000 acres.

Because a majority (66 percent) of the Bremer farmers buy their farm supplies in Bremer, it is important for the overall good of the community to make sure that their bills are paid in a timely manner. Yet selling at a time when the market is not at its peak means the farmers do not maximize their returns. This pattern of buying and selling is currently being challenged by some of the younger farmers. There have recently been a few farmers (8 percent) who have begun to play the futures markets individually. They buy futures, gambling that the price will go up and they will make more money.

Community Control of Bremer's Agriculture

Farmers are very conscious of what their neighbors think about how they farm. As one young farmer related, "How I completed the edges of a field was very important." To retain moisture in the soil, the farmers leave fallow, soil that does not have any crop planted on it, for one year. This portion of the land is rod weeded, using a large machine with rods running about three inches under the soil to pull out all of the weeds in the field and seal moisture in the soil by breaking the potential for capillary action that allows moisture just below the surface to evaporate. The operator of the caterpillar tractor pulling the rod weeder attempts to get as close to the edge of the field as possible. The edge of the field, or property line, is defined by a small row of rye grass, cheat grass, and wild roses. If a farmer is good in the eyes of the rest of the community, his field is weeded as soon as any weeds show and his edges are straight and even.

The young farmer explained:

I was having coffee at the local cafe when another farmer and his wife sat down beside me. We talked about the lack of rain, how dusty it was, and the difficulty of getting parts, and then they explained that they had seen me weeding. As the farmer explained, "You're not doing too bad, but I can see you are still getting used to the weeder. Now, after you've done this for 20 years you'll be able to clean your edges up."

The point of the conversation was to let him know that although his edges were not as even as they should be, it was okay for now because he was new to this type of farming, but he should concentrate on making the edges better or more even. This focus on neatness and what the neighbors think has a great deal of influence on how farming is conducted in the Palouse. The group orientation and the community-control mechanisms place a great deal of pressure on farmers to follow suit when it comes to farming.

When the farmers were asked who most influenced them to use a particular tilling method, 40.1 percent said their neighbors were the most influential. When asked, "Who would most influence you not to use a particular tilling method?" only 9.4 percent said their neighbors. These two findings illustrate the conflict between the community-control era and the mass society. In the community-control era one would expect to find the farmers relying upon one another for advice and directions on how to use a new method of farming. We do find that, yet at the same time, less than 10 percent of the farmers say their neighbors are most influential. Instead, an agent of the mass society, the university, is seen as the most influential in convincing farmers not to try a particular method of farming.

How do the two types of orientations exist simultaneously? At the level of personal interaction—that is, "How does my farm look to other farmers?"—the farmers in Bremer are very much influenced by the community. If the field, just as the yard at home, is unkempt, it is a negative reflection upon the farmer, his family, and his ancestors. As noted previously, when Bremerites speak of other Bremerites they speak in terms of the parents, grandparents, uncles, aunts, etc. Not to have a clean-looking farm would reflect poorly upon not only yourself but the other family members. As one farmer said, speaking about another's farming operation:

> He works hard, maybe not quite as hard as his dad did, but he's always out there working. I get up and you can hear the cat starting. He's always the first into the elevator with the first load of grain during harvest and the last to leave the field at night. Although his grandfather—now that was a working man—he'd farm all day, come home at night and tend his orchard (it used to sit on the hill there) and then go to town and sit on a board meeting several times a week. Now that man was a worker.

The Risk of Rape and Green Manure

Farming in Bremer is not just raising grain, selling it, and replanting for the next year. How one goes about farming has as much influence on one's standing in the community as how much money one makes. Risk taking is seen as illogical, especially since many of the farmers in the Bremer community have small test plots on their own land. To try something totally new places farmers in a position to be embarrassed in front of neighbors. One community-control mechanism that works to give farmers information about others is the practice of Sunday drives during slow times of the growing season. One wife explained:

> We work on the farm all week and then Sunday after church we take a drive. Where do you think we go? We drive around and look at how the other farmers are doing. Craig is always stopping and pointing and saying how stupid that farmer is because he is doing one thing or another. Like last year Ralph tried growing some rape. He got so much flack that I bet he doesn't try that again.

The fact that the local Bremer farmer keeps very close track of what his neighbors are doing is also reflected in the spring work. Depending upon the weather, the farmers begin in the fields in early- to mid-March. The farmers watch one another to see who will be the first in the field. A certain respect is given to those that push to be the first in the fields, although it is possible that the person who first gets in the field will get his equipment stuck in the soft north sides of the steep hills. This orientation reflects the community-control mechanisms that influence any change in agriculture in the Bremer community. To take a risk, trying something such as a new crop, or a new farming technique, places one in jeopardy within the community. If the risk fails, it is known by the total community. This makes it difficult for farmers to change.

The risk of trying new crops or techniques is enhanced by the strong tie to the federal farm-subsidy program. According to one farmer:

> You really have to pay attention to the federal regulations for the federal programs. Your records have to be in good shape. You see, they (the federal subsidy authorities) will fly over your land and take a picture and that is how they calculate whether or not you are within your specified acreage in the program. If you are over they can make you plow it under or drop you from the program. Then you couldn't make it financially.

This example illustrates the tie to the mass society for the farmers of Bremer. Over 80 percent of the farmers in Bremer participate in the federal subsidy program for their grains. When asked if they felt they could survive without the subsidy, only 34 percent said they could. Of those who felt they could survive, the majority (71 percent) were over age 50 and most of those were retired, with their land farmed by their sons or leased to someone else in the community. These data show that of those farmers still working at farming, two-thirds feel they could not make a go of it if they did not have the subsidies from the federal government.

These ties to the mass society are not the only force that is outside the control of local Bremer farmers. The nearly mono-crop production regime that takes place in Bremer has forced the farmers into a position where they rely totally upon outside agencies to market, sell, and transport their grains.

Keeping the Land in the Family:
Lawyers and In-Laws Don't Mix

Most farms are operated by a family member. Over 30 percent of the farms in Bremer are incorporated, but only 3 percent of these farms allow the owning of stock by people outside the family. Farm prices are difficult to establish because land seldom comes up for sale. Land that is available is generally leased out to local farmers. The negotiations that take place over land are indicative of the community-control era.

One instance of land that is about to become available involves Fred Hetzler, a farmer in his late fifties, who is about to retire. He farms approximately 800 acres adjacent to where his father and grandfather farmed before him. His farm is reminiscent of the traditional farms. He raises some sweet clover and alfalfa along with his winter wheat and barley. In the meadow below the prefabricated home are about 40 head of cattle and several large hogs. The original home is located near the corrals in the meadow and now houses a son-in-law and daughter. Hetzler has planned on retiring for the last five years and the other farmers in the valley know he is about to relinquish his land. Instead of placing the farm on the open market, Fred is negotiating with his sister's son, who farms the land adjacent to Fred's which is the original family farm. He wants a cash settlement for the equipment and payments over a ten-year period for the land. The son-in-law doesn't feel the equipment is worth the $50,000 Hetzler is asking but he doesn't want to see the land go to someone else. He says, "With the extra 800 acres I could afford to hire a full-time hired man." Hetzler estimates that his land is worth about $1,000 to $2,000 per acre. As he says, "I'm really not sure what it is worth. It's assessed for about $1,100 an acre, but there just hasn't been any turnover in land lately, so it's hard to say what the market really is."

Hetzler wants the land to stay in the family, but his son-in-law doesn't want to farm, so he either sells or leases the land to his sister's son or puts it on the open market. Farmland in Bremer is generally handed down to the eldest male son. If a retiring farmer doesn't have a son or if the son doesn't want to farm, he will approach a male relative such as son-in-law and see if a "deal" can be worked out for the purchase of the farm. The land often is split with a portion deeded to the daughter and a portion deeded to the son. Land that was part of the "original place" is often the land that is deeded over to the daughter. Most decisions about the farm and its daily operations are made by males.

According to Hetzler, "I've already had quite a few inquiries about it, but I've already planted, so I'm just waiting to see what John [sister's son] can come up with." The orientation toward the group in Bremer makes Hetzler feel guilty that he may have to sell to someone from outside the family or the community. The fact that he wants some things for himself and his wife during retirement places him in a position where he must go against some of the Bremer norms. He has talked of moving away from the area if he sells to someone outside of the community.

Eighty-three percent of the farmers in Bremer have relatives who farmed the land before them. Land is retained in the family in Bremer and the community-control mechanisms make moving land fairly straightforward. The community members of Bremer understand that to retain the family farm, land must remain in the hands of family members (Rodefeld, 1982). But as one retired farmer said:

> It's getting harder to keep it [the land] in the family. We are supporting myself and Margaret [wife] plus two daughters who live outside of the area and my son who does the farming. When I go he'd have to sell because my daughters will want their share of the farm. There just isn't enough money to be able to cash them out.

Although the farmers in Bremer make a good living (per capita income for 1984 was over $13,000), the escalating land prices in the 1970s made it difficult for family members to pay the other family members what the land was worth. For example, if the farm is 1,500 acres, which is just above the average county size, and the land sells for $1,200 per acre, the farm minus the equipment and houses is worth about $1.8 million. When the value of the equipment and the houses is added to this, the farm can be worth around $2.5 million. To pay the farm off in an estate the young farmer would have to pay out $1.875 million to his sisters.

Farms in Bremer vary in size from around 800 acres to over 5,000 acres. Twenty-six percent of Bremer farms are 800 acres or less, 19 percent are 800 to 1,200 acres, 23 percent are 1,200 to 2,000 acres, 28 percent are 2,000 to 5,000 acres, and only about 4 percent are over 5,000 acres. Those farms ranging in size from 1,200 to 5,000 acres are more likely to have a net family income of over $39,999.

Household income, as one would expect, varies with the number of acres farmed. Yet there seems to be a break-off in income at about 1,200 to 2,000 acres. When farmers were asked about their net household income, 43 percent indicated they made $39,999 or more per year. Of those, 31 percent farmed 2,000 acres or less. Of those farming more than 5,000 acres, 1.2 percent made about $30,000 net income per year and only 1.2 percent made $50,000 or more. In Bremer, while acres are thought of as income, overall the data indicate that those who farm average-sized farms have the highest net household income, while those who farm 800 acres or less have incomes around $20,000. These findings seem to go against the notion that if you farm more acres of land you will generate more income. In Bremer the federal grain subsidies dictate net household income more than number of acres farmed.

Land is the basis for agricultural production in the Palouse. If one does not own land, it is very difficult to become involved in agriculture. One farmer said, "If a person had $2 million dollars they would be much smarter to put it in the bank and just draw the interest instead of buying a farm." A person's status in the community is based on whether he or she owns land or just leases. It is one thing for a farmer to lease land if he is a local boy, but if he is an outsider his community status is ranked down with the farm laborers. As one lady, the daughter of one of the original homesteaders, said, "You know Barb, well what can she know. They just moved in five years ago and started farming." This attitude toward outsiders reinforces the value placed on retaining local ownership of the farmland.

Another form of land control is beginning to evolve in Bremer. As young farmers go outside the community to find spouses and then bring them back to Bremer, some of the older family farmers feel threatened with the fact that through a divorce a daughter-in-law could gain some control over the farming operations. To lessen this perceived threat, farmers are giving their sons lifetime leases with a stipulation that the land goes to the grandchildren. In this way if the son divorces, his daughter-in-law holds no title to the land and the family retains the rights to the farm. This instance portrays the influence of a legalized mass-society authority with which farmers must cope (Jansen, 1987). There is a great deal of embarrassment for the family members when this type of land ownership is discussed. It goes against the norm of family being very important to a community member. To use a legalized authority to control family members is in contrast to the traditions of Bremer.

Although lifetime leases are a fact of life in Bremer, the vast majority of married couples have not divorced. Eighty-three percent of adult Bremer residents are married and only four percent are divorced. The problem as seen by farm families and young single farmers is captured by one young male farmer:

> There just isn't anyone to date around here. When a girl reaches marrying age she either is already engaged or she leaves town. I've got where I actually take trips to Seattle trying to meet someone. Although as soon as you tell them where you live they go, "No way I don't want to be stuck out in the middle of nowhere." So what can I do? I have this farm. It's been in my family for 100 years and now I don't have anybody to pass it down to. Sometimes I wonder if its all worth it.

The difficulty of finding mates is a common problem for young males in Bremer. Isolation from other people their age has a great deal to do with why young women do not want to stay in Bremer. One young farmer's wife, from outside Bremer, explained it this way:

> I've been married five years. We've taken one trip. Most of the year he gets up before I do and goes out and sits on the tractor until dark. Then he comes in and doesn't say a word. I know after 14 hours by yourself you get where you aren't used to talking, but gawd I sit here all day with no one to talk to but his mom and sister and I need someone to talk to. In the winter he just sits around and broods about how bad the snow is or the price of barley. He just doesn't take me into consideration at all.

This young woman's story is not unique. The geographic isolation of Bremer places residents in a position where during the working year there is relatively little contact with other community members, especially for younger residents. As the population of Bremer has aged, the young farm women who do not work have become even more isolated. Farmers' wives in Bremer follow a national pattern when it comes to working outside the home. Over 48 percent of the women married to farmers work outside of the home and 5.4 percent of them work outside the community. Of the 32 women who work in Bremer, a majority of the jobs are part-time, while of the four women who work outside the community all hold full-time positions.

Are You with Us or Against Us?
Working with Government Agencies

Traditionally, the basis of personal power for a farmer in Bremer was tied to local authority. Sitting on the board of directors of one of the local churches, the school board, or the grain association was the means by which local farmers gained personal power. Since the evolution of the mass society this has changed. The newer power base is tied to organizations outside the community. One example is the soil conservation district. To sit on the board of directors of the soil conservation district makes one obligated to agencies outside of the community.

The change in the locus of personal power has several effects on the farmers. First, because the power base is located outside the community, the local townspeople do not see the everyday workings of what it is the farmer is doing. This outside obligation is in direct conflict with the need of the community members to know each other globally. Knowing someone in Bremer is knowing not only their occupation and family but also their volunteer associations. Community members who are not part of a particular organization such as the soil conservation district begin to question the community members who do sit on the board. In the words of one local farmer: "You know, you begin to think, Now, who is he representing—those of us here in Bremer or the government and its policies?"

Farmers who are not part of the outside organizations are not alone in seeing a conflict between being a part of the Bremer community and the organizations of the mass-society. Whereas in the community-controlled era the orientation is toward the continued existence of the group, it is not the case in mass society. To get ahead, say, as part of a larger group, it is necessary to focus on the rules as defined by the larger organization. These often come into conflict with the community-control era orientations, where the good of the group is the paramount concern.

Recently, a local soil conservation board member became aware that a local farmer had planted more grain acreage than he was allowed by the federal program. The board member had several options available to him. He could report the failure to meet program guidelines, which he was obligated to do as a member of the soil conservation board; he could speak to the farmer about the overplanting; or he could ignore the behavior. The farmer, who was a member of Bremer but also a representative of an outside agency, decided to ignore the behavior. His rationale:

He'll probably just use it for feed anyway. He's always followed pretty closely the guidelines set and his Dad's been sick so he might just be trying to pick up a little extra. And who can blame him given the circumstances.

This example illustrates the particularism that Bremerites use in dealing with individuals in their community. The board member knew the farmer and his family and felt that because of specific problems facing the family, overplanting onto land stipulated as grassland could be overlooked. While the board member was obligated by the mass-society organization to report the infraction, his obligation to the community and to another Bremerite took precedence.

Face-to-face relationships in Bremer reinforce the value of the community good over that of the outside organization. Although Bremer farmers are still very much tied to the community control, their actual income is dependent upon a mass society and its subsidizing of the grains grown in the area. One farmer explained the importance that the subsidies play in farming.

Under our present system it would be impossible for our farming industry to remain solvent without our federal subsidies. As long as the government controls the markets and the pricing, they are going to have a large part to play in the farm future in the form of subsidies.

As this statement by a local farmer illustrates, Bremer farmers are aware of their direct tie to the federal government. Bremer farmers still believe that they are community oriented and see the outside influence of the federal and state governments as infringing upon their rights as farmers.

Computer Farming: National Networks and Playing the Futures

In their everyday lives the importance of the community and their place within the community are evident in how Bremer farmers farm. As the new information technologies such as personal computers and satellite dishes have developed, farmers in the Bremer community are utilizing them.

A new association of Bremer farmers is a computer club. Farmers use their personal home computers to gather information pertaining to farming and then share this information with each other. The new club is formed similarly to the other volunteer associations in Bremer. Anyone is welcome to attend the meetings, which are held infrequently. At the meetings methods for gathering and evaluating agricultural information are discussed. Local farmers show others how to use spreadsheets for internal management of the farms. Twenty percent of the Bremer farmers owned a personal computer in 1987. A third of the farmers who own a computer are members of a computer network or club.

The primary use of the information gained from the networking is for internal management. Farmers use the information to prepare applications to specific federal subsidy and insurance programs. In the mass-society era we would expect the control of information to be retained by the large corporations and bureaucracies (Goe and Kenney, 1986). In the mass society, information is controlled by large hierarchical organizations that retain information for sale. Yet there are specific traits of the information technology that make the idea of "ownership obsolete" (Cleveland, 1985). According to Harlan Cleveland (1985), information is transportable. He points out that the new ability "to sit in Auckland, New Zealand, and play the New York stock markets in real time" indicates that rural is no longer equated with remote. In Bremer, farmers can now have certain information as quickly as large corporations.

Cleveland also points out that a key trait of information technology is the ability of users to share the information without much cost and without having the information deteriorate with use (Cleveland, 1985). In Bremer we also see examples of information technologies being used by larger corporations to standardize and centralize power. Yet we also see local business owners using the technology to play one corporation against another. One example of how information is being shared with local farmers occurred in the spring of 1988. A computer was placed in a local governmental office with the hope that it would allow farmers without computers to have access to large information bases such as AGNET. Soon after the computer was placed in the office, local farmers found ways to share the information. A LOTUS 123 template developed by the local state land grant university was purchased by one farmer. He copied the template onto a personal disc for himself and then passed the disc on to other farmers in the area. The information, unlike other resources, did not diminish but maintained its usefulness. In this way the information "leaked." Ownership of the disc became blurred and farmers throughout the Bremer area were utilizing the information. The template was developed to allow farmers to calculate their acres for planting according to federal rules for participation in the federal subsidy program. In this way the information became part of the public domain in the community.

This illustration demonstrates how local Bremer farmers use community-control era values to manipulate the rules of the larger society for their own goals of retaining local control. The farmers followed community values by making the information available to everyone. They broke a legal norm of the society, the replication of copy-protected material, but they increased their knowledge about the mass-society program. This example illustrates how the Bremer farmers retained at least a belief that Bremer can still operate in the manner of the community-control era.

The drought of 1988 in the Midwest increased the need for information by Bremer farmers. The December deficiency payment for farmers participating in the federal subsidy program was 7.8 cents per bushel (ASCS, 1988). To participate in the federal program farmers agree to leave one third of their land unplanted. Had the farmers stayed out of the program they would have had an additional third of their crop to sell at record prices. Now the local computer association in Bremer has recently begun collecting current weather information through a down-link system. The information will be used to decide whether a farmer should stay in the program or go out of the program and market all the grain he can grow. Current conditions make knowing the weather in the Midwest and perhaps other countries as important for area farmers as knowing how to remain in the federal subsidy program.

The everyday interaction patterns of the farmers still reflect the primary face-to-face interaction of the community-control era. At the same time, the less personal, secondary interaction with large governmental organizations is the norm when it comes to the growing of mass-produced grain. The use of personal computers has added another dimension to the interaction patterns of Bremer farmers. Previously they looked to local farmers, extension agents, and local universities for new information on farming. Now they interact with computers that contain data bases. This has a multiplication effect on the farmers, especially on those who are currently involved with other mass-society era organizations. The emerging values and orientations of an information era place the Bremer farmer in a position of working under a variety of rules at the same time.

As farmers begin to participate in the information age they use various technologies to maintain information on the futures markets, weather patterns, price fluctuations, and equipment sales around the country. One farmer has two mobile telephones in his farm truck. His horn blows when he has a call, and if it is his broker he is then able to call his wife at the main farmhouse, who can use their computer to look up information critical to deciding whether they should buy, sell, or retain their current level of activity in the futures market. The information enables the farmer to make decisions independently of how his neighbors are making their decisions. A major difference in the way this farmer is doing business is that it is anonymous. The rest of the community is not, as yet, able to monitor the interaction. In the past, citizen's band (CB) radios were the only form of communication between the farmer out in the field and the main farmhouse. These radios used public airwaves and were frequently monitored by others with similar equipment. A majority of the farmers in Bremer have CB radiosin their trucks, combines, and Caterpillar tractors.

During the grain harvest of 1985, a farmer was using a CB radio to tell his truck driver how to get to where the grain combine was parked. It was indicated by the conversation that the combine driver could see the truck driver but the truck driver was unable to see the combine driver. The combine driver told the young truck driver to go slowly and drive at the edge of the field they had just harvested. The truck driver misunderstood and drove at a fairly rapid rate through the center of the field. The combine driver began yelling into the CB radio for the driver to stop. The truck driver failed to respond and soon over the radio came a loud voice swearing at the truck driver. It became evident a few minutes later that the truck was stuck in a ditch in the middle of the field. The fact that other Bremer farmers were listening to the exchange was revealed when, during a rain break, the farmers were having coffee in the Bremer cafe. One of the farmers turned to the abusive combine driver and simply said, "You were a little rough on that truck driver the other day, weren't you?" The seven farmers, two laborers, and two wives who were sitting at the long table smiled and turned their heads down as the combine driver explained that it was hot, his equipment had broken down earlier in the day, and this was just one more frustration of a bad day. The explanation fit into the knowledge the others had of his day and nothing more was said of the incident.

Anonymity of action makes it difficult for the community to retain control over its members. As some of the farmers bypass the local cooperative grain-grower association to sell their grain, another community-control information channel is blocked. The local grain-grower association is managed by a local man, and his wife is the bookkeeper and secretary. Business is conducted here as it is in the bank. Transactions are conducted in an open office with community members who hold the community-control-era values. This enables information to be moved into the local informal network, the grapevine, where most of the community members know what takes place at each transaction.

The use of personal computers has enabled a few farmers to monitor storage fees at elevators in the region and now have their grain moved to where they can get the lowest prices. This is usually done through another agency so that the informal information network of Bremer does not learn that a local farmer is moving grain and the income that goes with it outside of the community.

Although these changes in how agriculture is conducted influence the knowledge available to the total community, the farmers have retained the norms and orientations associated with the community-control era. As a way of life the daily interaction patterns of the agricultural producers in Bremer have remained rooted in the norm that the good of the group is paramount.

Conclusion: Living in Three Eras

Agriculture in Bremer, at one level, is characterized well by concepts of the mass society. Mass production methods are used to grow a single major commodity on virtually all of the farms. Although small grain has been grown and shipped out of the region from early times, the growing of multiple crops, local processing (the flour mill) and the selling of locally grown food within the community have virtually disappeared. The choice of crop (wheat) and the acres planted are mostly out of the hands of individual farmers, being decided by the rules of a farm-production program operated from the nation's capital.

Much like in Henry Ford's mass production of cars, there is no individuality to the grain products once they are harvested. When wheat leaves an individual farm it is blended in elevators with the product of other farms, and any identity with the producer is lost. It is trucked to the river, where it is further blended with wheat from other communities, and loaded into barges for shipment to Portland where it is likely to be exported as a raw commodity. The end use of a farmer's crop, as well as the appropriateness of his wheat for that end use, is unlikely to be known by the producer or to be relevant to making any future production decisions. Plans for next year's production begin with the question, Are there any changes in program rules, and how many acres of wheat can I plant?

At the same time, agricultural production in Bremer is heavily influenced by community-control processes. Farmers are deterred from trying new ideas by concern over what their neighbors will think. It is common to go for Sunday afternoon drives to see how everyone else's crop is doing, and favorable or unfavorable comments are widely shared throughout the community. Neighbors are sensitive to and comment on a farmer's ability to keep the edges of his fields neat, whether he is a "hard worker," and whether his work gets done in a timely manner. Owning land is important to how one is viewed in the community, and when land is about to be sold, strenuous efforts are made to keep it within family and community. Particularism prevails in decisions, even the enforcing of compliance with the mass-society-oriented government farm programs.

The information era is attaining a foothold in Bremer as farmers have begun utilizing computers, and curious combinations of telephone/computer connections have developed to facilitate participation in commodity markets where decisions must be made in minutes. However, for the most part these efforts to adopt new technologies have not yet brought about significant structural change in the Bremer community. Agriculture remains the dominant occupation, and land, rather than symbolic, analyst-type skills, remains the most valued production resource. Researchers are beginning to admonish farmers to consider growing different varieties of wheat in different ways (Pomeranz et al., 1987), and the state Wheat Growers Association was soon to start advocating the growing of limited quantities of hard (rather than soft) white wheat and other changes to begin responding to specific targeted market opportunities. Nevertheless, as the 1980s decade came to an end, we could find no evidence that Bremer's farmers were starting to think that way, or to develop the direct contacts with consumers that might be expected in an information era.

In sum, agriculture, the main source of economic livelihood for Bremerites, clearly manifests attributes that characterize a mass society. These attributes are, however, shaped and occasionally controlled by social processes more characteristic of the community-control era. The interplay between these quite different forces is even more intensely demonstrated in the other businesses of Bremer, the topic to which we now turn.

5

Bremer's Other Businesses: Each in Its Proper Place

A few minutes after ten on any weekday morning, the doors of most of the businesses on Bremer's Main Street open and people exit as if cued by a conductor. The Main Street business people are going for their morning coffee. Many carry their own coffee cups, which they will fill free-of-charge at the insurance office. Others will sit and talk at the tavern/cafe, paying on the honor system for the coffee they drink. The three cars that pass by drive the length of Main Street, turn and then park in front of the tavern/cafe. The drivers know that little, if any, business will be done until the coffee break is over.

This morning, as the drivers leave their cars, keys still in the ignitions, they stand waiting for those stragglers who are on their way to the tavern/cafe. Greetings take several minutes, even though all of the parties will soon be sitting side-by-side talking over their coffee. By 10:30 the employees and owners have left in a group to return to work. This ritual will be repeated at 2:30 p.m., just as it has in past years and seems likely to continue for years to come.

The traditional patterns of behavior that are exhibited by morning coffee are duplicated in the everyday activity of doing business in Bremer. These businesses, stretched along the town's Main Street, include one bank, the hardware and implement dealer, the appliance store, the drugstore, two insurance agencies, the telephone and cable television company, another farm-implement dealer, the clothing store, two grocery stores, the tavern/cafe, the grain-growers' office, and three fertilizer and farm-supply stores.

These businesses make up the heart of the downtown of Bremer. Through examining representative businesses we will explore normal behaviors and whether these behaviors can be accounted for by the model posited in Chapter 3. We begin with how the residents of Bremer see their Main Street.

Main Street

A sign on Main Street reads, "Welcome to Bremer, Home of the Bulldogs, State Basketball Champions 1942, 1946, 1952, 1953, 1961, 1963, 1965, 1966, 1972, 1975, 1980." As one walks down Main Street, the traditional rural character of Bremer is inevitably apparent. Today, two pickups with diesel tanks fitted into their beds with mud splattered on their sides sit side-by-side facing opposite directions in the middle of the street as the drivers talk to one another. A large Oldsmobile and a Chevrolet sedan, just a year old, move slowly down Main Street, their drivers looking for parking spots where they don't have to parallel park. The outside of the businesses, many of which show the effects of the hot, dusty summer sun, reflect the town's name, most having "Bremer" written somewhere on their signs.

An unexpected sight along the north side of Main Street is a small flower garden situated between the single-story buildings lining the street. The daily care given to the garden is obvious, and near the back of the garden space—beyond the walkway, flowering roses, and begonias—is a wooden arch. Nailed to the small arch is an award plaque from Better Homes and Gardens. The award was given in acknowledgment of a beautifying flower garden in a small American town. This is not a concrete monument once built, forgotten, and neglected. The garden space reflects local community pride and contributes to the pride Bremerites have for their community.

A resident of Bremer sees Main Street as "pretty quiet, clean, and having a good variety of stores and services for a community this size." Business leaders are seen as "friendly and working hard to meet the needs of the customers." Yet, the desire to benefit from all that society has to offer is reflected in the residents' concerns about the same businesses.

Complaints include the fact that "grocery stores close at 5:00 p.m. and are not open on Sunday, while the other stores close at noon on Saturday." Residents know that prices are higher than those they can obtain 50 miles away in Spokane. Reflection of the national changes in employment patterns is illustrated by comments such as, "It is hard for working parents to be able to shop locally because of the store hours."

As residents have become more involved with people outside of Bremer, concerns over the cost of interacting with those people have become a focus for complaints. Some Bremer residents complain that "phone charges are too high, everywhere you call is long distance." Those few residents who live outside the local telephone company's range comment about not being able to use modems on their computers because "it is illegal to use a modem on a party line." The conflicting statements illustrate the ambivalence that exists between residents' desire to maintain their traditional business district and their desire to participate in the mass society with its large variety of goods and services.

The Bremer Bank: Standing in Line
for a Publicly Approved Loan

The Bremer bank provides a striking example of the community's desire to maintain old ways while still providing local residents with modern banking services. The bank is locally owned and controlled. On the right of the entrance stands the bank counter with metal bars separating the clerk from the customer. Old tabulating machines stand behind the clerk, and older men with white hair and bow ties oversee any transaction that is completed in the bank. To the left is a large, air-conditioned conference room that faces Main Street. Large, tinted plate-glass windows allow a soft light onto the deeply carpeted floor, on which stands a long, solid wood conference table with 14 chairs sitting around it.

The bank manager is the son of the previous manager, who managed the bank from 1938, when it was moved to Bremer from a nearby town, until his death in the early 1980s. Bremerites speak of the banker as "hardworking and honest, just like his father." As for the bank building itself, one local farmer told of standing on the road watching the bank, building and all, on the bed of a flatbed truck in the 1930s: "We were just waiting for the bandits to come out of the hills and take the whole bank, building and all." It didn't happen and the bank was set down on Main Street, where it has stood for over 50 years.

Two years ago the bank remodeled and put in a computer. Up to this point banking accounts were handled by the name of the account holder. No account numbers existed. Anyone who tried to transfer funds from another bank to Bremer was likely to be told just to "make up a number if the other bank insists." Monthly statements are not mailed to the homes, residents must come to the bank and pick them up.

Doing business in the Bremer bank follows a tradition that has been in existence since the bank was relocated. To obtain a loan the customer stands in line behind the other customers. When his or her turn comes, it is explained to the bank manager how much money is needed, why it is needed, and when it can be paid back. This transaction takes place in public view. The manager makes the decision about the loan while the customer stands at the window. One young man who wanted to buy a new car was not exactly turned down for a loan; he and the manager went outside to look at his car, where he was told that his car was in pretty good shape and he probably didn't need a loan.

The approval process, though considerably different from those found in urban banks, serves several important functions in the community. First, by having other community members stand and listen to the loan request, all community residents know how their locally owned bank is handling their money. If a loan is turned down, the residents are made aware of the reasons, and the public knowledge of such transactions reinforces the community-held view that the bank and its employees are conservative when it comes to handling money. Through making public any and all bank transactions, the community residents know, as do the local businesspeople, when someone is getting into "financial trouble." This public knowledge is useful because business owners will know that they should watch a particular creditor so that he or she doesn't get "in too deep."

The policy of the bank is to pay low interest rates on personal savings accounts and also to charge low interest rates on personal or business loans. Outsiders do not borrow from the Bremer bank. Decisions on loans are made on how one's family has traditionally paid back loans, whether or not people are borrowing "over their head," and whether a family member will be liable for the loan if the borrower fails to repay it. It is not uncommon for the bank manager to call a young farmer's father to clear a loan. This takes place even though the prospective borrower may be 40 or 50 years of age. Banking is a public function in Bremer and very little of the business is done behind closed doors.

Eighty-three percent of the Bremerites do at least some of their banking in town. They cite these reasons: "my money stays in the community," "the bank is stable, locally owned, and I'm known by bank personnel," "they are honest and they know my signature." Community residents also stress that "they [bank employees and owners] are people in the community." Knowing the bank employees in a variety of roles— bank employee, father or son, community club member, etc.—seems to reflect the basic idea among Bremerites that to trust someone you must know him or her as a complete person. According to one old farmer, "It's just hard to tell how honest someone is by watching them work. But now, if you know how they treat their kids, their wife, and their dog, you know how he'll probably be in the long run."

The Hartford Grocery Store:
Food but No Toothpaste

The Hartford grocery store's exterior is old red brick with large windows facing each street on the corner. The store has been in operation for 19 years in the current location, having been relocated from across the street, where it had been for about 20 years. The front door is covered with local announcements printed on white or colored construction paper. The use of small home computers with graphic packages is evident on the announcements for baby-sitting jobs, school fundraisers, and regional fairs. The inventory is primarily dry goods and some fresh vegetables, with a few meat items. The owner buys meat in the county seat "just for the convenience" of his customers. The other grocery store has traditionally had a small butcher shop, and according to the owner of the Hartford grocery store, "It's always been their job to provide meat." Hartford does not carry over-the-counter drugs, shaving cream, toothpaste, etc., because those items are "what keeps the drugstore open."

The strong group orientation among Bremer businesses is clear in the grocery store owner's refusal to carry products that other businesses sell because if he sold them the other businesses might not be able to survive. This commitment is also evident in an incident that happened when the new owners bought the other grocery store in Bremer. The young couple's freezer broke down, so Hartford loaned them a freezer. As he explained it, "We need young people in business in Bremer and if I can be of help I will." This egalitarian attitude is also a community norm among patrons of the local grocery stores. The retired mayor keeps an account book to be sure that he spends half of his grocery money at each local store. Among the community residents, 70 percent say they make a conscious effort to divide local purchases among Bremer businesses that offer the same products. Ninety five percent say they shop locally first, illustrating the existence of a strong group orientation among Bremer residents. The conflicting orientations of the Bremer residents and the business owners illustrates the difficulty in coping with the forces of different eras at the same time. The community-control based collective orientation is demonstrated by business owners' not selling products that other businesses sell, while at the same time Bremerites express a desire to have their local stores open the same number of hours that larger and more urban stores do.

Ninety percent of the business at the Hartford grocery store is conducted on a charge account system. Charge accounts were traditionally paid once a year after the grain harvest. Upon payment of the yearly bill the customer was given a half gallon of ice cream. Accounts are now paid on a monthly basis, although business fluctuates:

> In the spring things pick up and then by winter it slows down. That young couple down the street [at the other grocery store] are going to be wondering, "What did I do to make everyone mad at me this winter?" It gets slow. The credit will kill him. I don't want to be critical, but I don't know what he paid for it or how much he had to borrow but it'll be tough for them this winter. Before they bought that store they came in and spent three hours with me. I told them what the community was like.

The price of the store was stated in the local paper published in the county seat. This was the first lesson on the lack of anonymity in Bremer for the young entrepreneurs.

The group orientation of Bremerites leaves little room for anonymity. The norm of knowing everyone intimately makes knowing about business activities a necessity. Through a total understanding of all business, family, and personal matters of Bremer residents, it is possible to maintain conformity in behaviors.

As for having problems collecting from all of the charge accounts, the grocer laughs and says, no, he doesn't have many problems.

> Now, I'm lucky because as businessmen we talk to each other. Like, well, if somebody is getting into somebody too deep we'll tell each other and then we tell the person they need to catch up. But that doesn't happen often. Once in a while a new person will come to town and go to work for someone and then you might have them skip out. But that's only happened a couple of times over the years.

The dominance of face-to-face interaction accounts for the ability of the grocer to collect debts owed him by local residents. The mandatory-interaction expectation for Bremerites places pressure on all residents to meet obligations, especially those obligations to other Bremerites. The guilt associated with nonpayment is so strong that residents result to self-punishment. This punishment ranges from self-ostracization to an increased involvement in voluntary organizations. The collective conscience of Bremer makes the use of outside collection agencies unnecessary.

In the center of the store stands a post completely covered with pictures. When talking about his customers Hartford, the owner, points to these pictures of newborn babies, local birthday parties, school graduations, and wedding anniversaries stapled to a supporting beam located near the cash register.

> Those people are loyal. The older people are the most loyal. The younger ones, well, they'll go to Spokane for a loaf of bread. They just aren't as loyal. It's a sign of the times I guess...the young farmers, like your age, they want to live like city people and that means they want a choice of 10 or 20 types of bread and they change all of the time. The older folks—you know what they want so you stock it.

The influence of the mass society is exemplified by the grocer's explanation of why his younger customers shop outside of Bremer. Having been socialized by national news and advertising, the younger residents, according to the store owners, don't see the role of community tied directly to local businesses, as the older residents do.

The Hartford grocery store is undergoing change. The owner has recently cut his orders from four a month to two a month. As he says, "Larger loads mean less freight cost." He now uses an Accuradata machine to transmit his orders over the telephone lines to his wholesaler's main computer. Yet even with the information hook-up over the telephone lines and an increase in the size of orders, he still says:

> We just work together, not against each other. Like I could undercut Roy (at the drugstore) by 30 percent on drugs with the supplier I have now. But that would hurt him so I don't sell the stuff. We work together. It works. Flemington is dying [names several other dying towns], but we are still here because we work together. Now, Reynoldsville, they were bought out by some young Spokane kids; they are all trying to compete and outbid each other. It's killing their town. I don't know what they are thinking about. If I was to start selling drugs and Roy went out of business, that's three jobs. Now where would I be? Those people wouldn't have work so I'd lose three customers. Now tell me, is that smart business for some shaving soap?

Conducting a grocery business in Bremer is filled with conflicting norms and expectations. On one hand, the grocer exhibits a community-control orientation allowing residents to freely charge and carry many of them for months. On the other hand, he is also intimately connected to mass-society expectations. He controls his freight charges through ordering larger orders but less often than in the past through a large national wholesaler. These two conflicting roles create tension between residents and the grocer as their desire to maintain a rural personal grocery store collides with their desire for a variety of goods that are available in larger cities.

The new information age, which has ushered in a new type of interaction for the grocer, has also created some tension. Before, if he wanted a specific product, he would call on the phone and ask for it, and the truck would drop it by as soon as it was in the area. Now he can order only by interacting with the main computer of his wholesaler. This has created a few problems. In the past it was possible to order partial cases or lots because the wholesaler could spread the cases or lots among a variety of small stores throughout the region. Now the computer accepts an order and categorizes everything by cases or lots. The individual interaction of the past is no longer there. Consequently, the owner must play a variety of roles that were not necessary in the past. He must be a personal friend, know everyone's name in the community, control inventory that is constrained by ordering possibilities, and interact with a computer instead of the wholesaler he knew for many years. These quite varied roles place some psychological stress on the grocer that may not have been present ten years ago. So far he has been able to maintain the traditional primary face-to-face interaction in his business while adopting techniques associated with the information age.

As for the future, the grocer states:

> Well, we might lose a grocery store, and we might only have the grade school, but we'll be here. Somebody will still be growing grain so they will still need some beer and groceries.

The grocery is an example of a business that has attempted, with some success, to maintain the traditional way of doing business while still using much of the mass society's power of advertising and buying. The influence of the information age is somewhat more subtle. Whereas before the grocer made only four, then two, orders per month, he recently utilized the main computer at his wholesaler's warehouse to take advantage of a short-term but somewhat lucrative market.

A train of railroad workers recently stopped in Bremer, which they used as a main base. The workers wanted large amounts of doughnuts, specific types of beer, and several other items not generally sold in the store. That evening the owner made a special order to the computer at the warehouse and in the morning his order was delivered. The special order cost extra, but the money he made on the increased sales offset any loss due to the special order. This event illustrates the change in orientation that the grocer is undergoing as the new technology allows him to capture temporary market niches such as red beer for railroad workers passing through.

The Drugstore: Orders by Computer,
Delivery by Person

Confidence in business leaders in Bremer is tied to their length of service and to how their family fits into the community. This confidence is especially important to community residents when it comes to the pharmacist at the local drugstore. The drugstore is on the corner across the street from the Bremer Hardware Store. The shelves are partially filled, and often only one item is placed in the center of a bare shelf. The drug counter is at the rear of the store and it is not uncommon for customers to walk behind the counter and select the type of drug they are talking about. Prescriptions can be ordered by phone. The druggist calls the local doctor and verifies that the person needs a specific type of drug. The papers are usually filled out after the initial transaction. The druggist delivers prescriptions to Flemington at no extra cost to the customers. According to the druggist, "I've been doing it for 30 years and just feel it is my duty." The orientation of the community makes it impossible for the druggist to do anything but to continue providing the service.

While the face-to-face business is conducted on a personal level, other aspects of the business are conducted via computer and Accuradata machine, where prescriptions and other merchandise are ordered by telephone linked to a main computer in the Midwest. The owner is required by his wholesaler to use a computer to order merchandise. The wholesaler no longer accepts verbal phone orders or mail orders from retailers such as the Bremer drugstore.

The pharmacist speculated on the future of doing business in Bremer:

> Hopefully, I think it looks good for us as far as the local businesses. In terms of pharmacies since I've come, five pharmacies have closed in the area. The only small town that has one is Bremer.

The major concern for the pharmacist is that it is difficult to keep in business without a doctor. Bremer recently brought in a doctor to replace the retiring one, and the pharmacist is more comfortable about his ability to stay in business. Local business owners and employees are keenly aware that their business success is determined by the success of the other institutions and businesses in Bremer. Whereas in an urban area there are alternative services, in Bremer there exists only one of each of these key businesses. This fact has a great deal of influence over how business is done in Bremer.

The Bremer Hardware Store:
Teapots and Tractors

Conflicting expectations are not unique to grocers in Bremer during the 1990s. The hardware and implement dealer across the street from the Hartford grocery store faces similar problems. The Bremer Hardware implement dealer is a third-generation business in Bremer. It faces Main Street and has been passed down from father to son to grandson. The building front is painted white with Bremer Hardware in large red letters above the front door. On each side of the front door are large windows with rows of lawn toys, clothes irons, pots and pans, fishing poles, and miniature farming implements. The signs for babysitting, part-time jobs, and the county fair are displayed taped to the windows.

The Bremer hardware store is a franchise operation under several national corporations. They provide the parts and repair for the large combines and tractors used to farm the steep Palouse hills. Other goods sold are paint, hardware, and small household appliances. The people who work in the store know the patrons by name, house, and road where they live. The conversations at the parts counter—where two stools, generally filled, make it comfortable for the farmers, farmers' wives, or children to wait for their parts—focus on personal matters of other Bremerites. Those farmers who are in a hurry walk behind the counter and down the dark rows of machine parts to pick up the part they need. They wave the part to the parts manager and walk out the door. Those who have been sent in for parts but do not know the year or sometimes the make of the piece of machinery expect the parts manager to know the year, make, and so on. Generally this expectation is met.

The hardware store also sells fishing, hunting, and trapping licenses for the state. It is reported that the wives of farmers often buy the licenses and sign the spouse's name. Though this may run contrary to state law, it is commonly believed that farmers work when stores are open so they cannot be expected to come in to buy their licenses and sign their own names. Locals who have jobs in the town proper are expected to buy their own licenses and sign their own names. The practice of selectively administering laws is also followed by other businesses in the community. This situation illustrates the flexibility of the community in applying rules. The administration of rules is based on specific traits of the individual, such as whether one is a farmer or not. This norm is community-wide.

While Bremer Hardware participates in the traditional interaction patterns of small towns such as knowing everyone's name, participating in community organizations, and allowing flexibility when it comes to some laws, the business also orients to mass-society expectations. The paints, tractors, household appliances, and other items it sells are advertised nationally, on regional television and radio stations. The fliers that are mailed to local residents are printed at the national headquarters and the specials are decided on by national or regional marketing specialists. Recently, the Bremer Hardware Store expanded its operation outside of Bremer and now owns three other stores, covering about a 100-square-mile area. Behind this expansion was a reason that could apply to any business in the mass society. The owner explained:

> We needed to change. Our overhead has continued to go up but our purchasing power was limited because we could only turn over so much merchandise. Now we order for four stores and we can work on a smaller profit margin because we sell more. It's also easier for us to comply with the national advertisements. We almost always have the items in one of our stores now.

These two hats—that of being a locally owned business meeting the community's expectation of participation, which is face-to-face inter-action, and that of being a member of a multi-million dollar national corporation where corporate profits and standardized policy is the norm—are not the only ones the owners of the hardware store have to wear. The new role that has evolved in the last ten years is that of a participant in the information age.

As Harlan Cleveland writes of the information age: "The industrial era was characterized by the influence of humankind over things, including nature as well as artifacts of man. The information era features a sudden increase in humanity's power to think and therefore organize" (Cleveland, 1985, p. 185). To organize in such a way, businesses are using information technology such as computers, modems, satellite hook-ups, and videocassette recorders.

Bremer Hardware is no exception. It has been in operation for over 50 years and the owners bought their first computer in the 1970s. This system was a tape-transmission system whereby orders were placed by calling the national warehouse where another computer would read the tape and ship the order. The system became outdated in 1982, and since then they have been using a new computer system. According to the owner, "We have it for inventory control and we also do our billing with it."

The national corporation is requiring the store to hook up to the national headquarters via a modem. As the manager explained, "We will go back to using a modem by October. We've got a reprieve until then. We were supposed to be hooked up by now but it's gonna cost

$80,000 to tie all four stores together with the computer system." The contractual obligations the Bremer Hardware Store has with the national corporation require that the franchise be hooked up by computer.

The store also uses a videocassette recorder (VCR) that is supplied for training in new procedures and new equipment. In the past a representative from the national or regional headquarters would come to Bremer, or selected employees would travel to a central place where they would be trained in new procedures or on the new equipment coming out. Now this training is done with the VCR and tapes sent from headquarters.

The increased complexity of operating a hardware implement business in Bremer has changed operations on a daily basis. In the past the parts manager would estimate the age of most of the equipment that was being used by farmers in the area. He would guess when it was likely to break down and would order parts accordingly. As the mass society began to take hold Bremer Hardware was increasingly involved in corporate promotions, with free trips as the bonus for exceeding sales estimates. This changed the way business was done, as salesmen began to concentrate on short-term goals and bonuses instead of the traditional form of sales, which had as its aim the generation of future sales.

The mass society has also exerted other influences on the hardware store. Earlier in time, authority was based on ascription and the father passed power down to the eldest son. Now, with the mass society, there are specifically defined hierarchical levels. The corporation decides behavior as well as who has authority, which is determined by years of service. Currently, achievement within the corporation is based primarily on the number of sales an individual concludes. Familial lines no longer are important.

As Bremer Hardware ushers in the information age, other changes are taking place. Previously it dealt with only three vendors (companies who sell wholesale). Now it purchases from as many as 32 vendors. This increase in the number of companies that the hardware store buys from decreases the overall power of any particular vendor. Ordering merchandise is now done via computer. Problems are handled by another office situated hundreds of miles from the main office. Whereas in the past the owners, managers, and regional and national representatives interacted face-to-face, the primary form of interaction today is computer-to-computer. The owner is not sure that the new computer equipment will increase efficiency but is required by contractual obligations to buy and use the new system. The pressure to adopt the new equipment is not necessarily made because of cost effectiveness but because of increased standardization of operations nationwide. As the owner said, "If we want to stay in business, then we have to oblige."

The example of the Bremer hardware store points to several structural changes that have taken place as information technology has been used to increase the local power of the hardware dealer. The use of the telephone is no longer restricted to transmitting voice communication. The linking of the hardware store by machine to machines across the nation changes the interaction patterns from face-to-face, or voice, to machine-to-machine. While this interaction pattern makes it more difficult for the workers in Bremer to talk face-to-face with colleagues from the company, the machine-to-machine communication enhances the local owner's ability to compete in a regional market. Whereas the hardware store used to be only a part of a large corporation that dictated policy, the owners can now buy from vendors throughout the United States because of the lowering of costs facilitated by a reduction of personnel needed to take orders and prepare the orders for shipment. This empowerment of the hardware dealer changes his relationship with the original parent corporation because he can now, through quick information transmission and retrieval, play one wholesaler against another. In this way he is getting the best buy he can.

The Insurance Agency: Bring Your Own Cup

The front window is covered with indoor plants. The only identification is a small, 12-by-4 inch sign that reads "Insurance" above the door. Upon entering the insurance agency one sees a long counter that runs the 18-foot length of the narrow office. To the rear of the office is an open door leading to a small apartment with the TV playing. The owners do not live in the apartment, it just provides them with a place to "feel comfortable" and cook their meals during the day when business is slow. A single tall stool is next to the counter near the door. A stained coffee pot stands on the counter-surrounded by a variety of similarly stained coffee cups.

Community expectations in Bremer require that some local stores provide an area for patrons to socialize. Interaction in a business setting follows a pattern similar to interaction within families; people are expected to talk. Conversation centers on personal problems of the patrons as well as other residents in the Bremer community. The owner provides some of the cups, and other friends and businesspeople leave their cups there so that they don't "have to carry them up and down the street."

This insurance office is also a representative for the state licensing bureau. Local residents can buy and renew vehicle licenses and pay automobile taxes here. The owner says, "We do it more as a convenience to people than to make any money." The informal norms of Bremer often require businesses to carry products and offer services that are not profitable if examined strictly for cost-effectiveness. Because the businesses are the center of the community of Bremer, business owners have an informal obligation to maintain the downtown for the overall good of the community. These particular community-control-era traits help illustrate the level of community control over the everyday behaviors of doing business in Bremer.

Business at the insurance office is conducted on a person-to-person basis, with the owners seeing themselves as public servants rather than "uptown businessmen." Over 50 percent of the residents buy their insurance here or at the other insurance agency in town. Over 40 percent of the population buy their insurance from agencies located adjacent to Bremer, and 16 percent of those buy insurance from agencies more than 50 miles away. The impact of the mass society on conducting an insurance business in Bremer has created some tension between the owners, who have owned the business for over 30 years, and the local residents. The residents cite lower rates as their reason for changing agents from local to outside of the area, and the owners are concerned that local support for businesses is being taken away from the community by younger people who value only the dollar, not community pride and commitment.

Center Fertilizer and Farm Supplier: The Cost of Five-Cent Peanuts and a Misplaced Coffee Pot

Farm supplies such as fertilizer, herbicides, and pesticides and services such as tire repair are also a major focus of business in Bremer. The Center fertilizer and farm supplier is one of the largest employers in Bremer, with 15 men in the summer and three women bookkeepers. The Center sells hardware supplies and has a tire shop where mobile tire repair for farmers is also done, a bulk-fuel plant, and a fertilizer distributorship.

When one walks into the Center, the first look reveals rows of bolts, nuts, and screws, all stacked neatly on the stainless steel shelves. New lawn mowers are arranged in a row with their price tags saying SALE. At the rear of the store sit two older chairs and a twenty-gallon plastic bucket with peanuts in it. A large metal trash can sits next to the peanuts. On the wall above the peanuts and chairs are posters advertising used equipment, part-time jobs, and a mobile home, as well as a reminder that the Gun Club crab feed is coming up. One hand-written sign says, "Used 12 bottom plow for sale. Worked good for me. If interested call Jerry Long." No telephone number is listed. It is assumed that anyone who is interested in the plow knows Jerry Long.

As the employees greet each person that walks through the door they comment on his or her family, share any new gossip in the community, and then ask what the customer needs today. The community expectation of mandatory interaction forces business owners and employees to know each customer. Employees exhibit extreme signs of embarrassment if they do not know a customer. To gain information they will ask how your folks are, and what your wife is doing today. They hope the answers to these questions will give enough clues to enable them to talk to the customer in the expected manner. If residents new tires, they are asked to leave their car and explain where they'll be later that day. After the tires are on, the car is driven to where the customer is and the keys are left in the ignition in the unlocked car.

During the winter, store hours are shortened to half-days on Saturdays. The Center is inundated with car owners who want to have snow tires mounted when the first snow hits. If any are local business-people or work in town, they are scolded for not bringing their cars in during the week, when business was slow. If they work outside the community or are farmers, the tire store employees work late to finish their cars. The tire manager said:

> Now, we know that some people can't come in during the week because they're busy. So getting tires on today [Saturday] isn't a problem. But when I see you driving up and down the street all week and then you come in at 11:00 on Saturday I just say, "Bring it in next week."

Rules are designed and enforced in Bremer to enable the business-people to flexibly select how to interact with customers according to specific knowledge the employee or owner has of the individual customer. This attitude is accepted in the community, as are the free peanuts and coffee that sit inside by the oil stove. During the winter, farmers meet by the peanuts and discuss farming, the new school principal, the local basketball team's chances for a state champion-ship this year, and national politics. With spring, the chairs are usually empty except for an employee on break. Doing business over peanuts and coffee has been the pattern at the Center for over 30 years.

Yet all of the business at the Center is not local gossip and local control. The Center is a member of a national co-op and has much of its direction dictated by the national office. The advertisements are printed nationally and run on national television. The decision to bring on a new line of products is made at the national level instead of at the regional or local level as in the past. Following the corporate model found in mass society, managers are often moved from town to town to get "a better feel of the total business." When this was tried in Bremer, however, it failed. The new manager, an "outsider from the city," according to locals, attempted to "modernize" the business. Peanuts were five cents and coffee was placed behind the counter, where patrons had to ask for it. Although these changes may seem minor, the residents of Bremer felt they were an assault on their lives, one they would not accept. In an effort to maintain the "old ways," complaints began pouring into the national and regional offices. As one farmer summarized the problem, "After all, we're not Spokane." Soon the new manager was removed and a local was hired for the job.

Local residents believe that Bremer is truly different from a city. When a Bremerite talks about city people he or she talks about high crime rates, impersonal interaction, snobbishness, and the lack of knowing who you are dealing with. When a local person who was raised and attended school in Bremer was hired for the job, the peanuts and coffee went back out front. Charge accountswere again paid when the farmers had the money instead of within the 30-day period the new manager had put into place. Townspeople again stood around the barrel and talked of issues that border on town gossip. The violation of these community norms almost resulted in a loss of business for the Center. The ability of the community to act sometimes as one because of the informal information network enables the sanctioning process of shunning to work exceptionally well. It can also be carried past shunning to active participation in having the business return to the way it was. Community members were obligated to "at least say something" to one of the board members. Community expectations require the obligation of talking or writing a letter. The norm is that interaction is mandatory even if not formally called for.

Employing a local person is a community norm that had been violated when the new manager was brought in from the outside. When asked if a business should hire locally, 42 per-cent of the community residents said "all of the time" and another 57 percent responded with "some of the time." This high percentage of residents who feel that hiring locally is a community norm is an example of Bremer's businesses retaining Gemeinschaft, or traditional community behaviors and orientations.

Yet while this particular Bremer business seems to have been fairly successful in fighting off some influences of the mass society, the impact of the new information age is just now becoming apparent. In the summer of 1987, the new manager who had replaced the outsider explained why they didn't use a computer in their business:

> Well, the bookkeepers have been doing it this way forever and we just don't think it would be economically feasible. [Telephone company manager] tried to get us hooked up. But why? We don't need it to do business. It would just be more outgo with no more coming in. Now does that make sense? I don't think so. Hell, down at the fertilizer plant they spend a lot of time playing games on it. We don't have time to play games here. The regional office wants us to buy a computer, but unless they put up the money, we won't be getting one.

As of the summer of 1988, the Center had installed a computer-card-controlled gas-pumping system. The system allows customers to put their computerized gas card in a small machine. They can then pump their gas, and the billing information is fed into a central billing office in the county seat. The billing is done by computer. The computerized system enables local customers to have the same convenience as urbanites by being able to buy gasoline around the clock. Yet, the traditional rural character of doing business during normal business hours is the same as it has been for the last 30 years. This example illustrates the other side of the influence of information technology. Because the billing is now done in the county seat, a half-time bookkeeper had to be laid off. In this instance the technology allowed the larger entity, the corporation, to reduce labor without losing efficiency. This resulted in job loss within the local company and in the community of Bremer. Through negotiation with the parent board of directors the manager was allowed to have all the computerized bills sent to the Bremer office, where they are tabulated with the other bills customers may have incurred at the Center. In this way he was able to save one full-time position of bookkeeper.

The Kholer Tractor Company:
Outsiders with Names on Their Shirts

Just past the Center, on the eastern edge of the town limits, is a new business. It is a franchised outlet of a major national tractor company. The building has green aluminum siding and there are small landscape plants around the gravel driveway. The air-conditioned room is filled with classical music. The shelves are stocked with miniature tractors, implements, and grain combines. The prices range from $18 to $220 for a battery-operated miniature tractor with a disc. A new, shiny riding lawn mower sits in the center of the small showroom. The manager lives over twenty miles away in the county seat. This job was a promotion from parts manager.

The Kholer Tractor Company is characteristic of other mass-society business operations. All of the employees wear matching shirts and trousers, with their names embroidered on their shirts. The business uses a computer with a modem to control inventory and uses a VCR for training. The computer system is used to keep inventory and to order parts from other businesses or warehouses around the Northwest. The manager, who commutes to work from outside of Bremer, feels it is difficult to do business in Bremer because of the way locals treat outsiders. He explained:

> It's conservative. If you stop for a beer at lunch it's like you've broken the law. They just are somewhat cold to outsiders. There's people come in here who expect me to know what type of tractor they have. My gawd, I've never seen them before. How would I know what they have?

As the previous manager at the Center discovered, it is difficult to do business in Bremer if the residents don't know you, your family, and where and how you live. The manager of Kholer's is not an exception to the rule. Community residents speak of people as newcomers if they have lived in the community for only one generation. Other community residents who feel they are seen as outsiders voice similar statements:

> People are very cliquish and cold although there's an outward appearance of friendliness.

> Gossip can be a problem and it's hard to live down a bad reputation once you have one.

> As an outsider it takes a long time to get to know people if you don't go to town much.

> I feel that Bremer people who have lived here forever feel they can do no wrong. But God forbid if a newcomer does the same exact thing.

The town proper of Bremer has not grown or shrunk in total population since 1910; this has a great deal to do with the attitudes of the longtime residents toward those who are "new to the community," i.e., who didn't have parents or relatives that lived in Bremer. The stability of community residents is reflected in the naming of the graveled county roads that lie outside of Bremer, which are named after the families that have lived and still do live on them.

This orientation toward what constitutes an insider versus an "outsider" greatly contributes to the difficulty new business owners experience when attempting to do business in Bremer. One reason it may take so long to become an insider is Bremerite's perception of outsiders. They see outsiders as being cold, indifferent, and more aloof in the sense that they don't participate in all community activities. The outsiders, according to residents, don't "know enough to even say hello when they meet you on the street. They act like this is New York." Some Bremerites feel that it takes at least one generation before someone learns the norms and customs that make Bremer "country." These perceptions are similar with those that Louis Wirth found in Chicago in 1929, which lends credibility to the use of eras as a conceptual device in studying Bremer (Wirth, 1938). The apprehension and isolation that the Kholer manager feels point to some of the trade-offs associated with maintaining community identity in Bremer. Though residents enjoy the family-like atmosphere in the local businesses, that very form of interaction makes it difficult for new businesses and new residents to gain entry into and to participate in the everyday life of Bremer.

Bremer Telephone and Cable Television Company: A Co-op with Digital Switching and Optic Fiber Cables

The influence of the information age in Bremer is nowhere more evident than in the long, narrow office of the Bremer telephone and cable television company. Small personal computers sit at both of the desks facing Main Street. A stack of brochures is on the front desk. The brochures are advertisements for the community of Bremer and state that Bremer is a place of "Old Fashioned Values and Contemporary Vision." Inside the brochure, next to the picture of the golf course, are several graphs explaining the services offered by the telephone and cable television company. The graphs indicate that the services and equipment available for telephone customers are digital switching, touch-tone telephones, computer billing, long distance access, call forwarding, speed calling, conference calling, call waiting, mobile phone, and paging.

The manager, who is also the mayor and a local rancher, explains that the "telephone system could handle a town population of 1,000 to 1,500 people." Although Bremer has a population of only just over 500 people the reason for the large capability is that the available technology is built only for larger towns. The manager explains:

> We began updating our system in 1950. We were the first small town in the state with digital switching. The only problem that we have is that it is impossible to buy equipment for a town of our population, so we always end up buying equipment that would handle a town of two to three times our size.

The size of equipment isn't the only problem facing the Bremer telephone and cable television company. The Bremer company must also be compatible with the long-distance telephone carrier Regional Bell (RB). The manager explains the situation this way:

> As for the transmission of data over the phone lines, I can check to see if transmission is occurring and if it's reaching our trunk lines—if it's got that far we have to assume that the problem is at the other end of the call or at the T [the tie into the long-distance telephone lines]. It's usually at the T, where RB just hasn't upgraded like we have. They run on ten-year plans and it just isn't in their ten-year plan to add T's or upgrade their lines. If they would add another T I'd be out there tomorrow laying new cable. But that's not going to happen. Look at [names another small town]; they have a system that was outdated 30 years ago. They want to upgrade but RB just won't let them. It's up to them and little outfits like us just have to wait until they get ready to let us hook up. They just don't think it's worth it financially, but you know we have been doing some of the work for smaller companies around and you know we are making money at it, but the big regional company just thinks the jobs are too small to make money. I don't know, but I think a little outfit can do a lot of this better than they can.

The difficulties expressed by the manager indicate some of the problems faced by small independent businesses operating in the mass society. The constraints placed on them by large national corporations make it difficult for them to upgrade their systems. Bremer telephone and cable television company has "one of the most sophisticated systems in the state," but is not able to use many of its capabilities because they would not be compatible with the older equipment used by the national carrier in the rural areas of the state. The technical problems faced by the telephone and cable television company are compounded by the breakup of AT&T. According to the manager:

> You can't expect any help from the regional companies. They are so big they just don't have to worry about the little bit of business we bring them. See, our billing used to come to us and then to them but

now we have been bypassed with the breakup so we are going to lose revenue that we used to get. So we are going to have to raise our rates again.

The direct tie to a large mass-society organization such as the regional company has stymied the upgrading of the telephone system in Bremer and decreased the profits. Yet the locally owned co-op has begun to increase its area of technical support for smaller telephone and cable television systems in the region. According to the manager, the expertise they've gained in developing their system enables them to provide services to smaller, less sophisticated systems.

Although the Bremer telephone and cable television company is constrained by its need to be tied directly to a large mass-society organization, the business is financially stable. The co-op stock is the most difficult stock in the community to buy. Stock is usually handed down from one family member to another. If a family member wants to sell the stock after a death, then the board of directors goes over their list of people who want to buy the stock and decides who will be able to buy it. Individuals who live outside of Bremer are never considered when it comes to selecting new stock owners.

Positions on the board of directors are generally handed down from father to son. If that is not possible, then a long-term resident or business owner is asked to sit on the board. Expertise in telecommunications is not a prerequisite for sitting on the board; rather, a dedication to maintaining the community is seen as the highest priority for selecting new members.

The difficulties faced by the telephone and cable television company are indicative of the problems associated with a small rural business tied to large mass-society organizations. Although the business is constrained by the outdated equipment used by the national telephone carrier, it has accommodated the loss of revenue by providing services to other small towns in the area. The traditional categoric community attributes, such as ascription as the basis for selecting a new board member, are coupled with a new form of business, that of a service center.

Cafe by Day and Tavern by Night:
Bremer Caps and Other Local Rules

Across the street from the Kholer tractor store, past the large silver grain elevators, is the local tavern/cafe. A sign above the door announces, No one under 21 years of age allowed. Inside, a glass-covered counter faces the door. The counter is filled with candy and odds and ends such as aspirin and cough drops. On Saturday evenings and after 5:00 on weekdays the tavern is the only place open in town for the high school students to buy candy and cold drinks. Though allowing under-age individuals into the bar is illegal, the community norm of allowing specific enforcement of rules due to characteristics of specific individ-uals enables the bar owner and employees to selectively administer that law. A long bar runs back from the door to a darkened back room with older, retired farmers sitting at green-felt-covered tables playing pinochle, rummy, or sometimes poker. The stakes are inevitably low. To the right, cafe tables face a large front window. Ten or 12 men ranging from 55 to 85 years old sit with coffee cups, laughing and talking as they watch the activity on Main Street. It is quite likely that their fathers sat at similar tables years earlier. The chairs situated around the card tables are passed down from father to son, and members of the community know which chair is whose. Coffee is self-serve, with a straw basket near the coffee pot for payment: 30 cents a cup, refills free. There is no one drinking beer in the tavern at this time of day, an expectation learned the hard way by the manager at Kholer tractor.

The Bremer area was a prime beer-brewing area before prohibition, drawing on the expertise of many of the German emigrants, but since prohibition, public drinking has been frowned upon. Until 1920, the county supported 11 small local beer breweries. The influence of mass society can be seen in the loss to the community of the small, independently-owned breweries. The local patrons now drink beer brewed and marketed for a national market.

The men are dressed in jeans and plaid or dark cotton shirts, with a majority wearing baseball caps advertising the local hardware store, the Center, the Bremer Grain Growers, or one of a variety of chemical or seed companies. Baseball caps play an important role in providing instant recognition of one's status within the community. The caps are alternated from day to day and considerable time is spent discussing the best ways to clean them. The importance of cleanliness reaches even to the work caps that the men wear. The techniques for cleaning the caps range from the time-consuming task of steaming them over a colander and then blow-drying them to simply throwing them in the washer and hanging them on the line. While this effort may at first seem unnecessary, the symbols attached to these caps cannot be dismissed.

A young farmer new to the area explained that when he first began farming in the community, he was given a gift of a blue baseball cap with Bremer Grain Growers written on the front. He had seen blue-and-white caps with similar writings but not many of the solid blue caps. One day while in the Hartford grocery store he found people staring at him. He knew that newcomers were often stared at but still thought the intensity of the stares a bit unusual. Later, when he shared the experience with a longtime resident, he was told that the reason people were staring was that he was wearing one of 13 caps that had been ordered for the board of directors of the Grain Growers. The community residents were concerned that they did not know the new board member. The cap itself was a known symbol to community members, which they saw as separating them from "outsiders." The possibility that they would not know an important person such as a board member of the Grain Growers went against all of the community-wide expectations of saying hello and knowing each community resident by name, occupation, and family. The young man was not a board member of the Grain Growers.

Anthony Cohen, in his book *The Symbolic Construction of Community,* found similar uses of symbols in defining who was part of and who was an outsider in communities around the world (Cohen, 1985). These symbols are not often brought into play until a threat or, as in the example, an inability to recognize a "community member."

At noon, lunches are served from the deep fryer and grill to the local business owners and their employees as well as to a few farmers who may come to town. People sit in the front of the cafe, where it is well-lighted and people can be seen from Main Street. Around 2:00 p.m. is the unwritten coffee hour for the community leaders. It is during this time that the community leaders discuss how the community is doing, share any local gossip, and make general plans for any event that may be coming up in Bremer.

At 5:00 p.m. the cafe takes on another character, becoming a small local tavern. Beer is served to the employees of the local businesses and to the farmers who stop in. The jukebox is turned on and country music is played. Conversations are louder and the quiet, family-like atmosphere is replaced with the banging of balls on the pool table and the clinking of glasses being set on the long bar. By 7:00 p.m. the bar is usually empty, and the owners close whenever they "feel that everybody has gone home." About three times a year a live band is brought in and the tavern becomes crowded as the young people as well as the older community members drink beer, dance, and mingle.

Not drinking in public is a social norm upheld by the community leaders except for the rare instances when the larger community participates in a celebration of the end of grain harvest, New Year's Eve, or the weekend of the community fair. This norm is especially important for those members in the community whose roles are designed for the community's children and young adults. The schoolteachers in the community are very seldom seen at these public gatherings. When they are in public celebrating, they are quite conscious of the fact that they must be one of the first to leave and should not exhibit signs of intoxication.

The behavior of community residents remains overseen by the older Bremerites. If someone is breaking the norm against loud public behavior tied to alcohol consumption they will first be reprimanded by a simple statement and a smile. However, people throughout the community are likely to hear about the indiscretion in a day or two. The speed of the informal information network in Bremer makes it possible for the majority of the community to know of "serious" concerns, even on Sunday, when the downtown businesses are closed. The community members then take it upon themselves to "help." Because the incident was alcohol-related, if the individual is seen entering the cafe/tavern, other community members will alert the rest of the community if the individual drinks alcohol. The sanction of quietly shunning while continuously watching the violator is a tradition in Bremer. This type of informal sanction works in most other arenas of the residents' lives as well.

The atmosphere in the tavern/cafe reveals a traditional community-control mechanism of informal sanctions—public identification of any wrongdoing that may lead to months of being one of the topics of local gossip. Those who do not conform to public ideas of decency or behavior are sanctioned through quiet ostracism. To be ostracized in Bremer is to be labeled and then quietly ignored until the community feels a sufficient penance has been served.

The Requirements of Doing Business in Bremer: Complexity Hidden by Simplicity

The seeming simplicity of doing business within the community-control era is less than simple. To know all the customers by name, family, and other personal traits requires a constant updating of information about community members. Seemingly idle, nondirectional conversations about hearsay in the community that make one-minute purchases turn into 20-minute discussions are as essential for doing business in Bremer as the sale of the merchandise itself.

Business owners and employees must take into consideration the question "What will the community think?" That simple phrase has ominous meaning to most community residents. The community is a dominant force that guides the conduct of business. Yet conducting business in Bremer does not only mean being responsive to community control. It also means accommodating the forces placed upon the residents by the mass society.

The tension created between business owners and patrons has not at this time reached a point where community cohesion seems to be threatened, although considerable change has taken place in the way Bremerites interact on a business level. A local flour mill was still in operation until 1966. This particular business had been a cornerstone of economic activity in Bremer. During this period barter was an important form of economic exchange in the community. Whole grain was brought to the mill, where it was ground into flour and often exchanged for goods and services from the local businesses. The business owners would then transport the flour to Spokane, where they sold it for cash.

This traditional way of doing business has since been replaced with checking accounts and charge accounts. Although plastic credit cards have not replaced checks or charge accounts, the local fertilizer/feed store has recently changed the gas pumps to card-controlled. These small credit cards enable Bremer residents to place the card in a small computerized reader that automatically bills their account. Cards enable residents to use computerized billing at all of the co-op retailers throughout the region.

The strain of living within the two worlds of the community-control era and the mass-society era has left its mark on the residents of Bremer. The strong group orientation of Bremerites is threatened by the continued pressure placed upon local businesses to adopt practices that have been standardized and found successful in the mass society. The symbols of authority found in larger metropolitan areas are now beginning to appear in Bremer. Employees are now seen wearing identical "uniforms"—trousers and shirts with their names embroidered on them. Though the majority of the community residents know the employees, this allows regional sales representatives, franchise negotiators, and other mass-society representatives to speak to the employees by name. This standardization in dress has created some tension. Previously, clothing was not a symbol of success in Bremer. Businessowners and employees wore the same clothing and outsiders could not differentiate between them.

Adopting symbols to signify ownership and to differentiate employees from one business to another has occurred within the last three years. It is now possible to tell whether a person works for Kholer Tractor or for Bremer Hardware without the intimate knowledge necessary in the past. This is indicative of the movement from generalized roles to specific roles within the businesses in Bremer.

Whereas past (and in some cases present) roles were ascribed and a person received increased prestige in the community, roles now exist in the business sector that are based on achievement. This achievement is acknowledged through a change in title, such as a movement from floor manager to parts manager, and is indicated in the symbolic dress associated with the movement up the hierarchy of the corporation.

Doing business in Bremer means having to deal simultaneously with different types of social organizations. The insurance agent finds it increasingly difficult to practice insurance sales in a society based on mass production and sales of goods and services. The hardware and implement dealer is utilizing information technology to increase his power when negotiating with wholesale vendors. The manager of the Center must negotiate with the corporate board to retain at least one full-time position. In this way the community lost only one-half job instead of the one-and-one-half that would have been lost if he had not found a solution that helped fulfill a community expectation. The telephone and cable television company has begun to provide services to other small cable and telephone systems in the region.

Operating a business in Bremer requires that the owners and employees be conscious of expectations associated with all three eras. First, they must be participating members of the community; they must know all the customers by name and be willing to allow everyone to "know" them. Second, the business owners must deal with wholesalers who represent a mass society where standardization and mass production are the norm. Third, new pressures exist to adopt information technology that changes the flexibility that owners had in the past. Ordering is no longer a negotiated interaction with a manager or salesperson but is now handled computer-to-computer.

Conclusion

In contrast to Bremer's mass-production-oriented agriculture, the other businesses of Bremer remain strongly based in the era of community control. Virtually every business transaction, from obtaining a loan at the bank to ordering a beer for lunch, involves more than an economic decision. Seemingly idle conversation is expected, and has a purpose, that of conveying the information that becomes part of the shared information base essential to doing business in Bremer.

Lengthy conversations surrounding the purchase of a bottle of pop, the baby pictures attached to the post in the grocery store, the empty stores during coffee time, the five-cent peanuts—each is an integral part of getting to know one's customers and being able to serve them.

Also a part of this is Jerry Long's advertisement to sell his 12-bottom plow with the testimonial "It worked good for me" and his not needing to list a telephone number or address. Practically, Bremer businesses exist collectively, as part of the community, not as independent entities.

In this context, the external pressures being imposed by the mass society (as simple as names on uniformlike shirts) and the information era (e.g., submitting orders by machine instead of by person) become unwanted intrusions. They are concerns to be dealt with like any other threat to business.

If the Bremer way of doing business is threatened—for example, by bringing in an outside manager who doesn't know the customers and their needs—the threats are resisted. When the results are transparent to most customers and can even be turned to one's advantage—ordering by computer, for instance—such procedures are quietly accepted. In many respects the attributes of the information era seem less threatening to the businesses of Bremer than do those of the mass society, which to date have so often been resisted and rejected.

However, the reason that Bremer has been able to hold at bay many aspects of the mass society has less to do with individual business practices than with the unusual way in which business practices and governance of Bremer are clearly intertwined. Central to explaining the community-control orientation of Bremer's businesses is a powerful informal club with a deceptively simple name, the Community Club.

6

More Important than Government: The Community Club

County government responsible for law enforcement, rural roads, and other services is housed in the county seat, many miles away and mostly beyond the control of Bremer and its people. A city council and mayor, elected by Bremer's town residents, have direct control over day-to-day operations of the community's very limited services, including street repair, water system, snow removal, and sewer; but to understand how things of importance get done for the entire Bremer community—both town and rural—it is crucial to start in an old building that doubles as a gun club, on a side street near the outskirts of town.

On a Friday evening pickups and large Oldsmobiles can be seen pulling up to the old green building on the edge of town. The headlights reflect off the gray wheat stubble as they turn into the short gravel driveway leading to the gun club. Members of the Bremer Community Club are meeting to talk over issues facing the community.

Started shortly after World War II as a gun club, this is where local farmers and townspeople spent some time relaxing and shooting trap. After several years it became apparent to many of the participants that much of what was taking place within the community was being discussed in an informal way as members sat around drinking coffee on those days when it wasn't mandatory that farmers be in the field. The movement to a community club was informal and took years.

The organization and membership of the club is rather informal, yet the decisions made in the small (24-by-36 foot) building have long-term and far-reaching effects on the town and surrounding community of Bremer. It is here that members who represent almost all groups within the community, from retired farmers to business owners, meet to discuss, outside legal constraints, the needs of the community. Here, more than any other place, community issues are connected to one another and directions are decided. Whereas the participants see themselves as a social club, their ability to bring resources, human and economic, to bear on community-wide problems makes them the most powerful group within the community.

Tonight's meeting is seen as a "maintenance" meeting. An outsider quickly recognizes that this is a male-only activity and is not limited to those living within town borders. The fifteen people in attendance act like delegates for larger groups within the community, and this perception accurately reflects reality. The attendees include six local farmers, ranging from ages 38 to 72, and nine "town" residents, several of whom are seated at the round tables covered with green felt to facilitate card playing if time allows. The participants at tonight's meeting are also members of the school board, the national wheat board, the local city council, the county commissioners, church boards, the grain co-op board, the local telephone/television co-op, and the Main Street businesses. Historically, the president is usually a farmer. There has been a process of ascribed leadership in the club since about 1950, from which time members of one family, all male, have been the presidents. To an outsider it appears that this is strictly a social gathering.

At half past the hour the president—a young farmer who also attended Bremer High, worked as a volunteer fireman, and still maintains a working draft team of horses, as his father and uncle did—calls the meeting to order. The atmosphere is informal, with jokes and laughter common interruptions. Once the meeting is called to order, the president asks the secretary, the local banker, to report on last meeting's issues. The banker remains sitting and explains that the school board has hired a new superintendent, the doctor's committee is making progress, and the fairgrounds building group is also making some headway. When he finishes, the president asks if anyone has anything to add to the brief report. A farmer about 60 years old, a long-time school board member, leans back on two legs of his chair and says:

> We finally have a new superintendent. But it wasn't easy. Flemington has agreed to have him spend most of his time in the school here, but he will also spend at least one day a week in Flemington at the middle school. One thing we need to think about is how to make him feel at home here. You all know that he is going through a divorce and plans on moving in a double-wide [trailer], a nice one, and it will be down by the golf course. So we might want to make sure that when any of us go out to play we invite him along. I think it will make him feel more at home and also give us a chance to get better acquainted. The mayor

says that he plans on going tomorrow so he will call and invite the new superintendent.

A few heads nod and then another farmer, also a lifelong resident, begins speaking.

The doctor's committee has been working hard to get the additional money to pay for the doctor's house. We are still short about $4,000, so we need to put a little pressure on a few of the people who haven't contributed. Here's a list of donors [hands out list], so if you know of someone that is not on the list you can call them or let me know and I'll get in touch with them. I don't know why that last few thousand is always the hardest to get.

A pause occurs and then several people speak at once. The tone of the conversation is that the doctor is now trying to take advantage of the community by asking so much for his home. Several heads nod, but then the farmer who made the report indicates that the house is a major drawing card for a new doctor recruit so they just have to move on. Heads nod.

The next person to speak lives in town but is a retired farmer.

The fair-building foundation is about complete. Bill, Bob, George, Mike [names several others] spent last Friday and Saturday laying the concrete floor. We now need someone to help put up the girders.

Before he finishes, two men volunteer their labor and begin discussing what equipment they need to bring and whether the girders have been paid for. They have not. The volunteers agree to pay for the girders "up front" but expect others to "kick in" some money.

The meeting continues until about nine, when all but five members leave. These five members remain seated. A deck of cards appears, and a quiet game of low-stakes poker begins as the headlights of cars and pickups leaving the community club meeting flash on the gray stubble next to the building.

The success of the community club stems from several factors. First, it is a community club in all ways. Town residents, farmers, and others who live in the countryside are considered members. The club plays a critical role in binding together the community across the political lines drawn to separate town from countryside. The ability of the club to maintain itself—it has been in operation for over 40 years—is due in part to the mix of town and country members and to reliance on tradition. This has allowed for resources of rural members, including money, equipment, and skills, to be brought to town, where they are used for the benefit of the entire community.

In addition, the club provides a forum for discussion of the broad issues facing the community, with leaders representing most if not all of the major organizations in town. Decisions are made in this small green building about the schools, health care, and new city employees, as well as about potential changes that might help the community. Although it is an informal organization without any formal jurisdiction, the community club provides a glue that is critical to building the fabric of community.

City Council: Keeping Everyone Happy and Moving in the "Right Direction"

In sharp contrast to the community club, a different set of procedures prevails over the elected town council, which has official jurisdiction over public affairs within the city limits. Among those differences are the time and location of the meeting.

At 2:30 p.m. on the second Tuesday of the month, the local library is closed for business but the door remains unlocked. When the door opens, two men walk through wearing work clothes and unconsciously wipe their feet several times before stepping onto the well-kept library carpet. Within ten minutes six people are sitting around a small oblong table. The regularly scheduled city council meeting is about to begin.

The meeting is held on Main Street in full view of any citizens of Bremer who might be passing by. The council includes the mayor and five others, one of whom is a woman. The mayor, a man in his fifties, was socialized in the Bremer school system and has been involved in the guiding of the community for the majority of his adult life. About six feet tall, wearing a blue short-sleeved shirt, blue jeans, and brown cowboy boots, he sits down and opens the meeting. The first business to be discussed is whether a local resident should be allowed to cut down several trees near his home. The person requesting the removal, a long-time resident of Bremer, has said that he will cut the trees and haul away the wood if he can borrow the town truck. The council knows the individual and the discussion is not about whether he can be trusted with town equipment or whether the town's insurance will cover the use, but rather about who originally planted the trees and whether the council feels their relatives will object to the cutting of the trees.

Bill, a lifetime resident of Bremer whose father sat on the city council, leaves the meeting and goes to phone the relative of the person believed to have planted the trees. He returns after about ten minutes and reports that he couldn't reach the relative at his home but did find him at the local cafe having coffee. The relative had already talked to Bernard, the individual requesting the cutting down of the trees, and said he didn't have any objections. He had talked to his mother, whose father had planted the trees, and she said they were getting old anyway, so they should be cut down. The council then voted to provide a town truck, an extra chain saw, and the gas for the saws for Bernard to cut down the trees. The vote was unanimous and the council then moved on to other business.

The manner in which the business of the tree cutting was handled reflects the informal norms of Bremer. The community-control attribute of talking informally to community members before a decision is made follows a long tradition in Bremer. With the overlapping institutions within the community it is necessary that decisions be made by consensus within the community. This differs quite drastically from the formal norms of mass society, where legal mandates would dictate how tree cutting or other changes in the community would be handled. Bremer's political institution is working within the community-control era.

Council members are guided in their decision making by the values of the community. Relationships are based on primary face-to-face interactions, and family affiliation is important to the community. Therefore, the council is required to contact anyone who will be personally affected by its decisions. By phoning the relative of the person who originally planted the trees, the decision is public. The norm of making decisions according to community consensus is followed by allowing those who are historically involved in the situation a chance to participate in the decision. They then pass the word around the community that they were contacted and agreed to the action.

The next business to be discussed is the purchase of a lawn tractor and some hand tools for the town. Among the members sitting on the council is an employee of the local hardware store, which sells hand tools and lawn mowers, and an employee from the Grange, which also sells hand tools and lawn mowers. They both agree not to vote on the matter because it would look as if they were just trying to get a sale for their company. The discussion is led by the mayor:

> Those of you who are new to the council may not remember, but the last tractor we bought was from the Grange. And we buy almost all of our hand tools from the hardware store. Now, we haven't bought anything from the Kholer Tractor Company and they have submitted a bid. They are new to Bremer and I think it might be an act of good faith in them as a business if we buy the lawn mower from them.

The ascribed basis of power within the Bremer community is evident as the mayor uses his power to educate the new members on the way things are done in the town. As mass society has increased its influence over small local governments, the local city council members have lost much of their power in the community and it is now necessary for the mayor to explain the traditional way of conducting business. In the past this was not the case, as the members were actual power brokers in the community and had been trained in Bremer ways. One previous member explained:

> We have traditionally had an all-male city council, but now that most members are voted in unopposed, well, just about anybody can get on. The city council just doesn't have the support of the community like it used to do. I'm not saying that women shouldn't be on the council— it's just that it's been hard for women to get support politically here.

Political power in the community is based on tradition, with a background of power being handed down by ascribed status. A community member explained the appointment of the new mayor:

> We knew he'd be the next mayor. He's worked for the town for years and you just knew when he was a kid that someday he'd be a leader in the town.

This evening, the council is not in total agreement over the direction that the mayor was leading them, as their stern faces suggest. The two employees from the Grange and the hardware store suggest that the bids be opened to see what the cost would be. The bids for the lawn tractor are as follows:

> Bremer Hardware—$2,106
> Grange—$2,304
> Kholer Tractor Co.—$3,040

While the two employees from the Grange and hardware store abstain from voting, the other three council members are left to vote. The older member also abstains and the two newest members to the council are left to vote. The mayor makes a final comment before the vote: "We have to remember that business is important to the community and as representatives of the town we should make every effort to spread our resources around". The final vote is two to zero in favor of buying the most expensive tractor from the Kholer Tractor Company. The hand tools are bought from the hardware store, with the comment that the next purchase will be from the Grange. This representative meeting of the Bremer City Council illustrates several norms of the community.

First, while not voting, the mayor holds traditional power that was handed down to him personally from the previous mayor. Although he did not say, "We must buy from Kholer Tractor," he used his power to influence the other members in his way of thinking. It should be mentioned that prior to the meeting the former mayor and the current mayor held a coffee meeting to discuss the day's agenda.

Another important aspect of this meeting is the fact that the other council members followed the mayor's direction, even though they felt that the costs should be watched more closely. The council members are all aware that the "real" power base in the community is handed down by the previous leaders and that being elected to the council does not necessarily mean that Bremerites want them to go against the traditional power structure in the community. Though many of the new council members, with less than one generation of living in Bremer, have been trained in mass-society organizations where rational decision making is the norm, they were not selected to represent the community until the community as a whole felt they were well enough versed in community norms to follow the tradition of Bremer. As a long-time political leader said of a new council member:

> Well, he's lived here for a while now and has shown he wants to be involved. Now it's up to him to prove that he understands how we do things here. He's developed some community support, but it can go as quickly as it came. So we'll just wait and see.

As the meeting comes to a close, the final item on the agenda is the question of whether to apply for a federal grant to improve the local sewer system. The mayor opens the discussion:

> I know that the member who asked for this to be on the agenda has been working very hard with the County Planning Commission and he should be commended. But it should be remembered what happened to some of the other communities around the area when Mount St. Helens blew. They took the federal money to clean up the ash and they are still filling out the forms and paying employees because they took the money. Now in Bremer, we just got tractors and front-end loaders from local farmers and the city trucks and we cleaned up the town. Our final cost was over $10,000 less than what those other towns ended up paying even with the federal money.

The heads of the older council members all nod in agreement. The mayor then opens the floor for discussion. The discussion focuses on the

Mount St. Helens eruption and how the town of Bremer pulled together without any help from the government and cleaned their own town. A vote is taken and is unanimous: the city will not apply for the grant. The exception is the abstention, from the member who proposed applying for the grant. The meeting is then closed and the mayor says, "Well, it's coffee time."

Coffee Time and Necessary Explanations

Following a long tradition in Bremer, the council members move to the local tavern/cafe for coffee. The coffee hours are held, according to the retired mayor, to let the townspeople know as quickly as possible what the council has done at the meeting. As soon as the members begin moving from the library to the cafe the owner of the hardware store and the manager of the Grange walk in the door and pull up chairs, and after several minutes of small talk about the local university's football team's chance at a win this weekend, the owner of the hardware store asks what they have decided on the lawn tractor.

The mayor explains that they have decided to buy from Kholer's, that they buy most of their supplies from the Bremer hardware store and the Center, and that the reasoning behind the decision is to show the town's support of the new business. The owner of the hardware store asks what the price is. When one of the other council members tells him the price he says he can't believe that they would pay that much for a tractor when they could get it cheaper. He then goes on to explain how he has supported all of the community activities with donations of money and time. The mayor says that the tractor will probably only last a few years and then they will buy from the hardware store next time. This satisfies the owner and the conversation moves to topics for the next community club meeting.

Other Perspectives on Leadership

The current mayor holds power within both the formal and informal power structures of Bremer. When Bremer residents were asked to identify people within the community who they felt should make decisions for the community 15 percent identified the mayor. All other elected officials of Bremer were identified only by 11 percent of the respondents as power leaders. The informal power network in Bremer is quite evident from analysis of whom the community wants to help guide it. Other leaders identified were the banker, the druggist, the hardware store owner, and the retired mayor.   Using the reputational method of evaluating community leaders as suggested by Hunter (1953), it is evident that Bremerites see nonelected members of their community as their leaders.   Of the elected leaders, only 26 percent were identified in the community survey as community leaders. Seventy-four percent of all the people mentioned as leaders had no formal leadership position.   The traditional patriarchal system is also evident in Bremer's community leadership.   Although there are 3 women on elected boards of the city council in Bremer, 27 women (23 percent) were identified by the community and they received only 5 percent of the total designations.

The retired mayor was identified as a leader by 3.7 percent of the respondents.   In this way the traditional power leader, while retired, still wields his power and influences the decisions the council makes. The rules that the new mayor goes by are the same as those followed by the mayor before him: splitting buying and maintaining local businesses.   The actual dollar figure is not as important in the long run as keeping the businesses in Bremer, which illustrates the blending of goals and means.   Had the council voted to go with the lowest bid, the goal of keeping the city council fiscally solvent would have been met, but the goal of keeping all local businesses involved in city government would not have been achieved.   By explaining the past tradition and by mollifying the council members who worked for the competing firms, the mayor was able to meet all of his obligations.

Monitoring the image of the community is also the mayor's responsibility.   The previous mayor informally enforced a rule of no For Sale signs in front of homes.   The mayor explained that this informal policy helped protect the image of the community.   Besides, he would note, "They are advertised in the Centerville paper, and everyone who wants to know can easily find out."

Conducting business this way goes against the findings of some previous studies that have suggested that local decisions in communities are economically driven (Hunter, 1953).   In Bremer, decisions are often made with the good of the overall community in mind.   This group orientation is paramount when politics are conducted in the community. Although there are no legalized rules dictating that the city should split its buying among all of the businesses within the community, the informal norms stipulate that the good of the group must come first. This community-control orientation is evident in other political organizations in Bremer as well.

The city council has undergone substantial change in membership and local power base since 1980.   In 1980, those traditional power leaders who had sat on the council for up to 26 years began to retire.   In

1984, the mayor who had been born and raised in the community retired, and after 26 years of public service he handed the reins of power over to his "lieutenant." He briefly explained his past work, while sitting in a grain truck.

> I've spent almost 30 years working to keep Bremer a place where you could raise a family and feel safe at night. We've done all of this without any support from outside agencies and I wish the new mayor all of the luck in the world.

The retiring mayor had farmed for all of his adult life, as had his relatives before him and as his daughter and son-in-law continue to do. The changing of the guard on the local city council is not just a change in faces but in the local power base that the new members control. Traditionally, the city council members were male and had farmed or owned businesses in the community for several generations. Their goals were to maintain Bremer as it had been in the past, a locally controlled community that did what was necessary to keep itself solvent. The leaders were often farmers who retired and left the daily operations of running the farm to sons, daughters, or in-laws. They then moved to town, where they could spend their retirement working for the community.

One city council member explained the reason for city council meetings being public and held in the middle of the afternoon:

> We have a lot of older citizens. And the council had traditionally been made up of older people who couldn't see to drive at night. Plus they are older farmers who still go to bed early. So we still hold the meetings in the afternoon. That way the older people can get to the meetings.

It is not a problem for local businesspeople to take time off for the meetings, because the community knows which people are on the council and doesn't expect to contact them until after the meeting. To learn the events of the council meeting it is necessary only to go to the local tavern/cafe after the conclusion of the meeting, where the results of the meeting are discussed publicly over coffee. This is a tradition that has been in effect for more than 50 years and has been maintained by each generation of local leaders. Another function of having the meeting during the afternoon is to increase the visibility of the community leaders as they make decisions. Like most interactions, politics in Bremer is public.

There is substantial overlap between the city council and the less formal political groups such as the community club. The leadership of the community was traditionally controlled by the retired farmers and local businesspeople. As the power of the mass society increased, a change began to take place in who solved local problems. In the 1950s, the city council provided the guidance and leadership. This role has been taken over by other informal organizations in order to maintain local control and local ways of doing business. Even with the increased pressure from outside organizations such as the state organization of local governments, the city council has attempted to retain the traditional ways of doing business. As Floyd Hunter (1953) found, the formal leaders who sit on the city council are not necessarily the most powerful leaders in the community. In Bremer the mayor guides the less powerful community members who sit on the city council.

Authority in the political arena of the community is driven by local tradition and is focused on local authority. The power wielded by the mayor is handed down from one leader to another, and is restricted by the past history of the previous leaders. The success of a community political leader in Bremer is measured by how well the individual playing the role meets the traditional expectations of the community.

Public evaluation of even minor decisions made by the local political leaders is necessary because of the obligation and public nature of interaction among community members. The owner of the hardware store found it necessary to learn firsthand what had transpired at the meeting for two reasons. First, when a business owner would ask why the tractor was not bought from his company, he would need information to justify it to his employees and other community residents. After the conversation with the mayor, he had the explanation. Second, as an informal power leader in the community, he would be obligated to make his opinion known to the formal power leaders in the community. In this way he would be exerting his ascribed power and making sure that the decisions follow the tradition of Bremer.

This pride and the traditional way of maintaining local control have increased the control of the community club, the most powerful political organization in the community, and decreased the actual decision-making ability of the formal political structure, the city council. As mass society has increased its power over local city governments through regulations, the residents of Bremer have moved the major decision-making process from the formal political process to the informal political process. It is through the community club that the majority of "important" decisions are made, although there has recently been an increase in the questioning of how decisions are made by the power leaders in the community. An older leader explained:

> We've been getting some complaints about how decisions are being made now. But we just didn't make decisions before. The local leaders would decide on what they wanted to happen. They would go around the town and gather as much support for the idea as they needed and then they would present it to the rest of the community. We'd have a town meeting and those who didn't support it would complain and a large argument would result, but in the end the power leaders always got what they wanted.

The politics of Bremer are steeped in a tradition of local leaders guiding the community. Leaders have traditionally been trained in smaller, less powerful groups in the community before they have been allowed the power of leadership on the city council or on the even-more-important community club. The community leaders feel very strongly about maintaining local power even if it means a loss of revenue from state or federal agencies. One city council member re-marked after the last local election:

> I was kidding the new mayor. I asked him where the moat was. It's the only way I can see of continuing the tradition of isolation for Bremer.

The statement by the new city council member reflects the conflict between those who have been socialized in a power structure where ascribed status is the norm and those who have migrated into the community and have been trained in the systems of mass society, where status is achieved. This conflict is increased between the two factions primarily because of the difference in expectations that are associated with these two types of socialization. Whereas in Bremer interaction with other community members is obligatory, those who have been socialized outside Bremer see interaction as voluntary (Seeley et al., 1957).

Bremer has retained its traditional way of handling community problems. By separating their political groups into two categories—1) elected and 2) open to the public—they have been able to bypass many of the regulations placed on small rural governments by larger bureaucracies.

Political leaders in Bremer are trained from a very early age. While the prominence of athletics is a major feature of the local schools, athletics also play a role in training the future leaders of the community. Community members stress the role of training when asked about their local schools. Through the focus on community norms and working as a team, young residents are socialized to participate in organizations with the good of the group as the gauge by which all political activity is measured.

When a young man reaches his mid-twenties, he takes the first step in gaining political awareness, through association with the volunteer fire department. By fighting local fires and protecting the property of Bremer residents, he learns two things. First, he learns that he must remain visible to the community and show he has a desire to lead. Second, he learns the norms and orientations of the community. After several years as a volunteer, the young man will be asked to take a position on a board of a more structured organization. In this way the community as a whole has the opportunity to watch the individual in stressful situations and to see whether he maintains the values of Bremer as he works his way up through a prescribed system. The role played by the young man's father or other relatives in Bremer's past political arena has a great deal to do with which direction the young leader may take. There are several levels of political organization in Bremer, and the patriarchal system often dictates which of these organizations a young man will participate in.

The Community Club as a
Community-Control Facilitator

The primary goal of the community club is to maintain local control over the affairs of Bremer. In the words of a longtime community club member:

> We are here because we want to see Bremer survive. Too many small towns jump on any government program that comes along. We aren't like that. When we want something done we just get together and do it. When we came back from the war the school needed a swimming pool. There were some people who wanted to apply for some federal or state grants from the Education Department. Well, we [community club] just decided that if all [a] swimming pool took was some cement, pumps, and some small buildings, then we could do that, so we built a swimming pool. It's still there and it's one of the nicest pools in the area.

Although the complexity of the construction of a swimming pool was oversimplified by the community club member, the pool was constructed by local farmers and community members building the pool with local supplies and labor. This example of why the community club exists and what it does reflects the position that the traditional methods of maintaining local autonomy are still the best. Community-control orientations and norms are predominant in this organization. The community club president is the nephew of the previous community club president. Positions of power within the club are ascribed. While the club is open to anyone in the community, the primary power leaders within the club are persons who played on the athletic teams in Bremer and have continued or built businesses in Bremer.

An example of the ascribed nature of authority in Bremer is the newly elected president of the community club, whose mother is related to the family that has held the position for the last 50 years. In a letter mailed to all Bremer residents, he illustrated that he planned to continue the work of the community club. The letter read:

Happy New Year

As many of you already know, the Fair Board and Community Club have decided to start construction of a new community building. This project has been discussed for several years and nothing has been done. There is a great need for this building as the fair needs somewhere to house the arts and crafts displays. For the last several years these have been displayed in the old State shop but now the City owns the property and uses it daily.

The arts and crafts are a very important part of our fair. Not only do they add additional categories for our youth and adults to enter, they bring in much needed revenue from the state. Without this division in our fair, we would lose around $1,800 in reimbursements.

We currently have a small building fund that has accumulated over the years, enough to start. The building that is being proposed would have around 3,000 sq. ft. with restrooms. Plans call for plumbing and wiring to be put in to allow for kitchen facilities later.

Community Club is asking for your help. We need $12,000 more to see this project completed. We would appreciate your contribution, large or small, to allow us to finish this building by fair time. If you can help, please contact Bill Stanton, John Price, Fred Bingham, or send your contributions to Jim Olson, Box 108, Bremer, Washington.

Thank you for your support!!!!!

Sincerely,

Jack Dodson, President
Bremer Community Club

P.S. Most of the work will be done by donated labor, so if you can help at all, please do so!!!!!!

The letter written by the community club president illustrates two points. First, the president perceives the community club to be an important group in the community when it comes to bringing community resources together. Second, the mention of the potential loss of revenue previously provided by the state indicates the influence of mass society in Bremer. The community club is perceived to be beyond the influence of outside organizations; even so, it must take into consideration the loss of state money.

When the community residents were asked who they thought should make the decisions for the community, 25 percent chose the person who has lived in the community all his or her life, and 45 percent selected the person who has worked his or her way up through local organizations in the community. These responses indicate that the community shares a consensus on what and who a community leader should be. Traditional power is the basis of authority for Bremerites and they feel that the only way an individual can understand that tradition is to have lived several generations in the community. Other responses given by community members included the following: a person with the betterment of Bremer in mind, someone who puts the community interests above his or her own, and someone with a broad background of community attitudes who knows the community.

These responses to the question of who should make community decisions demonstrate the orientation of the community as a group. Leaders within Bremer are expected to follow the traditions of Bremer and to hold the community's interests above their own. In the mass society individual achievement is the norm; in the community-control era, as it is exemplified in Bremer, the good of the group is paramount in how the community wants decisions to be made.

The community club lies outside the reach of mass-society organizations. It accomplishes this by being an informal organization open to anyone in the community. Through the club's continued existence as a voluntary organization, its decisions are not formally voted upon by the public. It is much quicker for the community club to put its decisions into action because it is not required to follow all of the regulations from the outside that the city council does.

The overlapping roles among formal and informal political organizations within Bremer illustrate the overlapping institutional structure within the community. With the primarily agricultural focus of the community, the more formal political organizations, such as the city council, cannot have members who live outside the legal city limits. The community club has no restrictions; a young farmer is president of the club. The community club is made up of about half farmers and half community businessmen. This mixture of members increases the power base of the members. Whereas the city council, according to many of the community club members, can utilize only the resources of the residents of the town, the community club has the influence to gather resources from the more wealthy in the community, the grain farmers who live outside of town.

These overlapping institutional roles allow the community club members to have information from all of the other formal and informal political organizations in Bremer plus the economic and social resources available throughout the community. The overlapping roles allow the club's decisions to be accepted by the majority of the community.

Other organizations within Bremer such as fraternal organizations are operated as social associations. Although the members of the community club are members of the fraternal organizations, the decisions as to which way the community should move are decided upon by the power brokers who head the community club. Through participating in a variety of organizations, the power leaders are fulfilling the obligation of face-to-face interaction and association with the rest of the community.

This socialization pattern for training leaders lends itself to the maintenance of the traditional norms the community (Lynd and Lynd, 1929). The homogeneity of the residents of Bremer enables the socialization process to last throughout their lifetime.

Bremer: Contrast with Other Community Studies

The analysis of politics in Bremer is in direct contrast to previous studies of politics in rural communities. Loomis and Beegle (1950) explain their position:

> Political Scientists agree that the weakest link in government in the United States today is the local rural unit. It is inefficient in practically every phase. It fails to incorporate adequately the sentiments of the electorate into policy, and its responsibility to the electorate is indefinite. When the policy does reflect adequately these sentiments and desires, the county and township governing bodies are ineffective in carrying through the action necessary to realize the objectives involved in both short- and long-range policy. (Loomis and Beegle, 1950, p. 561)

When looking at the political arena of Bremer it is evident that the ascribed basis of power is still in effect. Leaders are appointed because of family characteristics such as the prior generation's participation in leadership. While who your relatives are and how they worked within the community is very important in being given a leadership role, an individual's background is also important. The community as a whole watches the young men as they participate in 4-H, FFA, athletics, and community projects. Through an understanding of how the individual behaves in these circumstances, the community begins to select future leaders when they are very young.

Upon either the recommendation of current community leaders or the historical involvement of an individual's relatives in community affairs, the young future leaders of Bremer are trained through involvement in organizations such as the local volunteer fire department. During this socialization period, future leaders learn what it is to be a political leader in Bremer.

Political decisions are made in the community according to flexibility of rules and particularistic criteria. The decision on which lawn tractor to buy for the town was not based on economics but on a community norm of splitting the buying among businesses within the community. These community-control attributes are exhibited among the residents of Bremer, and the community expects leaders to follow these norms. This finding is similar to the argument presented by Sanders (1977). Sanders argues:

> In almost any country today, the primary network of local government is the group of local people selected to serve as members of the local administrative unit. Some families are represented; others are not. Therefore, families in the same community will differ in degree of influence over and benefits expected from members of the local governing board. (Sanders, 1977, p. 122)

Sanders goes on to say that because of this fact those influential members in the community will come to expect favors from their kinship group or neighborhood. In Bremer this also seems to be the case; political leaders see themselves as sacrificing for the family. One retired political leader explained:

> When I sat on the city council I was not only giving my views but my whole family's. So they add a voice on the council. Because we donated a lot of time to the community I don't think it was out of line for us to borrow city equipment if we needed it.

The retired leader's sentiments reflect his justification of specialized treatment for his relatives because of his position in city government. The norm of public meetings being immediately presented informally to the rest of the community places a great deal of pressure on the local leaders to focus on the group, the community as a whole, rather than on any specific family. The example of the lawn tractor illustrates this point. A decision could have been made to buy the lawn tractor from a prominent city leader, but the good of the group was seen as the most important goal of the council.

Local authority is the norm in Bremer, as is maintenance of local control over community affairs. The community norms must be followed. Leaders who fail to follow a norm often find themselves relinquishing their position or adapting a broader community scope when deciding on community problems. The sanctioning process is public and is facilitated by the open, informal meeting held after the formal city council meeting. As in the bank, the norm in Bremer is that politics are open to the public. It is also necessary to remain public, as one community club member explained:

> If we weren't public and open about what we do then rumors would get started. Once that has happened it is hard to get everybody together again.

The attributes of the community-control era are very evident in the political arena of Bremer. The community has been able to bypass many mass-society regulations by having a political organization that is outside of the legal mandates of mass society organizations. Through a refusal to participate in federal and state grant programs, Bremerites have been able to maintain much of their traditional local control. As the community club has gained increasing power within the community, the city council and formal power leaders have been slowly losing their power. The direction of the loss is the opposite of what would be predicted by Vidich and Bensman (1958). They saw power being usurped by mass-society agencies outside of the community. In Bremer the power is being brought back into the community through the use of voluntary political organizations such as the community club.

The reason for the differences between this study and those conducted previously on political organizations in rural communities may be a reflection of the achieved position of the researchers. As agents of the mass society, they saw as most viable informants who were also agents of the mass society. Examples included by Vidich and Bensman were county extension agents, school administrators, etc., and these were seen as viable informants of the politics of the community. In this study it has been possible to move beyond the mass-society agents to the traditional informal power leaders in Bremer, and this movement may be reflected in the increased community control over local political institutions.

In sharp contrast, the influence of the information age, on the other hand, is minimal on the political institutions of Bremer. The influence of the mass society is diminished by the movement of political power outside the constraints of the legal formal political institutions. While out-networking has influenced business and education institutions, the politics of Bremer have remained consistent with community-control-era attributes.

Conclusion

The community club accomplishes for Bremer what no government can do. It connects the interests of town and country residents, thereby expanding the community's resource base. It has, in essence, solved the critical problem described by Galpin nearly 80 years ago, and which has frustrated local community leaders ever since. It is the separation of town and country resources. Galpin said:

> . . . farm people . . . are situated on the slopes of social watersheds draining into one specific village or small city . . . that . . . ignore township and county lines. No wonder it is difficult to get people . . . to work together. This maladjustment is perhaps the fundamental handicap of the farm home (p. 22). The farmer does not share in the control and responsibility . . . . The outlying farm population . . . come to town, stand on other people's streets, in other people's shops. The farmer pays in so much to the treasury that he feels he ought to have consideration; he pays so little directly toward the institutions that the villages consider that this rights are not compelling. (1915:26)

Through the community club's many actions, the resources of town and country residents are combined to provide benefits for the entire community that neither could achieve and maintain alone—a swimming pool, a golf course, fairgrounds, and even a doctor. More than any single entity or event, the community club is responsible for maintaining Bremer as a functioning community.

One farmer recalled his response when the idea of building a swimming pool was broached.

> How difficult could it be, moving some dirt and doing some plumbing? If you are going to farm you have to know how to do things like that. So, we brought our equipment to town and we did it.

Perhaps an oversimplification, but in essence that is an important part of what happened. Together town and country tax themselves through the private mechanism of community club solicitations, and separately they bring their complementary skills and labor together for their joint benefit.

The history of community centers and surrounding countryside in the United States has been one of political separation. Typically, county government draws resources and commitment from residents of the countryside, and city government draws resources and commitment from town residents. Bremer has found a mechanism for overcoming this separatist tendency.

The price, which many within Bremer would not call a price at all, is the rejection of mass-society overtures—in particular, government grants and loans. It is also, as illustrated through the city council actions, extraordinary efforts to legitimate actions (some of which may give priority to businesses having to "take turns" as good community citizens) over who submits the lowest competitive bid.

To the extent that processes associated with the community-control era characterize behavior in Bremer, what happens in the small green building at the edge of town on Friday nights bears much of the responsibility and/or deserves the credit. The community club, more than any other entity, gives shape to the umbrella of social control so evident throughout Bremer.

Through organizing and legitimizing a community club, the political organizations of Bremer have held most of the influence of the mass society at bay. When examining the political groups and organizations within the community of Bremer, patterns become clear. First, there are those political organizations that resemble political organizations throughout the mass society. These organizations follow standardized rules and legal mandates in their decision making. The city council is an example of a standardized organization that is guided by the community's norms of particularism and ascribed status. Second, the most powerful political organization within the community is not formed in accordance with nor does it follow the prescribed mandates required of mass-society political groups. The community club is an example of a community-controlled political organization.

The city council falls into the first category. While the city council responds differently to rules because of its ties to larger organizations outside of Bremer, they have, through the selection of leaders, attempted to maintain a responsiveness to the rules of the community rather than to the rules of the mass society.

7

Gender: Women's Roles Have Changed, Most Men's Haven't

The exclusion of women from the community club raises important questions about the role of women in the community of Bremer. We thought at first that women might play a larger role in the communication structure of the community, but our findings show that men move around the community—from farm to farm—and have substantial daily interaction with other male farmers; they seem to experience no disadvantage when it comes to knowing the everyday intimate details of the community.

At first glance the roles of men and women in Bremer reflect a Norman Rockwell painting of the past, where the father works outside the home and socializes the son to follow in his footsteps while the mother stays at home and nurtures the family. Yet at closer examination the roles of men and women in Bremer have two faces. The first is that of the Rockwell painting, the second is that of a community going through a transition, with women gaining leadership roles outside the boundaries that identify Bremer as a community.

A Wedding Anniversary in Bremer

The Bremer calendar that hangs in most homes, sometimes stuck with magnets to the refrigerator next to drawings by children and recent photographs of family members, shows that June 7th is the Livingston's 21st anniversary. Jan Kendricks, a longtime friend, observes the date and calls two other friends without any thought of first talking to Mrs. Livingston. Neither friend is surprised by the call; they too have looked at the June calendar and are aware of the Livingston's anniversary, although both know the approximate anni-

124

Figure 7.1 A Portion of the Bremer Calendar Showing Date of the Livingston's Anniversary

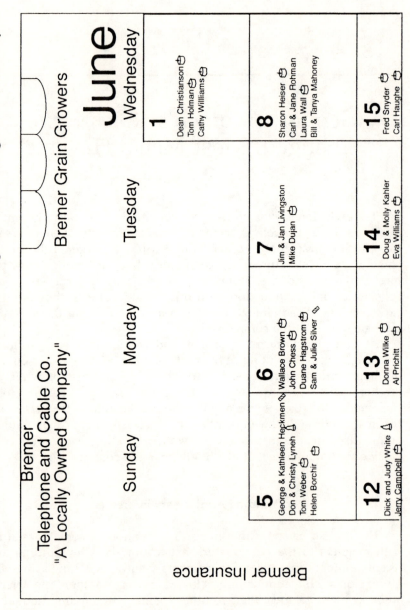

versary date without checking. Few who were at the wedding will forget the mistake of an outside relative who walked into the tavern in the middle of the afternoon, sat in the front, and ordered a beer.

The next day Mrs. Kendricks calls Mrs. Livingston and casually asks, "Your anniversary is coming up on the 7th. Do you and Jim have anything special planned for the evening?" even though she already knows from her husband that Mr. Livingston isn't planning to take his wife to Spokane for a short weekend as he did on their tenth anniversary. Mrs. Livingston answers with the expected no, and then Mrs. Kendricks asks if it would be all right if they came over to help celebrate. She adds, "Don't worry, you won't have to do anything; we'll bring everything."

It is as though a previously written script is being acted out, for all parties know that the Livingston's will be home the night of their anniversary. A friend plans the party with other friends before calling the celebrant, who is told that the friends will bring everything. That evening the husbands are told what they will be doing the 7th.

The night of the party begins with couples arriving and taking off their coats. The hostess, the woman who is celebrating her anniversary, takes the coats and places them on the bed in the master bedroom. The couples enter, then sit on couches and chairs in the livingroom, generally husband next to his wife, and talk about the weather and the pictures of the kids on the walls. After about an hour everyone has arrived and the gifts are opened. The women then go to the kitchen and bring the cake out to the men, who have gravitated toward one another and are talking about the new John Deere combines that have just come on to the market. The men talk about the size of the machine and the $200,000 price tag and complain about how the manufacturing companies who build the combines, although they are required to make parts for 20 years, generally subcontract out to foreign companies who make cheap parts that are not available. This, according to the men, forces many farmers to buy newer combines, which are increasing in size and cost, making farming more expensive and therefore less feasible for those with smaller and medium-sized farms.

The women who sit and stand next to one another on the other side of the room are also talking about the new combines, but the conversation focuses on not only the cost but also how many bushels of grain it would take to pay for the new machines. They also talk about the high interest rates and how that should be taken into consideration when someone thinks about buying any new machinery. These differences point toward the different but compatible roles played by men and women in Bremer when it comes to agriculture in the 1990s.

In a straightforward manner, a third-generation Bremer woman explains the change in her role in the farm operation over the last 50 years.

> When dad had the farm mom didn't even ask about the books. She talked about money problems but in a very general way. She never said, "Well, we paid too much for fertilizer this year." Instead, she talked about not being able to buy a new stove because Dad said we just couldn't afford it. Dad handled the money in secret, if you want to put it that way. It just wasn't a topic of conversation. Then when I married Owen we talked about the farm operation and money, but he handled all the checks and paying the bills. When it came to the end of the year Owen would just take all of the checks out and spread them around on the kitchen table, and for two or three days he would write "fertilizer," "seed," or whatever on them, put them in stacks, and it would be done. About, I'd say, 1960, we started getting pretty complicated. We had ground leased from Fred, my brother, and so I began taking care of just that part of the money. Then when we got involved in the farm programs it just got so complicated that I took over the books. You see, I just had more time to do those things. In 1973 we bought the other place and then we had to get an accountant. We had just reached a point where it was so complicated and complex that we needed outside help.

As this farmer explains, the diversity and complexity of agriculture have influenced her role in handling money on the farm, and they have also changed the male role. In the past women have always handled household money, but their handling of money for the farm has been a gradual transition tied to the increased influence of the mass society on agriculture. This woman's traditional role didn't change when it came to the house and the kids, but she felt that handling the books was just an additional duty.

> It was something extra I would do after the kids went to bed, and then when they moved out and got married I put in that little office over there and could do them at my leisure. Now I felt that I was more involved with the farm.

This pattern is not even throughout the community. There exist farms where women have always handled the farm and household money, and there are people who still see the control of the money as a male domain. As agriculture has become more complex and mass society has had a greater influence on production practices, the role of women has changed to reflect the increased need by the family farm to have someone continually collect and analyze the outgo and income. Yet it isn't just in agriculture that women's roles have changed in Bremer; education of the younger generation has also seen changes in roles.

While the anniversary party continues, the conversations in the room move to the local school. The superintendent has recently been fired and the high school principal has been given the job. The men, who have moved out on the back porch to accommodate the smokers, talk about the decreased emphasis on athletics and how that is going to make "wusses" out of the boys. One farmer expresses his view:

> I played football and I still could read. I just don't understand why everyone feels that you can't make a concession here or there for a kid who is putting his effort into sports. Learning discipline is probably the most important thing a person can learn in life and the football field is probably the best place in the world to learn that.

The men agree with this farmer but also talk about how they feel it is important to make sure the boys have a chance at athletic scholarships to help them pay for college. The conversation turns to how it is different today trying to prepare children for the future. According to one farmer:

> When I was five or six Dad started taking me out on the tractor and I knew then that I was going to be a farmer. I still take Rob with me, but we also bought the computer so he can get some other skills just in case this place won't support him and his wife. When Dad turned 59 he retired and we can make enough to support him and mom and Beth and I and the kids. But I'm not sure that is going to be possible when I'm 59. If not, Rob is going to have to find some other way to make a living. So he has got to have some other skills. Me, I played basketball and worked in shop but didn't pay much attention to the rest of school, but today things just aren't as cut and dried.

This change in the role of the father and the change in rural life is also reflected in the livingroom inside the house, where the women are talking about the new academic scholarships that the Bremer Women's Club has developed. Two students have recently placed high in the national scholastic completion and the scholarships are a response to that achievement. One young woman explains:

> Farming isn't a bad way to make a living, but most of the kids don't want to stay here after they graduate anyway, so we need to prepare them for the outside. College gives them an out. Otherwise they will end up trying to get the few jobs left in town.

These brief glimpses of conversations at a Bremer get-together illustrate several changes in men's and women's roles that have evolved over time. Control over the economic assets, once a male domain, now belongs to both adults in the family or to the woman. This change is also reflected in how the money from farming is spent and what criteria are applied to spend it. The role of fathers in the socialization process has also changed, and some of these changes are seen in the revised orientation toward education, as illustrated by the new scholarship fund. These changes are just a few that influence the role of gender in the community.

The planning of the anniversary is just one example of how traditional roles prevail in the community. Earlier in this book we talked about the values that exist in the community, but we have yet to examine them in the context of gender. We have discussed conversation that takes place at a social gathering and how gender appears to influence the content of conversations. Yet, the role expectations in Bremer need to be examined to understand fully the traditional form of the community.

Elk Season: A Ritual Stratified by Gender

Late fall, after the fields are planted with winter wheat and those that will be left fallow lie dormant from the frost, another ritual starts to take place in Bremer. Preparation begins for the annual elk hunt, a time for the men and young boys to bond and for the women to "have time for themselves." As the discussion of gender roles in the community has illustrated, men and women play different roles within many of the institutions that make up the foundation of this community. Elk-hunting season provides a ritual that may help in examining these differentiated roles.

As late October arrives, occasional rifle shots can be heard echoing down the valleys where many of the local farmers live. These reports are those of large-caliber rifles, not the flat booming of a shotgun. By following the sound of the reports, one can see that three males are standing next to a barn, holding rifles, several with scopes on them, talking, their breath visible in the cool air. Targets, white with a dark red center with surrounding circles, can be seen held by clods of dirt in the dark gray stubble halfway up a steep hillside. These men are sighting in their rifles for the annual elk hunt: a ritual where three generations of men place pack saddles on their horses and a rifle in the scabbard on the saddle, then make their trek to an elk camp in the high mountains of northern Idaho, where their families have gone to hunt the large dark animals, many as big as a horse, for almost 100 years.

While the older men oil their guns and prepare lists for items necessary for the trip, young boys, their voices almost giddy, ask questions about past hunts. Grandfathers and fathers laugh and talk about the "six-point bull" that they shot in '67 when the father was just a boy, and how they had to cut the animal into quarters to haul it back to camp, where they hung the animal's parts wrapped in clean white sheets in the trees.

One older farmer said:

> We try to do this every year. We trailer [horse trailers] the animals up there, ride in for two days, and then we set up camp. It's the same place that my Dad took me. It's one of the few times that we really get a chance to be with the young ones, without TV or telephones, or worrying about what's happening down here at the farm. And it's just not that; there is the danger. We have lost a few horses over the years because they would slip off the trail and fall into a canyon. Depending on the year we sometimes have to take the canyon trail. It puts hair on the chests of these young ones. Without it they would be just like all the other kids their age.

This annual ritual is seen by the local farmers as a time to reinforce their value systems, to help the young men become "men." The actual hunt lasts about two weeks and only males participate in the activity. The camps are made of large canvas tents stretched over pine poles. The poles are left year after year and, if the weather has been mild, are often still standing, so canvas is stretched over the poles from the following year. Bremer residents have their camps in the same vicinity in the mountains. In one way it is simply a movement of one group of Bremer citizens to another area for a short period of time. Yet the sense of community can be found even here. When an elk hunt is completed, the meat from the killed animals is shared. Almost every hunter returns home with some portion of elk. This meat is then generally made into German sausage and, if appropriate, elk steaks. The exchange of sausage leads to an informal competition over who makes the best sausage.

While the men are preparing lists for the hunt, filling the pack saddles, shoeing the horses, and sighting in their rifles, the women are also busy preparing for the hunt. Theirs is a time of "getting away" from the men. Phones ring in houses across the community as card parties, trips to the theater in Spokane, and Sunday brunches are planned. The activities for the women often exclude the younger females, who are hired to watch the younger children in the community. One woman explained:

> We just need to get apart. It's not like you live in a city, where both
> people work someplace else and then just come home at night. We
> are always around each other. Harvest, we are constantly tired and
> under stress. Bob gets to the point where he just doesn't want to talk
> to anyone and at times I just wish he would go off by himself and
> mellow out. Elk season is a time we can both do some things that
> maybe the other just doesn't want to do. I don't like hunting and he
> doesn't like theater, so now we both get to do some things we wouldn't
> do otherwise. Plus, it gives him a chance to be around Robert [son]
> without it always being a work situation. Just the two of them, like he
> did with his dad.

Other women expressed similar comments such as this: "It's a long winter with both of us around the house all of the time. He works in the shop, but he still is around the house a lot more than any other time of the year. Elk season gives us a break before that starts up again."

The ritual of elk hunting serves several functions within the Bremer community. One function is the reinforcement of roles and values of the community residents. The hunt provides an opportunity for the generations to get together, isolated from the rest of the world for a few weeks, reinforcing what Bremer residents see as the roles of men and women and citizens. The hunt provides items for conversation for the winter months. Yet the most important aspect of this particular community ritual may be the separation it provides for the farm spouses. Following harvest and planting, all parties in the relationships expressed a need to get away from one another for a while. It is a time of rest before they return to the farms, where they will continue with other rituals, such as preparing tax records for the upcoming tax year, working on the farm machinery, and waiting for the spring thaw, when the year is seen as beginning in the community of Bremer.

Role Expectations

Farming expectations are clearly tied to gender and age. Men drive the large grain combines and the women, young boys, and young girls drive trucks to the elevators. When a machine breaks down, the women generally go to town for the parts and the men do the mechanical work. At the grain elevators, men handle the actual unloading of the grain and young men weigh the trucks. In the home, the women generally write the checks and do the farm books. Yet when it comes to making the final decision as to whether to buy a large, $200,000 combine, the decision is generally made jointly with a variety of criteria used.

In other agricultural communities in the past, women had what is called egg money. The egg money was used for small household items and for spending money by the women, who had total control over this economic endeavor. In Bremer, where mono-agriculture has replaced diversified farming activities, the use of egg money is not prevalent. As women in the community have become more involved in overseeing economic business decisions, the separation of men's money and women's money has almost entirely disappeared.

Traditional roles still prevail in educating and socializing of young people. Men view their role as that of the disciplinarian and the provider. According to one businessman:

> My job is to make sure the family survives economically. I work at the shop here, although Mary [wife] comes in when she can. When our kids were younger I took care of all of the business by myself. When the kids were young I was the one who spanked them, although we didn't really use spanking much, and the one who said enough is enough.

This traditional role is reflected in the parent-teacher meetings that the school holds several times a year. As the principal said, "It's mostly the moms who come in and talk with us." Women in Bremer see their role as the nurturer and the supporter for their husband. One young schoolteacher was quite surprised when the conversation over coffee or lunch at the school generally focused on the teachers' husbands: "When we talked it was generally Bill did this or Bill did that, and everyone sat around telling what a good husband they had. I didn't expect that. I thought, with the women's movement, that the women stuck in these traditional roles would be angry, but I found just the opposite. They felt comfortable supporting the husband and the family."

When it comes to disciplining the students at the school, tradition also prevails. One female teacher explained:

> One day I had a senior boy who wouldn't do the work and kept interrupting the class. I told him if he didn't straighten up I would remove him from the class. At lunch I was told that I should leave disciplining the students to the men.

This model for role expectations is supported by the role of men in the school. Of the twenty-one schoolteachers who work in the school in Bremer, five are males. These males teach history and science, and all but one are involved in coaching at one level or another. The principals are all male in the Bremer school system, and men also hold the majority of the school board positions. Traditionally, one or two women have sat on the board. In the mid-1980s a woman became chair of the board, and community reaction was reflected by statements that pointed out that the "quality of school board members was decreasing, so their power should be limited." These comments and others similar to it lead one to assume that gender differences exist in the institutions within Bremer and that the change that much of the country has seen in women's roles is not necessarily reflected in the educational institution within Bremer.

The role of women in the school extends from the traditional role of nurturer in the family. Their status in the school system is amplified by the general status of women within the overall community. As noted previously, when residents were tasked to identify community leaders, the majority of all respondents named male members of the community.

In evaluating the role of men and women in the religious institutions in Bremer, tradition is the key word. Men are ministers in the community. The fact that men are ministers should not be construed as a move by Bremerites to look for male ministers; ministers are assigned by some of the churches for which they work. The church boards are entirely male. Women provide the food for the funerals and men are the pallbearers. This division of labor again illustrates the traditional roles of men and women in the community.

When it comes to local politics, men are generally viewed as the power leaders and sit on the local boards, while the women run the voting booths and count the votes. Local politics in Bremer follow a traditional form.

Health has long been viewed as part of the women's domain and in Bremer this pattern continues. The physician is male and the majority of health care is provided by him and his female assistants. Yet, in the home it is the woman who provides the health care, and women are also the holders of health information (as will be illustrated in Chapter 8 by the example of the nurse who understood why the young farmer didn't know much of his own personal health history).

A Change from the Outside

Up to this point in the evaluation of the role of gender in Bremer, the community does indeed follow the pattern of what has been perceived by many as a traditional, male-dominated community. Yet when we look outside the boundaries of the community, there has been a change in women's roles. The diversification of agriculture and the movement toward mass education has left its mark on the role of women in the community. An example is the Pea and Lentil Marketing Association, where the president and the treasurer are women. A woman also sits on the regional grain-growers lobbying group and women have organized several lobbying groups aimed at the marketing of local crops worldwide. These are not the traditional roles for Bremer women. In addition to the marketing groups formed by local women, an organization has also recently been formed aimed at maintaining the family farm, headed by women and for women.

Several local women are also involved at the state level in planned-parenting movements and hold positions on other regional and state boards related to health. These new roles have evolved, as one older woman explained:

> We all used to have four or five kids. Now two or three is the norm, so women have more time to be involved. Those home gardens have been replaced by extension telephones and lists with politicians' names on them. Today's woman is spending a lot of her time working the political system so we can keep this lifestyle for our kids.

The political power of the groups organized by local women is demonstrated in an event that took place during the fall of 1988. A state legislator canceled his talk to a group of male farmers to attend a meeting of local women who were organizing to lobby Washington, D.C., on the elimination of the farm-subsidy program. The state representative, after receiving calls from other groups, spent time with the new group and openly supported their agenda. This reflection of political power is not seen at the local level in Bremer but is seen by regional powers as viable.

The information age has also left its mark and has influenced the role of some women in the community. The few cottage industries that have developed in Bremer are directly tied to the use of information technology. The cottage industry that has developed is often a part-time occupation or business that is "wrapped around" other activities that are expected of women in Bremer.

Thus, the political power of women has grown, but this power is primarily outside the community. These and other changes have been felt by Bremerites at many levels. The traditional view of local women as those people who kept up the gardens, won national recognition for their work with flowers, and had bake sales for local scholarship funds still exists in Bremer. At the same time it is not possible to deny that when locals read the newspaper they see representatives of both genders from the community. The experience and contacts that local women have developed as they drive or fly to Olympia (state capital) cannot be ignored. These obvious changes in the role of women have created stress within the community.

Conclusion: Changing Roles, Added Stress

Stress from the changing roles can be seen in the school system as women teachers seek to be made principals. Several longtime teachers have raised the question at the school board and it has been decided that the board will attempt to hire a woman when a vacancy next occurs. As for local politics, there is a woman on the city council; however, no attempt has yet been made by women to join the community club.

The stress of changing roles can best be seen in the families, as men complain about their wives not being home to cook dinner because they are off to some meeting. As one farmer said when asked to describe his generation of farmers, "We are becoming the microwave generation." The joke is minor but the stress is great, according to some men who have grown up and been socialized with Bremer values. Although while men stand around machine shops they make comments similar to those found in the school lunchroom—men are speaking with pride of the accomplishments of their wives.

In Bremer, the face of gender roles in many aspects still resembles that of an earlier time, but with several twists. Whereas men control local politics and much of the local economy, it is women who have stepped outside their traditional roles and have become involved in the mass society as they work toward a political solution to many of the problems facing Bremer. The information technology now available to farm women and men has made it possible for networks to develop whereby women can get mailing lists from other organizations around the state by modem and can, without the aid of a secretary, conduct sophisticated marketing campaigns from their homes in the Palouse countryside. Up to this time there has not been much evidence of a change in the local power base because of these changing roles, and the question remains of when or if the local women will transfer these newfound skills to local institutions. Nor is it yet clear what the ramifications of such a change might be.

The role of gender in the Bremer community illustrates the trade-offs for maintaining community in the community-control era. It is also one reason why when urbanites hear discussion of gender roles in Bremer they say, "I could never live there. They should go in and force those people to come into the 20th century." The trade-off is that many of the advances made by women in the mass society have not been felt in Bremer. Yet, in examining the total impact of change on gender, it is quite evident that in Bremer women's roles are changing while most men's are remaining static. Some of the changes taking place within the community are a result of outside forces; but within the community itself, gender is still a primary factor in how much visible power one wields and who listens to what an individual has to say. The old adage "It's more important who said something than what they said" plays well within the power structure of the Bremer community, especially if that individual is a third-generation male. What impact the changing role of women will have on the ability of Bremer to maintain its traditional value systems and strong sense of community identity is a question that remains, for now, unanswered.

8

Medical Care:
Fulfilling the Old Doctor's Account
and Getting a Replacement

The one-page letter from the Bremer Community Club's Doctor's Committee was handed out by local merchants and community leaders to every household. It read as follows:

"Bremer Doctor's Account"

Dr. and Mrs. Hager will be retiring this summer and moving from Bremer. The medical practice and clinic they have run for the past 29 years has been sold to Dr. Fred McIntosh, who will be moving to our area this summer. He is planning to run the Bremer Clinic and begin a new practice in Centerville.

Dr. McIntosh has hired Dr. Bill Megar as his associate to take over the Bremer practice beginning next summer. Dr. Megar is presently in his last year of medical training in Portland, Oregon. He and his wife are the parents of three children and are expecting their fourth.

Dr. Megar and his family wish to live in Bremer provided they are able to purchase the Hager residence. In order to insure that Bremer will continue to have a physician in residence, the committee that was chosen by Dr. and Mrs. Hager to assist in bringing a doctor to our community is asking you to help loan Bill and Patty Megar the money to purchase the Hager house. A total of $70,000 is needed to purchase the house from the Hagers and cover additional expenses needed to finalize the transaction.

We are asking people [to] provide the loans in $1,000 increments which will be interest free. If you cannot give $1,000 but wish to help, you may try going together with friends, relatives or neighbors and

pool your resources which would be turned in as a $1,000 unit. Dr.
Megar will begin paying this loan back after he completes his second
year in Bremer. He will make his payments in 10 yearly installments
and, as the money comes in, it will be prorated so the lenders will each
receive a percentage of the annual payment.

A. "Skinny" Schneider and R. Billings are the trustees for the account.
J. Henry Sr., is the Administrator of the account. Donations or loans
can also be given to H.L., T.E., F.H., J.H., L.S., B.W., O.M., R.T., C.B.,
N.R., M.M., and P.H.

Any one of these people would be happy to accept your offering.
Checks are to be made payable to "Bremer's Doctor's Account."

If you wish to make a donation instead of a loan, checks are to be
made payable to "Bremer Community Club," with a notation in the
bottom left hand corner, "Doctor Account."

To insure that the residence is kept up and utilities and taxes are paid
Dr. McIntosh and his family will live in the house until Dr. Megar and
his family move up from Portland.

Thank you for any consideration you might give our request!

The Doctor's Committee

This letter caused a great deal of excitement within the town of
Bremer and the surrounding countryside. For two years community
residents wondered if a doctor was going to be found who would move to
Bremer to practice medicine. Recruiting and retaining health-care
providers in rural areas has traditionally been seen as a problem
because of the scarcity of available physicians or a weak local
economic base (Cordes, 1988). Several times during the two-year
period, doctors did come who expressed an interest in the practice, but
when the doctor's committee met and interviewed them they turned the
prospective doctors down. The major reason for turning doctors down
was the committee just didn't "think people would go to them," or
"they just didn't seem to fit in." An example may help to illustrate the
difficulty of selecting a physician for Bremer.
 One of the applicants for the position was a female physician of
Asian decent educated in the Far East. She wore traditional clothes
from her country of origin and was married to a native of the same
country. She had expressed interest in moving to Bremer and paid her
own expenses to come and talk to the doctor's committee. The town
representatives were unanimous in their decision not to sell the clinic to

this particular physician even though Bremer was only one of fifteen communities in the state searching for a local physician.

The basis of interaction in Bremer is particularistic. This is especially important for the doctor. To act as a physician in Bremer, the doctor must have the same knowledge that the other community members have of all members, as well as the same values based primarily in the Protestant ethic.

Medicine in Bremer is conducted in a manner reminiscent of the early 1900s. For nearly the last 30 years, one doctor has administered to the residents. He delivers the babies, comforts the elderly in their last days, fights with his clients over smoking and eating too much, and has been on call 24 hours per day for 29 years, with two weeks off in the summer. In his 30th year, the doctor notified the community that he was going to retire and that they needed to find a replacement for him. The community convinced him to remain for one extra year. During that period the community went to work finding a suitable doctor to replace Dr. Hager.

1958: The Arrival of Dr. Hager

Dr. Harold Hager, born in Switzerland, arrived in the Palouse in the fall of 1958. His hopes included finding a partner in this endeavor. The circumstances that led to his selecting Bremer as a site to practice medicine included his family's desire to live in a rural area. In Bremer they would be able to own the clinic when they retired, an attractive benefit. The Hagers came to Bremer with the intention of staying.

The Bremer people followed a pattern that had been developed many years earlier. The community club went together with the rest of the citizens in Bremer and signed bank notes in $1,000 increments to buy the clinic and practice from the previous doctor. These notes were interest-free and the farmers, businessmen, and interested residents signed them for reasons that were not economically motivated. As one of those who signed bank notes said:

> Yes, I signed a note. It was for $5,000. We had to have a doctor to keep this town together, and to provide the care for our parents we had to have one. When Dr. Hager came we just got together and decided that the only way to get a doctor and keep him was to make it so he owned the practice. It has worked every time. We put the money up. They [doctors] pay us back interest-free. But they earn it, don't let anyone kid you. To be a doctor here means being on call all of the time. The only time you can't get Doc Hager is when you see him and

his wife on the hills riding horses. But even then if it is an emergency someone will have seen them so we can almost always get him.

Being the only physician in Bremer in the late 1950s required long days and enduring patients who expected the doctor to know their past ailments. The town was undergoing a change as the baby boom was occurring. The doctor explained it this way:

> I was delivering babies all night, then I would be back in the office. I delivered many a baby in the back of the office here in town. But I always make an attempt to get them to Centerville to the hospital. Now it's quite different. I may only deliver one baby a month or so. Then it seemed that that's how I slept. Delivering babies.

The doctor explained that by 1959 he was looking for a partner. As we sat on a spring evening in the kitchen of his large white house with a small wood stove burning for heat, we talked about the difficulty of getting a doctor to come to Bremer. As we talked he finished his late dinner. About every ten minutes a siren would go off and red lights would flash. His wife is slightly hard of hearing and the alarm system is designed so that she doesn't miss any important calls from patients. These telephone conversations focused on whether the medicine he had given an elderly patient was having side effects, whether he thought someone's back was bad enough not to go to work tomorrow. The time was 10:00 p.m. and he was working again. Between phone calls and mouthfuls of food he talked about the process of getting a doctor and about deciding to leave the community after almost 30 years.

> I just needed help. But I couldn't find one. Then in 1968 I tried in earnest. Went through employment agencies across the country; we went national and local. We just couldn't find a partner. Then I decided this year that if I want to try something else in life, I'm not getting any younger. I'm 58 or 9. [Wife: "You'll be 59 this week. You have a birthday coming up."] Anyway, since I made the mental decision to leave we've been trying everything to get another doctor in. I had one interested but he was offered another job at $90,000 with no capital outlay. Here I am trying to ask a young doctor to come in, buy a building, and pay me for the practice. Young doctors just don't have to do that anymore.

A Physician's Plea for Help

Working seven days a week, 24 hours a day, for 30 years has been a drain on him. As rural populations have declined in the Palouse, the incomes of rural doctors have not kept pace with that of urban doctors. Doctor Hager also believes that young doctors just aren't motivated as the older doctors were. They can move to an urban area now and work four or five days a week, earn an income close to $100,000 the first couple of years, and not have to invest their own money. Being a rural doctor means something totally different.

> To practice medicine here you must be able to carry accounts for years. At times you have to take barter in exchange for your services. I've taken wheat, barley for my horses, a pig or side of beef. When you accept items like that you are placed in a difficult situation because you have to have some cash to pay your employees and to pay for the building. Plus the hours are long. I work or am on call every day of the week. Without a partner there isn't a break. Now in an urban area a young doctor is part of a practice with several doctors. This way there is someone to cover for him when he needs a break. I've tried to have doctors in Centerville cover for me, but the patients complain. They just expect Doc Hager to be there.

The belief that country doctors work hard and are very much a part of the community may be questioned in Bremer. The position of the town physician is indeed one held in high esteem among community members. Yet it is not a position that holds a great deal of political power. One reason for this lack of political power is the expectation that the doctor will at some time retire and leave the community. Being a member of the community of Bremer means that you and your relatives have lived in the community for several generations. The situation for the doctor and religious leaders is different.

The majority of power positions within the community are held by locals who have gained this status and power through a process of ascription. The doctor was not born in Bremer and had no relatives that had lived there prior to his arrival. He gained his status through certification from mass-society organizations such as a medical school and state medical board. Through this process he bypassed the traditional way of getting and holding power within the community. His status in the community reflects this position.

Needed but Not an Insider

Although the doctor is not seen as a traditional community member, after 29 years his presence in the community is considered a major necessity for its maintenance. Ninety percent of the residents go to Dr. Hager. When the possibility of a doctor not practicing in Bremer is discussed, almost 30 percent of the population say that they would move if there were no doctor. The position is important enough for the community that it is willing to create a special social role for the doctor. This status is outside the ordinary day-to-day roles that exist in the community. The role of doctor is given a special designation, especially by the elderly. The geographic location of Bremer, about 50 miles from a small city with a hospital and over 30 miles from the nearest hospital, enhances the local physician's status. Those who are particularly concerned about keeping the doctor in the community explain their position this way:

Community's priorities should be a full-time doctor who lives in Bremer.

Must have a doctor for the senior citizens. So many senior citizens live here, we definitely need a doctor here.

If we don't have our own doctor, Bremer won't be any better than the rest of the small towns around here.

On one level, the importance of a local doctor is based on older residents's fears that in case of an accident they would be without health care and could possibly die; at another level, the maintaining of Bremer's identity, that of being a "better place to live" in comparison to the other small towns in the area, is very important to Bremerites.

Life-bird, a helicopter dispatched from a major medical center, takes 35 minutes to fly to Bremer. This distance increases the fear that many of the older citizens have about their health care. This fear, which is valid, places the doctor in a unique position within the social structure of the community. The position of doctor is seen as a necessary part of the community without which many of the residents would leave. This leads to the second level of importance of having a doctor in Bremer.

Because of the strong group orientation combined with the long tradition of maintaining community control in Bremer, the economic viability of the community is threatened without a doctor. The retiring doctor speculated:

> When I leave, the hospital in Centerville will be in a bad way. I have 30 percent of the patients in the hospital now. Now in Bremer, if I was to leave without a replacement, a grocery store would probably go, the drugstore, maybe the new clothes business and a lot of people. Even if they [community residents] don't doctor with me they live here because in case of an emergency they could call me.

The survey data support the doctor's belief that the importance of the doctor goes beyond the medical support for the community. This belief is reinforced by a majority of the residents, who say they should "Pay whatever is needed for a doctor."

The community-control attributes that are so prevalent in Bremer have in the past and in the present allowed the community to pool their resources to buy a doctor. The retiring doctor explained his situation:

> I've decided to stay ONE more year. But it's up to some of the community members to help out if we are going to get a doctor here. We [wife and doctor] went to the community club and told them that they would have to buy the building and the practice and sell it back to the new doctor over time. Otherwise we just aren't going to get another doctor. If I'm making the sacrifice to stay another year they can at least become involved in getting this thing settled.

Following this meeting with the retiring doctor, the community club did in fact buy the building and practice from him. When that still wasn't enough of a drawing card to bring in another doctor, the letter at the start of this chapter was sent throughout the community. The doctor's wife explained another reason for the difficulty of getting a new doctor: "We had one young doctor who was sincerely interested, but his wife just absolutely refused to move out here in the sticks."

Indeed, the geographic isolation of Bremer has influenced the community's ability to recruit a new doctor. The importance of the doctor as a health giver and the importance of the availability of a doctor to the social and economic viability of the community place his status above that of most outsider positions within the community. A new doctor is handed down the reins when he arrives, yet it may take ten years or more before the local residents have enough faith in him to give extremely personal information about themselves. One elderly woman said, "I have to know someone pretty well before I'll take off my clothes for them. I don't care if they do have a medical license."

Where the other mass-society transplants in the community are required to abide by norms from outside of the community, the doctor must abide by local norms. The superintendent of schools gains his status from organizations outside of Bremer such as the Education School District (ESD) and through the utilization of information technologies. He can enhance his position statewide and overcome to a certain degree the geographic barrier of living in Bremer. The doctor is unable to follow suit. One reason for this is that the hours required of him place him in a position where he does not come into a great deal of contact with people outside of the community. The other mass-society positions in Bremer are positions that are required by the state or federal government. Examples such as soil conservation officers, school superintendents, bank auditors, and health inspectors indicate that those positions do exist in Bremer. The doctor's position does not fit into any of these categories. Although he is certified by outside organizations over which the local residents have very little power, he must live his productive years as a servant of the community.

This isolation increases his tie to the local norms of the community, but because of his unique position within the community, he holds very little political power, for this position is outside the local power structure. Yet when asked, "How important do you think having a doctor live in Bremer is to life in the community?" 89 percent of the residents reported that it was very important. This indicates that although the doctor is outside the normal range of community status for insiders, his position is seen as very important to the overall livability of Bremer.

Hippocratic Oath Versus What Were They There For

The community norms of Bremer are the predominant guiding factor for behavior within the community. The doctor is placed in a precarious situation because of the conflict between his societal role, which dictates that what goes on in his office is confidential, and the norms of Bremer, where all information is public. To meet both sets of expectations, the doctor and his staff interact outside the office as citizens of Bremer, and therefore, knowledge of patients is placed in the information base of the total community. Although providing information to the public about specific individuals is illegal from a societal point of view, in the community-control environment of Bremer it is necessary for all members to have information about all other members for the community-control mechanisms to operate.

One recent summer a young farmer injured his hand. He called Dr. Hager, who said he should come to the office for an X-ray. He drove to the doctor's office and parked outside. As he entered, patrons of the local grocery store across the street from Dr. Hager's watched as he held his hand. When he entered the office an older lady and her granddaughter were seated in the waiting room. The receptionist told him that he should fill out the rest of the form and then they would talk to his wife about the things that he didn't know, such as addresses of relatives, etc. This is a normal behavior in Bremer. Males are not expected to know certain necessary facts such as insurance company names and addresses of relatives. These are seen as within a wife's realm of knowledge. He was soon attended to. The farmer, with a fully bandaged hand, left the office and returned home.

Two days later when the farmer was shopping in Bremer, the owner of the grocery store walked up to him and said he'd heard that the injury to his hand wasn't bad. He thought it funny, though, that a young man would injure himself pounding in stakes for a game of horseshoes when he works around dangerous equipment all day and never is hurt.

The point of this brief example is that information about health is seen as public knowledge and that while the doctor may or may not pass the information on to the rest of the residents of the community, the staff, as members of Bremer, are expected to share the information. The staff, like other Bremer women, have a major role in providing information through informal means to the rest of the community. Health is perceived to be within a woman's field of knowledge, and information about the health of other community members is transferred over coffee and on the phone lines and is incorporated into the overall knowledge of "who you are" within the community. The particularistic orientation of Bremer residents is observable as residents explain why Bill doesn't help with the heavy lifting at the community fair. "Bill has a bad heart" or "Fred hurt his back on the tractor last week" is a particularistic means by which the health of an individual is taken into consideration when evaluating him or her.

The medical institution, then, is not outside the normative structure of the community. When it comes to respecting the norms and expectations of the mass society or the community, the doctor is expected to follow the norms and rules of the community.

Payment procedures are handled on the basis of particularistic norms, with deadlines for payment reflecting differences among community residents. Whereas a 30-day limit is placed on teachers, business owners, and large farmers, those who do not have insurance or the income to pay their bills in a timely manner are given a great deal of flexibility.

There are two reasons for this. First, health is held in high regard among the residents of Bremer. Second, medical expenses are not seen as a luxury. The traditional values held by the community residents place luxuries such as new cars, motorhomes, boats, satellite dishes, and trips in a different category than necessities such as health, food, and shelter. Because of this hierarchical system of needs, the use of the doctor's services is seen as a necessity, and therefore, payment should be based on the individual's resources. This is reflected in the cost for office visits, which ranges from $15 to $25, with exceptions made for elderly on fixed incomes or young families just starting out.

A Helicopter and the Loss of Control

The development of information technologies and the use of a Life-bird helicopter have influenced the position of the doctor. In the past if an individual was seriously injured, the family or a member of the volunteer fire department would take the person by car to the hospital, 30 miles away, or an ambulance was called and the individual was then transported to the smaller county seat hospital. With the use of Life-bird, injuries that are serious enough to require the helicopter are generally taken to one of the hospitals in the city 50 miles away. Through telecommunications the hospital is notified in advance of the injury, age of patient, and any special circumstances so that they can be prepared to help the individual when the helicopter lands.

As the helicopter picks up the individual, the authority of the local doctor ends. The helicopter usually lands on Main Street in front of the doctor's clinic. Once the patient enters the helicopter, the doctor is no longer the primary caregiver. This is in direct conflict with the doctor's traditional power over health services in the community. In the past the doctor would follow in his car to the county hospital and administer to the patient. He is now placed in a position, in emergencies, of making the original diagnosis and then being relieved of his position as a health-care giver.

Conclusion

The medical services within Bremer, which consist of one doctor, a nurse, and a combined secretary-bookkeeper-receptionist, stand in direct contrast to other community health-care systems in the region. Two communities adjacent to Bremer have lost their physicians and have not found replacements. All of the staff in Bremer are "locals" and have been socialized to follow community-control rules. The female staff are active in health care to the extent that community norms permit. The doctor holds a unique position because he is an outsider, but possesses a skill necessary to maintain the social as well as economic viability of the community. The community perceives, with a great deal of validity, that without a local doctor they would lose businesses and the older residents would be forced to relocate to where they could have medical care. Because of this unique position, the community follows a tradition of using large economic incentives to recruit a new doctor about every 30 years, and because of these economic incentives can be quite selective when choosing who the new physician will be. Not long ago a new doctor was brought into the community to replace the retiring doctor. The new physician is a father of four (family is important in Bremer) and has just graduated from medical school. Because the gross income of rural doctors has lost parity against urban doctors, an added incentive, the interest-free loan for the home, was used to recruit a young doctor. The age of the doctor is stressed whenever the community talks about recruitment. It takes about 10 to 15 years for a doctor to pay off the clinic, house, and practice. Bremer residents believe that to learn what it is to be a Bremerite takes at least one generation, so with a young doctor it is more likely, according to community residents, that he will learn the basic values of the community.

As the career of one physician ends, the retirement of Doctor Hager was recognized with a large going-away party. The following week the new doctor was welcomed. In 20 years, perhaps a new letter will be passed around to local residents reading "Doctor's Account."

9

Education in Bremer: No Dropouts and a Winning Sports Program

A full year after the merger, students in the Bremer school can be seen mingling in the long hallway, oblivious to the class pictures that hang above their heads. When many of them first entered school they had walked the hall looking for pictures of their grandparents, uncles, aunts, and parents, but today the walls are simply a part of their daily environment. The new students who are from Flemington Junior High look at the pictures as simply "old" pictures. They have no reason to search for relatives' pictures hanging on the walls. The cooperation agreement between the Flemington and Bremer school boards seems to have little impact on the everyday lives of the students except for the long bus rides as they move from community to community and back again.

Half Bird, Half Animal: The Mascot That Didn't Work

Following the public meeting to discuss the consolidation of or cooperation between the Flemington and Bremer schools, the local paper's front-page story was entitled, "Flemington, Bremer boards approve school co-op plan." Though the school boards had agreed to cooperate on an experimental basis, some residents of both communities continued to feel that the cooperation was ill conceived. Some organizations such as the Grange, with its aging membership, were leaning in the direction of ignoring the problem of decreasing enrollment. In the same newspaper, a story discussing enrollment projections for the local schools made this statement: "Another bill that has been proposed, and that appears to ignore results from a lengthy study of small rural schools about three years ago, would consolidate any school district with less than 1,000 students." The school administrator quoted in the article believed that the bill would never pass. However, the pressure placed upon the schools of Bremer by mass-society organizations are having a very real effect on the community of Bremer. Enrollments in the local schools in the Palouse are decreasing. Newspaper reports indicate that schools are consolidating or cooperating. Community-control organizations such as the Grange do not believe that the mass-society organizations will force consolidation of small rural schools. To expound on the social reality of the loss of a high school from another small town, regional and local newspapers featured stories on the loss of Flemington High School as the "end of an era." A former Flemington student that was interviewed said, "They [another small community] did the same thing we did 20 years ago. They got rid of their high school and they [the town] died. I hate to see it happening." And the newspaper descriptions of Flemington include statements such as this: "The place that churned out 1,008 Bulldogs in eight decades, and cleaned up on Future Farmers of America awards, now is to send its high school students to former rival Bremer."

The cooperation with Bremer created a perception in Flemington that it was losing an important feature of the community: the high school sports program. To reduce this loss, the residents of that community tried to get the Bremer school district to change its athletic mascot from the bird to a griffin, an animal that is half bird and half animal, but the Bremer residents felt that they were already giving up too much when their school board agreed to cooperate with Flemington. So the name has remained the same for Bremer and with the name remains the history of a winning sports program.

"Westsiders" or Locals: Who Controls
the Bremer School?

The Bremerites' perception of who controls the school influences their perception of how their other institutions are controlled and their community identity is maintained. Since the 1950s, the federal government has had an increased voice in what remedial courses should be offered and how federal money should be spent in the schools. At the state level, the schools are overseen by a state superintendent. This is an elected position and is controlled by the majority of the state population, which resides on the western side of the state. The locals feel resentment toward "Westsiders," who are "city folks" and don't understand the problems facing small rural schools.

At the regional level, an education school district (ESD) oversees the implementation of state and federal directives. The hiring and firing of local superintendents is directly controlled by the ESDs. Although the school is controlled by extra-community agencies of various levels, the ESD gives the impression of the school being controlled locally. This enhances the feeling that Bremerites have control of their school system. A demonstration of who controls the hiring of a new superintendent for the Bremer school system illustrates that Bremerites may not have the power they believe they do when it comes to selecting who will guide their school system. Several years ago, the ESD office provided a list of eligible candidates. The ESD staff prioritized the list of candidates. The Bremer school board then selected and interviewed potential superintendents from this list. This system for selecting heads of school districts allows the state to maintain control over the employees while giving the final say in selection to the local boards. The employees of the ESDs are generally previous teachers and administrators.

The Bremer superintendent is responsible to an elected school board. It is at this level that the Bremer residents exert the most influence. School board membership has traditionally been passed down from father to son. One father explained:

> I was on the school board when my kids were in school, but when they graduated I quit. I thought my son would take my position now that he has kids in school. But he didn't run. Now we have people on there who are new to the town. They all have visions of what the school should be like, but hell, they haven't lived here long enough to get any support. It's no wonder that they can't get anything done.

The tradition of ascribed status as the norm for participation in the guidance of the school is now undergoing a change. School board members don't hold the high status they held in previous years, and the lack of community support corresponds to the opinion of many residents that the quality of board members has suffered. In the words of one farmer:

> We need to take away some of the power of the school board. Over the years the quality of board members has gotten worse. They are not aware of what has happened in the past, so they read these state reports and think they can make decisions. It just doesn't work that way.

While achieved status has become more prevalent in the election of school board members, those community members who believe that traditional authority works better in guiding such an important institution in the community as the school have withdrawn from participation in the process. No woman had served on the Bremer school board until 1979. Since that time some members of the community have perceived the movement of women and a few new residents onto the board as a sign that the power of the school board should be reduced. Traditionally, the role of women in education has been in the realm of teaching, socializing children, and working with auxiliary clubs. The women's club is an example of the role women have traditionally played in educating Bremer citizens. The Bremer General Federation Women's Club handles fund-raising for scholarships for local students. As one member said:

> We handle the local scholarships. We plan fund-raising events and our goal is to provide every Bremer student with some sort of financial assistance if they want to go on to college. We are generally pretty successful at that. Sometimes it isn't a lot, maybe $500 or so, but every bit helps so they know that the community is behind them. We also plan local banquets and make sure that every community resident who is in the hospital receives a visit and a card. We are the glue that keeps the thing together and at the same time we have a good time and play cards and have a nice lunch.

The combination of the changing roles of women in society and the changing demographics of the community have placed the school in a precarious position. The traditional power leaders have withdrawn and newer leaders have replaced them, resulting in diminished power for the school board.

The most heated public meetings held in Bremer are the local school board meetings. Tension among community residents increases dramatically when their school is threatened, as discussed in Chapter 1. Cohen has found that "the boundary encapsulates the identity of the community and, like the identity of an individual, is called into being by the exigencies of social interaction" (Cohen, 1985). In Bremer, the boundaries of the community are based on people's perceived similarities with each other and are called into being when a threat is posed toward one of the visible organizations, such as the school. This interpretation of why the residents of Bremer become enraged over a threat to their local school gives some insight into the importance that the school plays in their identity. Community-control attributes such as the orientation towards the group rather than the individual are evident in the way Bremerites perceive the role of their school. Any threat to the school is seen as one not just to the school but to all in the community, whether they have children in school or not. Most Bremerites had relatives who attended the school, and so they have an emotional and sentimental tie to the institution. And, because of the family orientation of the community, a threat to the school is perceived as a threat to the future of the family and the tradition of their community.

The School: 50 Years of Maintaining Identity

Fifteen teachers teach the 180 students in the long, flat building of the Bremer school. Currently 25 percent of the students are from Flemington. The hallways of the school hold Bremer's memories, memorabilia, and ties to the past. Because of this strong tie to the majority of residents, the school holds a special place in their hearts and minds. The pictures hanging on the walls above the lockers and exhibited in the high school library portray the young faces of the current students' parents, grandparents, uncles, and aunts. The awards that sit in the trophy case are engraved with the names of the parents and relatives of the current students. The constant reminders of the past reinforce Bremer's sense of identity. Therefore, an external threat to the school is not only a threat against a local institution but is seen as a threat to the very past of the people who make their home in this Palouse community.

As many of the small schools that historically surrounded the Bremer community were closed and the students were moved to the Bremer school, their pictures, awards, and memorabilia were brought to the school and integrated into the history of the Bremer school. This pattern has not been followed with the cooperation agreement with Flemington, for the experiment is seen as temporary by many of the Bremer residents. During the past 50 years the school has been the photographs in this public place have served to maintain Bremerites' ties to the past. Yet despite the community's attempts to retain local control of their schools, the influence of the mass society has increased.

The Importance of Knowing Each Student

At the level of local control the opportunity exists to examine the difficulty of living in at least two eras. The superintendent and elected school board are tied to the community-control era within Bremer because they live, work, and for the most part grew up in Bremer. The importance of the school to the overall identity of the community places a great deal of local pressure on the school board and superintendent to maintain the values and behaviors associated with the community-control attributes among Bremerites. When residents were asked what they liked about the Bremer school system, these community-control attributes became evident in statements such as the following:

Help kids in all situations. Take time with them.

Take a personal interest in individual students.

They do have the small-town support of everyone and every student.

Close contact with parents and children.

Encourage athletics! Encourage leadership and teach young people to work physically.

Kids interact with kids of all ages—learn to know each other and accept for what they really are.

They teach community pride and tradition. Attendance is very important. They back the schools and support each other.

They [the schools] exert peer pressure.

These statements indicate the values associated with education in Bremer. The group orientation of Bremer is especially strong when it comes to the socialization of Bremer youth. The importance of the group is evident as community residents speak of the school's teaching community pride and tradition and of the mechanisms used to maintain community-held norms. Peer pressure is applauded as a positive part of education in Bremer. The value of hard physical labor is seen as one of the lessons learned in school. These values had a direct tie to the community-control era, when schools were controlled locally and the teachers taught only what the locals felt should be taught. The informal norms that are so much a part of the community of Bremer are seen as being taught not only at home but in the schools as well. It is believed by the locals that if the school fails to socialize the children and to reinforce the informal norms and sanctions, they lose control of the next generation.

Face-to-face personal interaction is considered very important in educating the youth of Bremer. Instead of listing strong academic subjects, the community residents focus on interpersonal interaction with the students, parents, and rest of the community as the strong point of their schools. It is these values of the group and "knowing everyone" and the value of hard work that the local authorities must deal with as they report to the mass-society organizations such as the ESD and the state school superintendent.

Teachers balance these two interests in a variety of ways. First, they spend much of their energy supporting extracurricular activities in which the "hard work" of the students can be shown to the public, i.e., the community. The strong focus on athletics is another way the educators in Bremer reinforce the values of hard work. It is not uncommon for students who are failing classes to be given special privilege to participate in sports because "that's where they're going to learn discipline and hard work."

To meet the academic standards of the mass society, teachers rely heavily upon standardized workbooks that students can use to prepare for SATs or for their senior exams. A few community residents have complained recently about the heavy use of workbooks, but the teachers explain that it is one way to standardize what their kids get and what the kids in the city 50 miles away receive.

School Levies: We Could Pay More

One indication of the importance of the school to the community members is their desire to pay more for their school than the state currently allows. Bremer residents value education; 24 per-cent of the residents have a college degree or have done postgraduate work. The state limits school levies to 6 percent of the annual school budget. The rationale behind this limit is to "force schools to maintain a similar environment," according to a retired superintendent. The particular-istic orientation of the Bremer residents is especially evident in the fact that 40 percent of them believe that the parents and other community residents should have the final decision on the ceiling for school tax levies, while 37 percent believe that the elected local school board should be given the authority to decide this issue. When it comes to funding their schools, almost 80 percent feel that they should make these decisions at the local level. The strong group orientation of Bremer is reflected in its desire to maintain local control of the most important institution in their community and to pay for it.

Residents voiced these opinions and concerns:

The state should stay out of funding for our school. If we want to pay more than the current ceiling allows then we should be able to do it.

When the school goes the town will die so why can't we put a little extra money into it to keep it going?

If we don't have our kids close who will watch them? Someone from the outside?

Without our schools close we just won't be able to pass on our heritage. And it's a heritage that should be passed on.

These sentiments reflect the community-control-era attributes associated with a past where geographic proximity was a deciding factor in guiding how and with whom one interacted. Community residents continue to believe that by having a close geographic proximity to their children during the school day their values will be passed on; if the students are removed from the community, they fear, those values will be lost. Parents of children attending Flemington Junior High often comment on the different values being taught by some of the Lutheran teachers there. Others point to the nontraditional teaching techniques used by some of the teachers. As one parent put it: "All they do over there is take field trips. You'd think that they are afraid to sit in a class and teach those kids."

A secondary reason for the importance of passing on the values of the community is based in the community-control role expectations. In Bremer, roles have traditionally been developed to fit the individual. To do this it is necessary to know the person throughout his or her life. Bremerites feel that if they lost the local school they would then lose access to important information they deem necessary to develop roles for the next generation.

Athletics: Ritual or Sports?

Specific rituals have been developed over time to reinforce the community identity of Bremerites. One ritual is mandatory participation at athletic events. Attendance is mandatory for parents, as it is for all of the students' relatives. Conversations over coffee in the local tavern/cafe often focus on how the team is doing and what their chances will be to make it to the state championship this year. The community supports the athletes through a variety of mechanisms. A grocer donates the meat and cuts it for the concession stand at the game. Local residents volunteer as parking guides, as labor to set up bleachers, and as maintenance personnel. They speak of the players as representatives of Bremer and the values that Bremerites hold. Sitting

on the hard bleachers watching local youth play basketball, one hears
snippets of a conversation that give some insight into sports in Bremer:

> Well, our kids out there are honest, they play hard, and they follow the
> rules. You can pick out a Bremer player just by the way they act.

> Yeah, Bob plays just like his dad. With a lot of heart. His Dad wasn't
> the best player either but nobody tried harder.

The values that Bremerites hold to be the most important in their
lives—hard work, honesty, maintaining a tradition—are exemplified
by athletics in the community. The ritual of attending the athletic
events and reaffirming their identity as a community is very important
to Bremerites. This behavior pattern reflects the community
expectations of mandatory interaction. Not to attend a public function
tied directly to the socialization of the future residents of the
community would place one in a position to be sanctioned. This
sanctioning could be something as simple as not being able to interact at
coffee on Monday morning because the conversation would focus on the
previous Friday night's athletic event. When the basketball or
football team plays in the state championships, which is quite often,
the town closes its doors and moves in mass to where the championships
are held. Residents elaborated:

> Well, you can always tell when Bremer is playing. No one is in town or
> at home.

> If anyone ever wanted to rob the whole town, that's the time to do it.
> It's about the only time of year that someone isn't around to see if a
> strange car pulls up. It's getting so bad that some people stay home
> just in case a group of city people come down to take advantage of
> everyone being out of town.

The residents of Bremer and the store owners close the doors of their
homes and businesses and go to participate in a ritual where they
reaffirm their identity. This is an illustration of the blending of goals
and means. For business owners to turn down business does not fit into
the mass-society norm of doing whatever it takes to make a profit. The
goal of Bremer businesspeople is to make a living while at the same
time supporting the group and the community, and this support at times
takes precedence over the economic reason for being in business.

While Bremer persists in the community-control era, it is also
participating in the mass society. The ritual traditions in Bremer
reinforcing the community identity include sports. The importance of

sports programs comes into conflict with the mass-society orientation of the federal and state organizations that have authority over the Bremer school.

Hiring Within or Hiring Outsiders?

Local residents perceive the schools in Bremer as being under direct control of the community, and yet they are quite aware that their teachers are members of a state teachers' union and also members of national teacher associations outside local control. To maintain their values in the schools, Bremerites have traditionally hired locals as teachers. The majority of the teachers at the Bremer school are from the Bremer area or some community in eastern Washington. There has been a specific effort made to retain the traditional authority associated with the community-control era. As a retired school administrator explained it:

> We try to look for a young teacher who has a background in small towns. Especially small German towns. This way they have an understanding of the way this town operates. They [the community] support us totally, but there are some things that we have to do too. We have to make sure that we teach the values that they [the community] have. We just couldn't do that by bringing in city people to teach these kids. The values just wouldn't be the same.

This way of handing down authority is very much indicative of the community-control era. Traditional authority is the norm and the schools follow that norm. Although the Bremer school system is maintaining some degree of local control through hiring locals and participating in the rituals of the sporting events, the impact of the mass society cannot be overlooked. While the schools are part of a hierarchy of educational institutions within the state and the nation, Bremerites have attempted to maintain local control over their curriculum by hiring people "like themselves."

The mass-society norm of legalized rules and authority changes the way the community can control teachers. Bremer relies primarily upon community-control mechanisms to control its residents, but because teachers are members of a large legalized organization outside the control of Bremer, the community must rely upon peer pressure to control them. The importance of hiring teachers who know the norms and expectations of Bremer is manifest. The state has specific requirements for teachers, yet there are ways to bypass the rules of the mass-society organizations in a rural community. The Bremer school board and superintendent have traditionally bypassed some of the state's legalized rules through a statute that allows small rural schools to apply for waivers of specific requirements of teachers. The superintendent can formally request a waiver of a teacher's certification requirements to teach a specific class, backed by the argument that it is difficult to convince new teachers with current certification to relocate to Bremer.

When residents express their ideas about changes needed in the school, they focus on the very behaviors that they applaud when asked what they like about their school. For example:

Don't "pigeonhole" kids because of parents' social or economic status, or siblings' ability in school.

Enforce rules uniformly.

Make sure teachers do not "sluff off" just because they are a Bremerite.

More emphasis on education and less on sports.

Spend less time on classifying values, more on educational skills.

Be more realistic as to what is going on in society and needs for the future.

The impact of living in a mass society is evident in the problems that Bremerites see with their school system. The conflict between relying upon traditional authority and authority based on achievement is evident in the desire of the residents that their teachers not be given special treatment just because they are from Bremer. Whereas a majority of Bremerites believe that interpersonal interaction is very important in socializing their children, they are also concerned with how their children will fare in the mass society. This change in orientation is reflective of mass-society influences and is caused in part by the realization that many children will move outside the community to make their living or pursue higher education.

But I Can't Read

One reason for this change may be the fact that as agriculture has become more mechanized in the last 50 years and fewer jobs have become available for young Bremerites, some young people have left

Bremer to try to make it on the "outside" and have returned unsuccessful. One returning youth explained: I went out of here thinking that I was a leader, had good educational skills, but boy was I surprised. While I had been spending a lot of time in P.E. [physical education] classes those other kids [from outside Bremer] were studying business and math. I'm mad now. Some people are saying that I should sue the school for not teaching me to read. But I can't do that. They were always so supportive of me. I'm not sure what I'll do now.

Although this young man's story is not the norm for Bremer, graduates' stories similar to this one reflect a failure in their favorite institution. Information travels very quickly, and when it was discovered that a star football player had been dismissed from the military because of lack of minimal reading skills necessary to be in the infantry, the community became upset. In the past, a role would have been found for this young man. As one resident recalled:

> When I was a boy there were a few students who couldn't read well and jobs were found for them around town. You didn't have to read well to be a mechanic in those days.

Now, as agriculture has become mechanized and tied to the mass society, employment is difficult to find. Recent graduates who remain in Bremer talk of the few entry-level jobs available. According to one recent graduate:

> There are only so many jobs. You can't even work at the fertilizer plant unless you have a state applicator's license. So if you can't get the license then you are in a really tough spot.

Many of the larger employers in the community are working within a mass-society orientation, where roles are achieved instead of ascribed. This places individuals such as this young man in a position where they must move outside of the area without many of the skills necessary to compete with better-trained youths. When the high school students were surveyed, only 6 percent said that it was "very likely that they would remain in Bremer after graduation." Of those 6 percent, 90 percent said they would probably farm for a living. The Bremer students are aware of the changing employment picture in their community.

During the last 50 years it was generally expected that young men would return to Bremer and farm, while young women would marry a farmer or move out of the community. These expectations are no longer the norm. When high school students were surveyed about how they felt about the possibility of being a farmer or a farmer's spouse after graduation, only one percent said they would prefer that more than anything else. Another 18 percent said they would definitely like it. These attitudes about staying in Bremer and being tied to agriculture reflect the reality of the outmigration of the community's youth. The anecdote of the young Bremer graduate who felt betrayed by the community and school because he was not prepared for the "outside" illustrates the pressure being placed on Bremer by mass-society organizations outside of their control.

It is not only the differences in expectations that create problems for the Bremer schools. The increasing average age of Bremerites and the lowered birthrate are creating structural forces that are also influencing the institution of education in Bremer.

The mass society has influenced how Bremerites deal with authority in their schools. Whereas in the community-control era teachers were brought in by the school board and were hired on one-year contracts, the legalized rules and norms of the mass society have changed that practice. Membership in the state teachers' union places the hiring and firing outside local control. Bremer residents explain the situation this way:

> We've got some bad ones in the first few grades, but what can you do? Once they have tenure they basically have to physically abuse a child or drink in class before we can get rid of them.

Responsiveness to rules within the Bremer school district is primarily particularistic. It is difficult for Bremerites to work within a system such as a state school system without maintaining at least a semblance of that flexibility. This particularistic manner of interacting with individuals is indicative of the community-control era. Teachers who have been educated and have lived their lives in Bremer reinforce this norm. Students are treated differentially according to criteria that are not always school-oriented. As the comments of the community residents indicate, the fact that their children are evaluated on criteria that are not always academic poses a problem. The students must take with them the legalized grades given by the school district. The average grade point average of Bremer high school students in 1988 was 3.19 on a four-point scale. When asked why the average was so high, the teachers explained that colleges were now asking for students with higher GPAs so there might be "a little grade inflation" just to keep their kids "competitive."

The mass-society norm of standardization and mass production also creates some conflict within the community. Grades have traditionally been given for the student's total performance, not just the academic side. If the student works at a job and is visible to the teachers, this work is taken into consideration when giving grades. If the student is a good athlete and adds to the cohesion within the community, the student is given good grades. The rationale here is that the student is adding to the group identity and is a worthwhile community resident. Particularism is the key in Bremer when it comes to evaluating students, and this is in direct conflict with the rational authority found in the mass society. One of the reasons that particularism is the norm may be that over 70 percent of the Bremer High students have had relatives that lived in Bremer most of their lives.

The ambivalence that local residents feel toward elected school board members is also evident in their changing attitudes toward the schools. As parents understand that most of their children will not remain in Bremer as adults and that the "outside," or mass society, requires different skills from their children, they are attempting to deal with the conflict between an education that perpetuates the norms of a community-controlled era and the skills necessary to survive outside of Bremer. This conflict is evident in the contradictory statements about what the residents like and dislike about their school system. They like the personal interaction, the fact that the teachers often know children through their parents' and grandparents' experiences and the fact that the norms of the community-controlled era are taught. On the other side of the coin, they dislike the favoritism they see taking place in the school, which is a result of teachers' knowing the students outside of school.

These conflicting views of what people would like their school to be has placed the Bremer community in a position where they are not sure which direction to go: toward rational authority and achieved status, or toward retaining traditional authority and ascribed status. The conflict over cooperation with the Flemington school district illustrates the problem as the residents see it.

Classes by Satellite: Cost Isn't the Problem

As Bremerites attempt to deal with the conflict between the community-control era and the mass society, another potential problem is facing the community. This problem is how to deal with the increased use of information technology. During the last several years there has been a great deal of discussion about whether it might be possible to gain some additional local control over the schools while still preparing their students for the "outside" through using information technology such as a satellite dish. The local teachers have been against such a move:

> We [teachers] just feel that [a satellite dish] wouldn't be worth the extra money. Also, you understand that they wouldn't need a teacher in the classroom, just an aide. So here you would have a teacher located at a university someplace else, where the kids have to use a telephone to interact with them, and you would only have an aide to answer questions. It looks to me as a way to cut down the number of teachers and to cut costs, not necessarily a way to increase the offerings to students.

The position taken by the teachers is that through the use of information technology such as classes offered by satellite, their status in the school and community would decline. Teachers have historically been held in high regard in the community, although the influence of the mass society has diminished this status. Their fear is that through the use of aides and classes taught by someone outside of the area, their status and authority would diminish even more. Administrators in the Bremer school are already in direct contact with the ESD through personal computers with modems. They send and receive reports and information about budgets, teacher accreditation, and so forth. Although the administrators interact over telephone lines with computers from their offices in Bremer, as a norm they still interact with the teachers and parents on the community-control and mass-society level. The threat the school board members and teachers feel from the telecommunication equipment is that their power will be usurped by state agencies and their creativity and freedom to teach will be even more standardized.

In the mid-1980s, the Bremer school system bought eight small personal computers. Three of the computers were set up in the typing room and the others were left in their packing crates. As one teacher explained:

> None of us [teachers] know much about these things [computers] but we'll be taking some courses next summer. Right now the kids are using them to type on and they are using some of the graphics that came with them. In time we'll all have our grades on them and then we will be able to prepare for our yearly evaluations much quicker.

Use of personal computers came slowly to the Bremer schools. Within three years, all of the computers were in use and two classes were using them: (1) typing and (2) computers in business. The adoption of the new information technologies started with the administrators and then slowly worked its way down to the classroom.

Increased use of personal computers at the Bremer schools has not brought a major change in the way teaching is conducted. The teachers use textbooks that date back to the mid-1970s. Although 100 percent of the students at the high school have used a computer in the past, only 45 percent of the students surveyed indicated that understanding how to use a computer was very important, and another 45 percent reported that understanding how to use a computer in getting a good job was only slightly important. The students report that learning to work hard and to do homework is the school-acquired skill most important in getting a good job. The responses from the students coincide with the beliefs of the teachers and the community—that is, that community-control attributes are the most important aspects of being a success. It has been speculated by several sociologists that orientations of how individuals see themselves as part of the overall society may change as the influence of the information age is felt (Dillman and Beck, 1986). Evaluating the Bremer schools makes it evident that the mass society has greatly influenced how the school system operates, yet the community-control attributes still dominate how students are socialized.

Attributes associated with the mass society are paramount in how administrators interact with those outside the local school. Administrators work for accreditation to work up the hierarchy within the local school as well as within other state organizations such as the ESD. The use of information technologies now allows these rural educators to interact with others at their level in the hierarchy of the state education system. They now have current reports as quickly as their colleagues in the urban areas around the state. Through constant interaction with the regional centers, they are able to keep their names and achievements in the minds of their superiors. This reliance on information technology indicates that as use becomes more prevalent, networks may form that decrease the importance of power at the local level. This may be especially important as it pertains to the mass-society institutions such as the schools.

As for the skills necessary to participate in the future of the information age, one school administrator related:

> The future? Well, for my boys who stay, they will work the farms. Now, for those that don't, well, they are going to have to learn other things like how to run a computer. But we just aren't able to teach them all of that here. They'll have to get that later on.

The school administrator was basing his prediction of the future for his graduates on the students' desire to get more education. Ninety-two percent of the Bremer High School students plan on getting more education after finishing high school. Of those students who plan to get further education, 49 percent plan on attending a university in the State of Washington, and 30 percent plan on attending a community college.

Conclusion

When evaluating education in Bremer, we see a community that continues to exist in the community-control era while at the same time existing in the mass society. The stress created by the two forms of social organization develops as the norms associated with local control, face-to-face interaction patterns, ascribed authority, and particularistic behavior must be modified to accommodate the legal norms of the mass society.

Bremer has attempted to retain local control of its school through hiring locals, while at the same time state and federal organizations attempt to standardize the schools throughout the state and the nation. The increased power of a hierarchical organization supported by state and federal tax dollars has led to a perception in Bremer that "school board members are no longer as competent as they were in the past" and that their control over the school should be limited. This has also led to fewer of the informal power leaders participating in the school board.

Residents want the traditional values of Bremer taught but are also concerned that the skills necessary to participate in the mass society are not being taught. They focus on the quality of teachers and administrators and the restrictions placed on the school by state law as the reasons for the conflict. They are in a position where they wish to retain a tradition of community control but also want to selectively use resources provided by the mass society. This brings to the forefront the fact that many of the values the residents hold are in direct disagreement with their desire to better prepare their students for the mass society.

As the influence of the information age is being felt, the teachers feel threatened because they believe their power is being usurped by a satellite dish and videocassette recorder. The administrators of the school are using technology to gain more power within the mass-society organizations, but the teachers themselves feel they are the ones losing in the use of the new technology.

The significance of the sports teams is an indicator of how important group orientation is to Bremer residents. As the sign entering Bremer declares, the sports teams at the high school provide a focal point for community interaction. The tie of agriculture to the school system is exemplified by a former school administrator. When asked what the future held for most of his students, he explained:

> Well . . . again, it depends on what area they pick. A lot of my boys go into agriculture because their dads are farmers and they're not having ten kids any more, they're having one or two. I think the kids in agriculture are going to come back and farm. The other kids, I couldn't say. I think the technology is so diversified now that they are going to have to look for it someplace else if they want to learn about it.

As the form of interaction desired by the residents in their everyday life is placed in conflict with that of the mass society, cohesion among members of the community begins to break down. At this point in time, a process of negotiation is going on involving formal and informal power leaders in the community. The outcome of these negotiations, which are discussed over coffee, are still unknown. Factions have developed supporting a movement toward a standardized education system similar to those in urban areas, while other factions remain convinced that to truly educate their children and grandchildren the school must retain the values and norms associated with a traditional rural community. Several questions remain: Whose pictures will hang above the lockers in the school hallway 20 years from now? Or will there be a school in which to hang any pictures at all? What impact will information technology have on the current ability of Bremer's schools to teach values first and academics second?

10

Religion:
A Tradition Bypassed?

It is Sunday morning at 10:00 and a light snow is dusting the surrounding hills. Outside the flat brick building housing the Methodist church, 21 cars are parked. The many Oldsmobiles and Chryslers sit beside small foreign cars, some with bumper stickers reading "Member Washington Association of Wheat Growers." Inside the church, about 45 people sit in the well-polished pews. Those in attendance are primarily gray-haired and dressed in dark suits and dresses. The choir stands on the varnished stage and sings several hymns from the well-worn hymnals. The pastor, a young man in his early 30s, still near the beginning of his ministerial career, opens the services with a prayer. Sunday-morning religious services at the Methodist church—the largest church in Bremer, with a membership of over 300—have begun.

Two-and-a-half blocks down the street from the Methodist church stands the taller spire of the white wooden building of the First Christian church, with a large white cross adorning the peak. Seven cars, older Chevrolets and Fords and one new four-wheel drive, are parked in front. Inside the church, simple benches are placed in rows facing the small podium at the front of the hall. Those in attendance are primarily young couples in their 30s with their children. Twenty-eight people are attending today's services. The membership rolls, according to the pastor, number 38 members. The hymns are accompanied by a young woman playing a piano. There is no carpet and no large organ on which to play the music. The pictures on the walls are simple pictures of Jesus Christ. Small crosses are spaced evenly around the long room. The pastor opens the services with a prayer, his voice echoing in the long hall.

Leaving the Christian church and driving the 13 blocks to the edge of town, one finds 25 vehicles, the majority of which are pickup trucks, parked in lines leading to the long green Bremer Gun Club. Men with brown hunting jackets and down-filled winter coats are walking toward the building carrying shotguns. A few young children with excitement registering in their voices are following fathers toward the building, which has smoke curling from the chimney. Shotgun blasts can be heard echoing off the snow-covered hills. Sunday-morning activities are underway.

Churches and Their Role

In 1950, two churches were situated in the town proper of Bremer, and another three churches were within easy reach of the town. By 1988, the variety of religious institutions in the community had nearly doubled. Five churches are now in the town proper, with two churches outside the town limits. Although their roles differ and the predominant church in the community is the Methodist church, the churches have begun to work together. Of the five churches in Bremer, only two, the Methodist and First Christian, hold Sunday-morning services. The other churches hold services in buildings in small towns within a 30-minute drive of Bremer. The reason for not holding services in these other churches is that their memberships are small, and the religious leaders felt it was better to hold services where church members could interact with other members of their church who lived in the region.

In Bremer, 44 percent of the residents report that they attend church twice a month or more. The impact of the mass society and the improved roads can be illustrated by the distance many of the residents currently drive to attend church. Over 60 percent of the Bremer residents say they attend church in Bremer, while 31 percent attend a church outside of Bremer but within a 30-minute drive. The impact of the information age is only slightly visible in Bremer church life. With the availability of satellite dishes and cable television it might be reasonable to expect many of the rural residents of Bremer to be members of an evangelical church that is broadcast on television. This is not supported by survey data. Only 1 percent of the residents report that they are members of an evangelical church.

Reasons that people give for attending church in Bremer range from current-value orientation or support to attempting to retain traditional values. As two residents explain:

I send my kids to church because they need to know the basic values of their neighbors. Plus, at Sunday school the younger kids get a chance to socialize with their friends in a structured manner. I want my family to live by the same values as we did when I was a kid. You have to go to church if you want to get added support for these values in today's society, although it's harder and harder to get the men to church. I think Sunday football is the cause of a lot of the problem.

The traditional role of the church in Bremer was to provide a cohesive fabric for the maintenance of the community values. A religious observance of saying grace before large public dinners was traditionally a pattern but is seen less and less today. One older resident recalls:

My Dad was a minister, so I was always asked to say a prayer at meetings. We almost always opened meetings with a prayer. Now, you have people who have different religions and beliefs living here. So you just never know if you will say something that will make them uncomfortable.

It appears that the increased number of religious organizations in the community creates a difficult position for the person asked to give the prayer. The pattern of not saying grace at large public dinners is also found in other small communities surrounding Bremer. The question that arises here is, Does this decrease in formal observance of religious rituals reflect a decrease in religiosity among rural residents? There are two conflicting views of whether Bremerites are less religious than they were in the past. The first view is expressed by a long-term resident:

Basically we are just honest, hardworking people here. Most people here have always been religious, but it just isn't something that you wear like a flag. It's a personal thing. We don't push religion here. People are about the same as they've always been.

The view expressed is that religiosity has remained about the same over time. Religion, according to this resident, was always important but wasn't a major guiding force when living in the community. A local religious leader supports this view. He explains:

Are they [Bremerites] religious? Well, yes, I'd say they are. But it's not quite what it was. When you look down the aisles on Sunday you see a lot of older faces and not many young ones. I think the younger people just don't see God as a driving force in their life like their parents did.

A conflicting view is expressed by another resident:

When I was young [1920s] religion was very important. We said prayers in school and always went to church on Sunday. Now, people just aren't concerned about life after death. They are just living for today. You can see it in the kids too. They just don't have the respect for God, country, or each other. I'm concerned about my grandkids; they just aren't being taught God's word. It looks to me as if the town is just turning into a town of atheists.

These two views illustrate differing perspectives of the importance of religion to Bremer in the past. Both views indicate a perception that religion was a part of the history of Bremer. How important religion was in guiding the everyday lives of Bremerites is still unanswered.

The residents in the past attended church within the community and donated their money to local churches. As transportation problems decreased, the new mobility of the residents led to a loss of status of the traditional religious organizations in the community. Determining where Bremerites donate time and money to religious organizations should give some insight into the importance of the local religious organizations. When we examine whether Bremerites donate a majority of their money to local churches or organizations outside of the community, we find that 65 percent of the population sometimes donate to local churches, while 41 percent of the population sometimes donate to churches outside of Bremer but within a 30-minute drive. Only 6 percent of the population sometimes or always donate to church organizations broadcast on television.

Religion within Bremer is still viewed as a community activity and the impact of televised religion is minimal. The community-control attributes of Bremer are no longer reflected in the religious institutions. Local control is seen as paramount in maintaining an institution in the community. The pattern in large mass-society religious organizations of moving their religious leaders from community to community every three to five years has had an influence on how the church is seen within the community. A longtime church leader [board member] states:

Twenty years ago a Methodist minister would be placed in Bremer and would be expected to live there for most of a lifetime. Now we have a minister placed and he and his family may not even get unpacked and settled before they are required to move on. Now, in this town you just have to be around for quite a time before you are known by the town. Where it used to be that the minister was consulted on most problems the town faced, now a lot of people don't even know the minister's name unless they've been to church in the last few months.

The decreased role of the church can be partially attributed to the length of time spent in the community by religious leaders associated with the larger mass-society organizations. Remarks such as the one by the Bremer woman about sending her children to church illustrate the point that there are some residents who believe that traditional values are not being supported community-wide. An example of the movement from religious observance to leisure is the large turnout on Sunday morning at the Bremer Gun Club. This may also be a pattern that has continued to evolve since the Lynds were conducting research in the 1920s and 1930s—a time when religious gatherings were being replaced with leisure activities (Lynd and Lynd, 1929).

Sunday-Morning "Men's Time"

On this Sunday morning, the road running to the Bremer Gun Club is lined with pickup trucks. Inside the club is a large gun rack, a long bar where drinks are "serve yourself," and four or five tables covered in green felt, where some older members are playing rummy. This is "men's time," while their wives and children attend church or sleep late. Although the gun club has been seen as "men's territory," in 1979 women were allowed to attend the annual crab feed. Women generally do not participate in these Sunday-morning outings, although some children do.

The sound of shotguns firing is muffled by the double-paned glass windows, where those who come strictly to socialize stand commenting on the accuracy of the shooters. Those firing at the clay pigeons stand at the firing line wearing down jackets over plaid wool shirts. The baseball caps worn today are not those worn in the field but are "dress" hats. These are the hats that have not been accidentally dropped in oil or had sweat stain their bills.

Generations of farmers mix in the relaxed atmosphere of the gun club. Fathers stand watching their sons teach their grandsons the art of firing a gun. With the changing role of women in society, young women are now also being brought to the club to learn how to shoot. Previously, the gun club, with its Sunday-morning meetings, was strictly a men's club. Women are now admitted to the club, although on Sunday mornings all the participants are usually male, with the exception of an occasional young girl.

The gun club has taken up the slack allowed by the increased variety of churches in the region and the decrease in influence of any particular church.   While other residents are attending churches, these residents are gathering in an informal, noninstitutionalized place with the primary goal of socializing. As a past president of the gun club explains:

> It didn't really start as a club. Just a few of us would get together while the wives went to church. Well, now we have quite a few members, as you can see. We have the crab feed each year and a few card nights scattered through the year. We began to allow women to the crab feed in the early 70s and that has been fought by a few old-timers, but I think it was a good thing. That way the women don't think we're just sitting out here drinking and playing cards.

The success of the gun club can be partially attributed to decisions made by the larger religious institutions. Religious leaders at the local level are moved from one community to another every three to five years. In a community with Bremer's tie to the past, three to five years is not long enough to develop relationships with the locals. The community-control norms are often unseen by the new religious leaders.

Cooperation Among Churches

The role of religion in traditional communities, in the words of a Bremer resident, was one of helping individuals attempting "to cope with the too-bigness of life." As Bremer enters the 1990s, religion plays a much more social role. In the past, religions were separated on the basis of specific beliefs. Now, religious organizations work with one another to share the limited resources available in a small community. An example is the summer Bible school. The school is held for young children in the Methodist church but is a combined group including all religious denominations in the community. A generic Christian religious message is presented at this summer school. One mother expresses her opinion:

> I think Bible study is important, but the Methodists are liberal when interpreting the work of God. But it is still better to have a Bible study group for the children. They need to share their beliefs with one another, even if the interpretation is not what I teach at home or what our pastor preaches.

Cooperation among the churches in providing a summer religious program for the Bremer children is an example of the community's working together to attain common goals without infringing upon others' rights. The socialization aspect of the summer programs is important enough to the parents and community for them to support a generic but Christian religious presentation for their children.

The development of alternative organizations to take the place of Bremer's traditional organizations, such as its churches, does not mean that religion is unimportant to these rural residents. In 1988, 94 percent of the residents reported that religion was very important (60 percent) or somewhat important (34 percent) to life in Bremer. Only 3 percent of the residents said that local churches were not important to overall life in Bremer. With a consensus that local churches are important to life in Bremer, the status of church leaders is also specifically defined, if not formally, then at least in the normative understanding of Bremer residents.

As a whole, the community believes that clergy should lead in personal religious matters, but only 29 percent of the residents feel that they should be consulted before the community changes. Community members interact with outside political organizations in a secondary manner, and they interact similarly with outside religious organizations. Bremerites make a distinction between outsiders and those who are part of the community as a group. They interact in a familylike interaction pattern with members of the group and in a secondary, more distant manner with outsiders. The distance individuals can trace back their heritage is one measure of how others in the community interact with them.

The fact that the religious leaders who are brought into the community are a temporary authority influences the power they hold and how they are accepted by the community residents. Like the doctor, the local religious leaders are held in a special regard by community members. Their contribution to the maintenance of traditional values is seen as important by the community. However, as short-term residents they fail to learn the local values and belief systems.

The values of sharing and yet maintaining a strong individual system of beliefs imparted by the religious leaders fit well with the traditional values of Bremerites. The conflict between the community-control attributes of group orientation and homogeneity and the mass-society attribute of assigning religious leaders according to achieved status instead of the traditional ascribed status is manifest in the marginal position held by religious leaders, especially in the political arena.

In the 1930s the Lynds wrote, "Like art and music, religious observances appear to be a less spontaneous and pervasive part of the life of the city today, while at the same time this condition is being met by more organized, directed effort to foster and diffuse these values" (Lynd and Lynd, 1929).

The findings of earlier researchers indicate that in urban environments social life was dictated less by religious observances, which were found to be less tied to churches than to other organizations in which the traditional values were imparted. In the past decade in Bremer, we have seen a pattern similar to that which took place in the urban areas 50 years ago, although the reasons for the similarities may be different.

Religious Leaders: Knowing Them Is the Problem

In Bremer, where face-to-face interaction is the norm and community norms are the predominant rules, the role of the church reflects the change in the mass society. The increased availability of leisure activities in urban areas decreases the ritualistic observances of religious organizations. In Bremer, satellite dishes and cable TV provide a similar function to that of movie theaters in the 1930s, although the reason given by Bremer residents for changing their religious observances is tied to the lack of "knowing" the religious leaders.

To overcome this lack of knowledge about local religious leaders, residents have developed community-control organizations in which they can foster and pass on their traditional values. Within the religious organizations of Bremer, the tie is to the mass society and the larger bureaucratic organization that is governed from outside the community. Community norms dictate that religious leaders must have a unique position within the structure of the community. The lack of local control has a dramatic influence over the power of the church in local affairs.

Community norms and values and the local responsiveness to rules place the church in a position of following the local norms, which stipulate in unwritten form that religious leaders should guide only in personal religious matters, not in the overall direction of the community. The structural interactions governed by community norms have allowed Bremerites to bypass many of the impacts of the mass society, and remain in the community-control era. As the heterogeneity of the community members increases we might expect to see group consensus over religiosity decrease. At this point religion is seen as a very personal matter that lies outside community control, although the norm is to practice a western religion. The female doctor (discussed in Chapter 8) who wanted to set up a practice in Bremer was not only from a foreign country, but also practiced an eastern religion. The doctor's committee gave this as the main reason for having turned her down, although her gender undoubtedly also figured in the decision. In the tradition of Bremer, doctors are male, white, and Christian.

Conclusion

Religion is important in the everyday lives of Bremerites, but it is not the primary guiding force for community activities. The social fabric of Bremer and the everyday life of its residents support the maintenance of community, and it is these interactions and behaviors that must be examined if we are to gain a complete understanding of the conflict that exists when people have one foot in the community-control era and one foot in the mass society, and are faced with a changing society that focuses on information and its handling. Bremerites have adapted to the changes in their religious leaders' status by creating other organizations, such as the gun club, in which to pass on their values.

Are they religious? The answer is yes. The qualification is that to be successful their religion must be tied to their community norms and beliefs. The existence of the Bremer Gun Club and the Sunday-morning ritual of trap shooting indicates the strong orientation toward the group in Bremer. When their churches become controlled from the outside, Bremerites devise community activities that continue to bind them at the community level.

Religion in Bremer is viewed by the residents as a private matter. The influence of the mass society has reduced the influence of the churches in the community, according to the residents. There is little evidence of the intrusion of the information age on Bremer's churches. Social class does influence some religious interactions in the community. The predominant church in Bremer is the Methodist church and the longtime residents attend this church, whereas a few while newcomers and less well-off Bremerites attend the local evangelical church.

The primary finding in this analysis of religion in Bremer is that religion is not a critical factor in maintaining community in Bremer. Religious leaders face a variety of barriers when working in the community, many of which are the direct result of the strong community-control orientation of the community. The mass society may have played a role in the reduced impact of religion on community cohesion, yet this is speculation on the part of the authors. Reconstructions of the past history and importance of religion to community residents also revealed less impact of churches on community organization than one would be led to believe by previous research on the church and rural communities.

Traditionally, the role of religion within Bremer was to pass on values. As the mass society began to become predominant, religion increasingly became seen as something from the outside. Bremer has created its own informal organizations to maintain its perceived "different" values. The question that remains is, Will Bremerites be able to control their value system through informal means as some newcomers and poorer residents foster a coalition at the nontraditional churches?

11

Class and Social Life

Returning from someplace outside of Bremer in the company of Bremerites, it is not uncommon to hear them say, "You can always tell when you're getting close to home. Everybody waves." Waving a hand, raising a finger, or nodding your head in acknowledgment of drivers of other automobiles, pickups, trucks, or large tractors is an expected behavior. When Bremerites talk of getting close to home they are speaking of passing these boundaries within which their vehicle is recognized. This expected interaction while driving on the public roads is just one of the behaviors that is informally required of residents of the community. The norm of waving is socialized into Bremerites at a young age.

Engaging in extensive and frequent communication when meeting another person on the street is a behavior of Bremerites that is also learned at a young age. When encountering someone else on the street it is not acceptable only to nod and move on. The norms for such interaction are to stop, say hello, and explain what you are doing downtown. This behavior of overcommunication is evident in almost every face-to-face interaction on the streets. An example of this behavior follows:

Jan: How are you today?

Sally: Fine. I'm just getting some tin for Sam and picking up some cold medicine for the kids. I've got two that have been having this cold hang on for weeks now.

Jan: I know. Jean's kids have had one too. Well, I should be going. I've got to get the mail and then stop by the Grange. We need a little bit more of 16-20 [fertilizer]—I've been getting the lawn taken care of before it gets too cold.

The two women part and walk in opposite directions down the street. Face-to-face interactions among men follow a similar pattern. The required interaction indicates the need for knowledge among community members. The lack of anonymity among community members places individuals in the position where they must divulge personal information to feed into the informal information network to counteract much of the gossip that moves through the network along with factual knowledge.

This mandatory interaction stems from the community-control era. Hans Bahrdt observed, earlier this century, that when people from a rural community are lost in a city and find it necessary to ask for directions, they feel it necessary not only to inquire for directions but also to explain why they need the information and why they were not able to find their way (Bahrdt, 1966, p. 83).

Both the lack of anonymity and gossip are seen by many community members as unpleasant aspects of the community-control era, as indicated by comments such as the following:

[A problem is] people who gossip.

Everyone knows your business before you do.

Everyone knows (or thinks they know) what everyone else is doing.

Near total lack of privacy and anonymity.

Small town social life equals gossip.

People don't mind their own business.

Everybody wondering what his neighbor is doing.

The rumors and gossip! Everyone knowing how to live your life.

The expectations of community members' participating in face-to-face interaction and sharing information with the other community members through the informal information network lead to overcommunicating. With community norms paying a great deal of attention to the rules of interaction, Bremer has over time maintained these community-control-era attributes.

The importance of overcommunicating cannot be overlooked. Without it, the knowledge base of community members would be greatly diminished. Knowledge of everyone in the community is important in maintaining local norms. Without the knowledge the informal information network provides, it would be difficult for businesspeople to follow the norm of interacting with customers as individuals and not as a group.

Several questions remain to be answered. First, how does living in at least two different eras influence the social life of the community residents? Second, as the impact of the information age begins to make itself felt, does participation in the information age influence with whom and how a Bremerite interacts within Bremer? To examine these two basic questions we need to begin at the beginning, with the birth of a new Bremer resident.

Birth: Expectations and Orientations

Traditionally, the birth of a baby in Bremer is a community celebration. The residents share in the excitement of the new child. Baby showers are not formally advertised, but the time and location of the shower are passed by word of mouth throughout the community. Photographs of the child are placed in public places such as grocery stores and the doctor's office. It is expected that all community members should provide a gift for the new child. This exchange is reciprocal and the community expectations are that once you have a child you are also expected to buy a gift for all other new children born to the community.

The importance of new babies to the community is evident in the many pictures tacked to the centerposts of the grocery stores. There are several reasons for the importance placed on new children. First, becoming a member of the community begins at birth. To be an inside member of the community it is important that a person be born into the community. When community members speak of one another they often refer to when someone was born in relation to when other people in the community were born. An example is this description of a Bremerite's birth:

> I was born just after the war. Number two. Harold's mother was in the maternity ward with my mother and he was born the day after me. It's funny because my mom and his mom were born in the same month and had the same doctor deliver us as delivered them.

The importance of a birth in its designation of who one is can be illustrated by this resident's comment about who he is and how he is related in birth order to other members of the community. This birth order will be influential the rest of the person's life in whether he will be the leader in a political organization or a support person.

Birth order is an ascribed status and cannot be changed. The competitiveness of the community members, especially of the younger males, is often based on these ascribed statuses. The hierarchy that is developed early on is evident in the sports teams. Older players are always the first-string players. People don't move up in any organization until those who were born before them retire or pass on the power.

Birth in the community isn't just the basis for a hierarchy within the community, nor is it just a celebration of new life, as is the case in tribal societies. A new birth in Bremer is an informal means of confirming the goodness of the community as a whole. With a new birth the community feels that it is guaranteeing the survival of the group.

Party Lines and Community Information

Technology has reduced the ability of Bremerites to have up-to-date information on all residents. In the past, telephone party lines provided a means for community members to keep up-to-date on the more intimate matters of other members of the community. An older woman explains:

> My ring was two longs and a short. My son lived just over the hill on the other side of the ranch and their ring was one long and two shorts. We knew everybody's ring, so if it was someone in the family we would just pick up the phone and listen. It wasn't really an underhanded thing to do. Everybody knew that others on their line were listening, so you tried not to say anything that would make them mad while they were listening. It gave me a chance as a grandmother to hear what my grandkids were up to. That way if I heard they were going to do something that would get them in trouble we could do something about it. I miss the party lines. It was a way for older people to still be involved.

The eavesdropping of residents on others' telephone conversations was another way to gain information on community residents. The use of this technology as a means of community control has diminished as private telephone lines have replaced the party lines of the past, despite their continued prevalence in other nearby communities. Knowledge of community members must now be gained through other means. Bremer residents also see the use of television as influencing their everyday lives. The recollection of one older resident:

When I was a boy going to school here, we knew everyone in town and would walk around in the evenings and visit with folks. Summer evenings everyone would sit out in their yards and wait for neighbors to walk by. Now, everyone has television and they just sit inside and people don't visit anymore.

Bremer Friendship Calendar: Whose Birthday Is It Today?

Over 1,300 names of Bremerites decorate the Bremer Friendship Calendar. The reason more names appear on the calendar than there are people is that the names indicate both birthdays and anniversaries of local residents. The calendar was developed, as were those in many other communities in the Palouse, to make it easier for residents to know who is celebrating what. To collect the exact dates of important occasions, volunteers agree to ask all of their neighbors for their birthdays, anniversaries, and other important days in their lives. These are then incorporated into a calendar and distributed at no cost to all of the households in Bremer.

The importance of the Friendship Calendar is similar to the importance of the pictures located in the grocery stores. It is one more symbol of "who we are," according to Bremerites. The knowledge contained in the calendar adds more information about community members that helps tie the community together.

Recreation: Work and Play Blend Together

Leisure activities in Bremer form a basis for relaxation from work while at the same time enhancing one's tie to the community. Typically, leisure activities of residents have little, if any, work related to them. Upon closer examination, the orientation toward the community as a group is paramount in most leisure activities. An example is a simple day of boating, water skiing, and tubing on a local lake.

The hot summer days before the grain harvest provide an opportunity for Bremerites to get together and enjoy the water at Bremer Lake. While some boats with water skiers gliding behind them turn circles on the blue water, other boats can be seen moving slowly near the steep banks of the lake—these boats carry farmers who are examining the rough dirt roads located near the lake at the edge of the wheat fields. They are looking for large rocks that will need to be moved before the trucks loaded with grain will be able to drive down the roads. When a large rock is spotted sitting on one of these roads, a yell goes up from those in the boat. Several boats soon pull up to the bank and as many as a dozen young men jump out to move the rock. Although those who move the rocks will not benefit personally from having a clear road, their strong tie to the group makes it mandatory that they help, even on a day set aside for recreation.

Reflections on the Past

Many residents talk easily and with feeling about earlier times and how Bremer was once a center of growth.

> We were close. All those little towns that you drive through as you get here were full of people. Most of them had a high school, and everything that made them a town. Like Lincoln, for instance; they had a blacksmith, post office, two churches, a small store. They even had a twelve-man football team and a good baseball team. When it burned down [1920] everybody moved to Bremer. After that the town changed. I think that was the thing that started the town [Bremer] to become the center of everything.

During this period of Bremer's past, small communities were situated about every 10 to 15 miles throughout the Palouse. Transportation was difficult. The dirt roads and hard winters made travel from one small place to another difficult. As the farmer explains, the small town's decline led to movement from these small hamlets into Bremer. Yet the population of Bremer did not increase greatly. Another farmer expresses his ideas of this phenomenon.

> Look down the valley. See all of those windmills. Well, there was a house filled with kids at every one of them. There were one-room schoolhouses every 10 miles or so or wherever they could get enough kids to put up a building. Now look at them. All you see is open fields with an old windmill every once in a while.

In the past, everyone was involved in either growing wheat, transporting it, or providing services to the farmers. As a retired businessman puts it:

> When the [flour] mill was still in operation [it closed in 1966], you'd see people bring in a wagon or truck full of grain and have it ground into flour. They'd then go around town and pay their bills with it. We [businessmen] would get together and take loads to Sterling [to the north]. Everyone was involved with the grain in one way or another.

Agriculture was the center of life for most of the residents of Bremer during this period of time. The social life of the residents was dictated by when farmers were working and when they were not.

Social-Class Differences

Throughout our interviews with Bremerites, we looked for evidence of social-class distinctions. We concluded that such distinctions exist but are small. The size and homogeneity of Bremer are such that social-class differences are a minor basis of who interacts with whom in the life of the community.

The first indication of class differences was historical. In the past, women's clubs were designed in part to give the "town women" something to do while the "farmers' wives" were taking part in harvest. During the long Palouse winters, the farm wives would come to town, when the roads allowed, and participate in the meetings and catch up on any local information they had missed while working on the grain harvest. During this period in the history of Bremer, the town women were seen as superior to the farm women. The reason for this is explained by a farm wife:

> Well, I'd work every day during harvest from about three in the morning, when I'd get the stove going and get breakfast ready for everyone. Dad would go feed the pigs, get the cows milked, and feed the teams. After that I'd clean up and get the wagon ready. I'd take the cook wagon out and set up for lunch. I was feeding over 20 men three times a day, so it didn't give me much time to go to town. The town women saw us [farmers' wives] as poor and not too cultured. But they knew that without the farmers their husband's business wouldn't last long.

This stress between farm women and town women was caused by the idea that farming was dirty work and if your husband had a business you were above that type of work. The interaction patterns between the two groups slowly changed as farming became more mechanized and the farm women were able to participate more fully in the local clubs.

When Bremerites speak of their community and what they like best about Bremer, they use comments such as the following:

> Knowing everyone, being able to leave the keys in your car without fear of it being stolen.

Low crime rate, nice neighbors ready to help if needed. It is nice to know most of the people in a small town.

Everyone is friendly, everybody knows you and speaks. People come to your aid in a crisis. Good loyal people.

It is a typical small town with caring people more like a close-knit family.

A high percentage of "good" people and a strong pride in community.

These comments from Bremerites illustrate the strong pride that exists in their community. "Knowing everyone" is a major feature of their perception of what makes Bremer a special community. Yet the perception that Bremer is a tightly knit family and that everyone is known is running up against the change taking place in agriculture. As farms have increased in size and agriculture has become more mechanized, fewer people are needed in the growing, transporting, and selling of the grain grown in the Palouse. This change has caused friction among the Bremerites and the farmers who produce the grains. As farms need less and less labor to produce their crops, those individuals who had previously held jobs as farm workers are now no longer able to maintain their status within the community. One previous farm worker explains:

I worked for nine years for William [farmer] and then they bought two new combines. They used to have seven smaller ones, but now they only need two combine drivers and two truck drivers. So now I work driving truck in the harvest, and during the rest of the year I commute to the university and work as a janitor. Now everybody treats me different. It's like, well, "You couldn't make it here, so you aren't part of us any more."

In the past in Bremer if you farmed or worked for a farmer, the community residents treated you as a member. But as agriculture has changed, the definition of who is part of the community and who is not may be changing. Two Bremerites expressed their feelings as follows:

If you aren't born here or your kids aren't from the BIG farms here, you make a mistake, they never let you forget it. Nonfarm kids don't get a second chance.

The people are extremely cliquish—there is a very real caste system here.

The stress between farmers and nonfarmers has increased in some ways as the availability of transportation has allowed farmers to go outside of the community to spend their money. In addition, more people are working outside of the community and this also has created stress. As of the spring of 1988, 33 percent of Bremerites reported that their spouses work outside the community. Outside employment challenges cohesion of the community and the perception of its members as part of a large family. This is especially true for women in the community who need to work to help support the family farm or just to keep the family solvent if they live in town. One problem that has developed is the inability of those who work outside to participate in the business community in Bremer. As they explain:

It is hard for working parents to be able to shop locally because of the store hours—no groceries after 5 p.m..

The store owners do no offer enough services, the grocery stores close at 5 p.m.. The other stores close at noon on Saturday.

Nothing open on Sunday and lots of businesses closed on Saturday, especially during fall and winter.

In the past, community members worked and shopped in Bremer. But as farms increased in size and the labor force necessary to maintain the level of production decreased, local jobs were not available. As people began working outside the community, the amount of daily face-to-face interaction declined. Those who work outside of Bremer complain that the businesses don't understand their problem and still close at 5 p.m.. This reduced face-to-face interaction has added to the division between who is a community member and who is not.

"Welfare People": No Place to Go

Increased out-of-the-community employment isn't the only change that has influenced the community of Bremer. As housing prices have fallen, the residents have felt that outsiders have moved in who have no regard for the good of the community:

As the housing prices dropped people began moving in who just don't have the good of the community at heart.

Almost all of the activities that were once enjoyed here have all been done away with. Because there's not much employment people have to move. Now welfare people move in for cheap housing.

The perception of the "new" people in Bremer is that they are here because the cost of living is low but do not want to be part of the community. This perception leads to a distrust of new people and the ideas that they may express. Those who see themselves as outsiders explain their situation this way:

As an "outsider" it takes a long time to get to know people.

Outsiders are not seen as a person, just a function, i.e., farmer, farm wife, good housekeeper, good gardener.

There are a lot of people who think money and name [family] are everything. If you don't have either or both, you're left out of a lot of things.

As an outsider my opinions are distrusted.

If you don't fit their norms usually you and your family are shunned as undesirables, i.e., wrong color, wrong name, wrong income bracket, etc.

This feeling of being outside the mainstream of community inter-action has created some conflict between the "insiders" and the "outsiders" in Bremer. Those who are insiders feel threatened by the newcomers and have perceptions of them being "on welfare" and not wanting to contribute to the traditional interactions in the community. As one insider explains: "They don't even know enough to say hello when you see them on the street. This isn't New York, you know."

Those who are new to the community, either through marriage to a local farmer or a move to the "country," feel that the old-timers are "stuck in a rut" and that it is "the old-timers who have let the town decline." Friction has developed as more and more people work outside of the community and new residents move in from the outside.

At this point in time it does not look as if a great influx of "welfare" people are moving into Bremer, but data obtained from the Washington State Department of Social Services do indicate that there are a growing number of families in Bremer who participate in some form of state or federal assistance. Yet the numeric increase (4.5 families) is so small that one cannot tell objectively whether the community perception is correct. In March of 1985, the average yearly caseload for Bremer was 13 families on welfare assistance. By 1987 that number was 16, and by July of 1988 the average caseload for Bremer was 17.5 families. These data do not support the perception of Bremerites that their community may be declining and that a lack of local employment is a major factor influencing this decline. This pattern of increased participation in assistance programs is also taking place in the communities adjacent to Bremer.

As these changes have taken place, "knowing" someone has become more difficult. The traditional orientations and values held by the Bremer residents are threatened as they no longer "know" everyone. The change from daily face-to-face interaction to interaction on a weekly or even monthly basis breaks down the ability of the community to control its members and to retain its traditional values. The newcomers to the community feel isolated and shunned and believe they are not wanted in the community. Even those who have traditionally been members of Bremer but who now work outside the community feel they are shunned because they no longer participate fully in the daily life of Bremer.

While farm size has increased, so has the per capita income in Bremer. Yet as per capita income has grown, those who do not own or have the ability to lease large portions of land have moved down the social ladder. During the same period that per capita income was increasing, the number of families requiring federal or state assistance to survive also increased. This has resulted in a magnification of the class system between the haves and the have nots.

Conclusion

The structural changes that have taken place in agriculture have influenced almost every aspect of the Bremerite's life. The employment base has shifted and an outmigration that began in the 1940s has continued, leaving behind a large percentage of the population who are retired. This change in population structure has influenced the educational institutions, which have been forced to consolidate. Some residents feel that this has led to a decrease in community identification. In the past, a community expectation was that residents interact face-to-face, and this is true to an extent today. Face-to-face interaction is tied to a tradition of informal norms and diffuse roles. As the economic structure of the area has changed, we are beginning to see a change in how people are perceived within the community. The class system that existed in the past, based on land ownership, is now being changed as agricultural producers become more involved in the mass-society organizations.

The complexity of living within eras simultaneously is reflected in the desire of Bremerites to retain their traditional ways of interacting with one another while maintaining a viable community. Their belief that knowing everyone is important in maintaining a viable "rural" community is reinforced through their continued overcommunication and use of a Friendship Calendar to identify everyone's birthday and anniversary.

Not everyone who lives in Bremer feels included in community activities. Those who are considered to be outsiders, either through self-identification or community identification, feel outside the flow of most community affairs. The norm of interacting face-to-face within Bremer is currently being threatened by the perceived movement of "welfare" people into the community and "insiders" who now are forced to work outside of the community. These new stresses and how the community members deal with them will affect whether it will be possible in the future for Bremerites to "know everyone" in their community.

12

Community Expression and Renewal: The Bremer Fair and Stock Show

The Bremer Fair, as women refer to it, or Bremer Stock Show, as men usually describe it, seems an unlikely event at an unlikely time of year. Mid-April weather is unpredictable. Rain mixed with the season's last snowflakes is a possibility, if not a probability, for this special Saturday in April.

A day-long series of events—outdoor breakfast, five-mile run, golf tournament, parades, potluck dinners, and community dance—constitute a schedule that, rain or shine, will take place. For a Bremerite not to participate is akin to declaring that being a Bremerite is unimportant. Nonparticipation is a statement stronger than words can articulate. Thus, for one Saturday in April fieldwork stops and stores are closed for a day-long celebration of being a Bremerite.

In a region where fairs are typically scheduled during the still-warm-and-sunny post-harvest days of September, Bremer has chosen a time of year that maximizes the likelihood of local participation. School is not yet out, planting is generally completed, retirees have returned from the South, and, as one resident said with unintentional understatement, "There's not much that competes with it."

The Bremer Fair and Stock Show is nothing less than a renewal of community and a reminder of what it means to be a Bremerite. It is a cultural event that distinguishes Bremerites from members of all other farming communities in the Palouse hills. It is an annual ritual that helps motivate Bremerites to defend the boundaries of community and makes such matters as school consolidation a dramatic issue of concern. Above all, it is the renewal of commitment to the community. It is the one day of the year that residents of the community spend together and that attracts former residents back for a renewal of roots.

Participation is no less mandatory for most residents than are baby gifts, attendance at funerals, and support of the basketball team. To be working in the field, planting the last of the spring wheat or peas, is not an acceptable excuse for failing to participate.

Preparations

Preparations for the Fair and Stock Show begin the day after the previous year's event is over, as neighbors converse about what was good and bad about this year's fair. Like other important Bremer issues, this too is under the control of the community club. A subcommittee of the community club, the fair board, is responsible for organizing the event. Although planning goes on throughout the year, it is in the final weeks and days it reaches a fevered pitch and leaves few members of the community untouched. Decisions are made on who will hand out awards at the Wheat Fete (although everyone knows that it will, according to tradition, be the organizer), who will sell raffle tickets for the quilt, who will have dinner at whose home, who will play in the golf tournament, and who will be in the parade. There is a role for almost everyone in the community and in some cases many roles. Few who are asked consider declining.

The center of activities is unquestionably the fairgrounds, a cluster of seven buildings on a few acres, just off Main Street near the edge of town. The largest building is a 70-foot-long beef barn with an adjoining shed where horses can be tethered. Two smaller metal buildings serve as sheep and hog barns. Next to these buildings is a show ring bordered by bleachers that might seat 100 people. Nearby is a small (15' x 15') cookshack, and somewhat farther away a new craft building, which, like the others, was built by volunteer labor with contributed building materials. Adjacent to the fairgrounds sits a community golf course, of which much was built by volunteers.

The buildings are mostly unused during the remainder of the year, save the hog barn, where the fair board allows a youngster to keep his hogs for the fair year-round because he has nowhere else to raise them, and the new craft building, which houses golf carts except during the fair.

For a few people the Fair and Stock Show starts on Thursday evening as they bring their animals to the fairgrounds. Other participants will arrive early Friday morning. Children with fair animals are excused from school for the day to bathe and groom their animals and attend the judging and awarding of ribbons. During this day of preparation the fair is attended mostly by parents. The downtown cafes do a booming business, including take-out orders, as parents shuttle back and forth with burgers and drinks for their kids. In the nearby craft building, flowers, quilts, needlework, canned goods, and other expressions of people's work are delivered, judged, and awarded ribbons. However, for the most part, Friday is a quiet day. The energy of participating in the Bremer Fair is saved for Saturday.

Symbolic of the entire event, no fair book announcing classes, entry requirements, or prizes is distributed. Because of past experience, people simply "know" what to bring. And when people show up with unexpected new entries, as did the exhibitor of llamas, new classes are made up on the spot. Participation takes precedence over formal rules to govern it.

Frying Cakes and Turning Eggs

At 3:00 a.m., as if on cue, headlights from all directions can be seen coming down the roads toward the Bremer Fairgrounds. Their destination is the tiny cookshack in the center of the fairgrounds. Some of the men driving there at this early hour have repeated the ritual for much of their adult life. To be asked to "turn eggs" or "fry cakes" is considered an honor, and once they have been asked, the role is theirs to keep until willingly turned over to someone else, often another family member, but always a male. The role of "money taker" is an interesting exception. The superintendent of schools, whoever it might be, is expected to perform that role.

By 5:00 a.m. the last of the food is carried in, grills are heated, and breakfast is being served. The earliest customers are young people from Bremer, brought to the fairgrounds by their parents to feed and brush their animals. Although the judging has all been completed, this is a day for community residents to walk through the barns, and the animals are expected to be neat and clean. As dawn approaches, the pungent but pleasant aroma of animals, soap, coffee, fried eggs, pancakes, and sawdust envelops the entire fairgrounds. Cooking breakfast is a social affair, with more attention given to exchanging jokes and good-natured barbs than to the size of the pancakes, the hardness of the egg yolks, or the crispness of the sausage.

An occasional bottle of bourbon has been known to be placed under the counter between the extra supplies of paper plates and ketchup, out of sight so that "wives won't suspect a thing." Yet, as the morning progresses and the conviviality within the cookshack heightens, wives who stand in a small group nearby eating their breakfast speculate about how much of the bottle has been emptied and whether their husbands will feel up to going to the dance that night. This is a day of fun and celebration, and a few Bremer norms will be violated.

Other small groups of early-morning customers can be heard talking about the new John Deere combine that will cut grain at nine miles per hour and comparing how this fair measures up to past fairs. The crowd continues to grow and includes some strangers who have accompanied out-of-town runners participating in the Wheat Fete. They have assembled here both for breakfast and to watch a portion of the race. Even these early-morning customers, as they cross the bridge between the parking lot and cookshack, are greeted by two women seated in front of a handcrafted quilt, prepared to sell raffle tickets to all those interested.

A stranger to Bremer, having just dropped off a participant across town at the starting point for the Wheat Fete and now standing in line at the cookshack, illustrates the difference between a Bremerite and one who is not. The half-dozen people, adults as well as children, ahead of him are greeted by name as they pay for their breakfast and start through the line. When it is the stranger's turn he is momentarily puzzled by the lack of a posted price, and to keep from having to ask he offers a $20 bill for his $2.75 breakfast. The cashier finds he needs change and asks no one in particular if they have some ones. Instantly, two men behind the serving line and two customers in front reach for their billfolds. The cookshack worker who was about to put into the pancake batter a long wire stirring rod attached to a half-inch electric drill, which yesterday might have been used in a construction project on his ranch, gets money out first. There is a flurry of activity as the cashier collects ones from three of the five people who offer.

Next, the stranger is taken aback when the man in charge of the pancake griddle holds up an empty plate in one hand and a pancake turner in the other and says with enthusiasm, "How many will you have this morning?" His uncertainty on how to answer isn't helped by the fact that the ten-year-old boy ahead of him, called Bret by the cook, said "None" and moved on down the line. The stranger concludes that two is appropriate, and with them in hand proceeds down the line.

Meantime, Bret has responded to the sausage turner's question of how many with "Five," and his plate is quickly filled with five large link sausages. He declines eggs and is given a cheery admonition to "enjoy breakfast." The stranger accepts two of each, and then looks puzzled as he is confronted with a large metallic tub affair, actually the bowl of an ancient cream separator, with no signs. He looks at the butter beside it and then gingerly touches the handle. After a test to confirm its contents, he adds syrup to his pancakes and looks for a place to stand and eat, only then realizing that he has picked up nothing to drink, as those in line behind him ask for coffee or milk while taking their turn at the syrup bowl.

Locals know the fundamentals of getting breakfast: they know the unposted price, they know they can ask for whatever number of cakes, sausages, or eggs they want, and they know milk is out of sight under the counter. Signs about breakfast are as unnecessary as it is for them to ask; most who need to know already know. The stranger gets the same friendly smile as the others, as well as idle comments about how cool the morning is and what the weather will be like later today, but what isn't said is perhaps the question on everyone's mind: "Who are you and why are you here? Are you someone's relative? Are you a former resident who went to college and came back for the day and I just can't remember what you looked like 20 years ago? Are you just here awhile for the Wheat Fete?" The question never gets answered, as customers keep coming, most of whom are greeted by name and know the rules.

The Wheat Fete

Across town, in the park by the Bremer school, the first of perhaps 300 runners are assembling for the annual running, jogging, and/or walking of the Bremer Wheat Fete.

The Wheat Fete is five miles long. Because of the lack of cross-roads in the surrounding hills, it is set up for participants to go through Bremer, past the fairgrounds a scant 20 yards from the cookshack (the main center of activity at this time of day), and up a long hill a mile and a half from the start; entrants then turn around and return the same route to the finish line. The starting line doubles as the finish line.

Running is a popular activity throughout the region, and many small communities sponsor runs, or jogathons, as they are sometimes called. The Bremer Wheat Fete appears on listings of the times and places of those events, and the Bremer event attracts numerous outsiders partly because it occurs just two to three weeks before Bloomsday in Spokane, where some 50,000 people will participate in one of the nation's biggest running events. The Bremer Wheat Fete is a tune-up, where serious runners can expect to compete against a few other serious runners as they prepare for the "big one." Bremer leaders have frequently asked radio stations in the region not to announce the Bremer fair, or Wheat Fete, to keep it locally oriented. Still, the message gets around, some years more than others, and Bremer accommodates, even with instructions along the route.

Those runners who arrive early and decide to drive the route chosen for the run (which is always the same) to get a feel for it are greeted by a series of homemade cardboard signs that locals have attempted to make interesting—one more role for a local person.

In one recent year, the first of the signs—handwritten magic marker on white poster card stapled to a pointed lath for posting—made this simple statement:

One mile; that was the easy one.

And only a few yards farther down the road, a more elaborate sign:

Mile number 1 is now complete. The scenic view can't be beat! But look ahead, there's Heartbreak Hill. What a challenge and a thrill!

And near the top of a hill:

Okay you've made it to the summit, now to say Hey, I've done it.

A few yards farther, and apparently influenced by the Boston Marathon:

Two miles. Summit. Wheat Heart-break Hill, elevation 2,090.

At the turning point, a water crew has a table already set up and a car backed into the ditch so that the road will be clear. Out here they serve the extra purpose of being able to stop drivers from nearby communities who may be unaware of the event, and then keep them from interfering with the run. The sign reads:

You're halfway through so turn around, let's all head back to town.

The next sign, a scant half-mile away, reads:

Three miles and here comes that hill again. Here it is, a little slope, keep on going, there's still hope.

At four miles:

Hang in there, one to go. Whew, mile four is history, repeat no more this misery.

And for good measure, as runners approach the fairgrounds for the second time, a hand with extended finger points straight ahead:

This way to go to the finish.

The difference between a Bremerite and an outsider is that the latter probably thinks, and even smiles, about the unusual spacing between signs and uneven wording. A Bremerite, we suspect, thinks more about who has made the effort to construct the signs and makes a mental note to comment with appreciation the next time they meet. Someone has performed an important community service.

Back at the park across from the school, in the hour prior to the race, there is an unlikely congregation of experienced runners wearing nylon warm-up suits and nylon headcoverings and once-a-year-joggers in unmatched shorts, sweatshirts, Bremer Grain Growers caps, and occasionally a cowboy hat. Some of these latter are there as a result of a bet or a dare, or just to support the community, about to start their only "run" of the year.

Neighborhood residents keep an eye out for locals and offer them coffee or use of the restroom, or just talk with them for a moment. The locals, in conversation, and the serious runners, methodically and quietly limbering their muscles, provide a striking contrast on what has turned out to be a crisp morning.

The back-to-back park restrooms are busy: soon a long line extends in front of the women's side and no one is using the men's side. A man addresses the line of women in a clear but casual voice, announcing, "The men's side is free and some of you can use that. I'll watch out for you." When no one moves, he says in the same tone of voice, as if continuing the previous announcement, "There is also a restroom in the school building—it's available." A couple of locals who apparently know where that one is then leave the line and head toward the school building. Bremer has its own way of solving problems, whether it is temporarily "changing" who uses which restrooms, or using a school facility for a community club event. These boundaries, like so many others in the community, are in a gray zone of changing to meet the need, whatever it might be.

As the time for the race draws near, the stranger, now back to the park for the start, stands well in front of the runners and holds a small camera above his head in an inadequate effort to take a picture of the crowd of runners. A local person sizes up the dilemma and says, "Go ahead and hop in the pickup beside you—you can get a better picture from there." A second person says, "Yeah, no one will care about something like this—do it." He does. Meanwhile, the woman with the starting gun has come to the starting area. A few runners continue to warm up by jogging forward from the starting line and back. Without warning, the starter raises the pistol and fires, with three runners still several yards in front of the line, where they are suddenly astonished to see the crowd of runners coming at them; they turn and join the race. What the start lacks in orderliness is more than made up for by spectator enjoyment, and no one seems to mind.

A half-mile away, a dozen or so fairgoers, knowing the race is about to begin, keep a watchful eye on the road. A few breakfast eaters carry their plates to the white rail fence at the side of the road and wait in anticipation.

The first runners, the ones in fancy nylon shorts and jersey tops, whip by almost before anyone notices they are there. There is no clapping, cheering, or other sign of acknowledgment, except that conversations momentarily stop. Only when the first few locals come by is there a response from the growing throng of observers, with "Thatta way to go!" and "Go for it!" being punctuated with the runners' first names. Mostly, though, people continue their conversations and keep eating. The connectivity of observers to local runners is perhaps best illustrated when a single woman runs by midway through the pack during a moment of complete silence. Another woman, who is balancing her breakfast plate on a fence post, says simply, between bites, as if in normal conversation, "Did your husband get home last night?" The runner, after a quick look to identify the person behind the voice, says, "About 11 o'clock. He was really tired." Both the race and the breakfast continue.

The serious runners reach the turnaround point while the last of the walkers are still near the fairgrounds, and as the watch for returning runners begins, the crowd grows more interested and some start to speculate about how high someone from Bremer will finish. When "he" shows up on the horizon, the word gets passed, and both applause and cheers greet him as he passes the fairgrounds for the second time, a few minutes after the lead pack has gone by to the sound of appropriate but less-sustained applause.

At the finish, T-shirts are awarded even before walkers have reached the turnaround point, and prizes to the top finishers are announced and presented well before the last walkers arrive back at the start. Most of these out-of-community runners are well on their way home before the run is officially over.

Bremer Golf Tournament

The lack of success of locals in the Wheat Fete is often reversed in the second competitive event of the day—the Bremer Golf Tournament. It is played on a course built by locals for locals. First-time visitors to the Bremer Golf Course are often surprised, if not confounded, by the layout. During the regular season, one walks up to the small "clubhouse" only to discover it is unattended. A sign explains that in order to play, one should put five dollars into a small envelope and drop it into a green mailbox. A computer-printed sign stuck to the wall with a thumbtack reads, "If you fail to pay, Marshall Bob will come looking for you." Marshall Bob is a retired resident who lives across the street and has voluntarily agreed to watch the course and supervise the teenagers who mow the lawns and keep up the greens.

Even more baffling is the scorecard, as players discover that it is divided into three sections and that to play 18 holes one must complete the course three times. One out-of-bounds line is described as Jenson's field, and another is the road leading out of Bremer. Even with these instructions it is not surprising in the summer to see local players in blue jeans, and on occasion cowboy boots, playing by their own rules, using a pitching wedge to lift an errant shot out of six-inch wheat stubble.

The extremely narrow fairways and postage-sized greens result in shots straying into adjacent fairways and occasionally the next fairway over. It is a course built for community enjoyment, as evidenced by the occasional "farmers' day," when local farmers show up in work clothes and carry one iron, a wood, and a can of beer as they make their way around the course.

Today's golf tournament is scheduled to start at 10:00 a.m. and to be completed when the parade begins, although in the history of the tournament, play has never actually been completed by the beginning of the parade. For this day, out-of-bounds markers are observed and the play is somewhat more serious, partly an accommodation to the few outsiders who participate in the tournament. However, it is a golf course on which experience counts and the locals are most likely to take home the top prizes. Winning scores are often in the upper sixties.

The Parades

As the noon hour draws near, those members who are around the stock barns begin to make their way downtown, walking down the road toward Main Street, to where the annual parades take place. Pickup trucks pulling horse trailers and others with antique cars can be seen frantically looking for a parking spot so that they can unload their cargo. Many of the farmers who were up at 3:00 a.m. to cook the breakfast have since finished their shift and rushed home, put on a clean western shirt, loaded horses into their trailers, and returned to town. While horses are being unloaded and wagons are being attached to the large draft horses, young children, some dressed in clown outfits and others in bib overalls carrying pitchforks, are running and laughing as they too make their way toward downtown.

There are no No Parking signs placed on Main Street to tell people they should not park there, because everyone in Bremer knows that the parade begins at noon. Those who have parked there earlier follow local custom by leaving their keys in their cars or pickups so that someone else can move their vehicles if they are held up at the stock barns. After the parade any residents whose cars were moved simply walk around until they find them, without concern. However, problems arise when nonresidents park on Main Street and lock their cars. As the parade volunteers frantically look for the outsider, others attempt to gain entry into the locked car so that others may assist them in pushing if off the street.

The Bremer parades are ad hoc affairs. There are no entry forms. Children who want to participate in the children's parade, which is run first, simply show up. Prizes will be awarded for ingenuity and style. The children's categories, though not specified in any written rules, are under four years of age, four and five, six and seven, and eight and above. Once children reach the age of twelve, they are generally expected to participate in the adult parade that follows. The children, who usually number over 100, are lined up by volunteers from the community club just off Main Street; there they impatiently stand— some by their bicycles and plastic trikes, others holding their pet dogs, and still others propping up two tall walking stilts. Cameras click as the parents, grandparents, and neighbors take pictures of the participants waiting for the starting signal, which is generally a loudly yelled but clearly informal, "Okay, you can go now!"

The strain of waiting is apparent as the first children on bicycles shoot out of the side street and turn left down Main Street. Inevitably, community club volunteers have to run out to slow them down so that the parade moves along in an orderly fashion. The children's parade makes its way down the two-block downtown area until it reaches the grand parking lot, where other volunteers guide youngsters around the turn to make their way back toward the other end of town, following the identical route. As the children reach the downtown area for the second time, they slowly melt into the crowd where relatives stand waiting to pick them up. They are now ready to watch the main attraction—the adult parade.

It takes about 20 minutes for the main parade group to become organized as some who watched the children's parade hurry to take their positions. During this time residents mill up and down the crowd talking about the weather, new births, tonight's dinner, the dance at the local tavern, and invariably how this year's celebration compares to past ones.

The adult parade begins near the east side of town and this year, as always, the first participants are three horsemen riding abreast, one with the American flag held in a leather holder on the stirrup, another with the state flag, and the other with a white flag that has the Bremer Horse Club insignia embroidered on it. All the riders wear cowboy hats that are worn only on this occasion and the Fourth of July; baseball caps are the norm for headgear for the rest of the year.

Next comes the elementary, junior high, and high school marching band. Because of the size of the school, all grades must participate to have enough people to form even a small band. The band consists of about 20 students and baton twirlers (majorettes) wearing matching green uniforms, a new addition to the band bought with donations from local residents. Although the quality of their music is sometimes questionable, no one doubts the enthusiasm of the participants. No frowns can be seen and the music is not criticized, even by those with musical ears.

A large group of horses and riders follows the marching band, and riders can be seen pulling their fidgeting horses back as they nervously stand and then move a short distance to stand again. Their nervousness is understandable. After the parade some of the horses will be hurriedly reloaded into the backs of the horse trailers and returned to their fields, where many will wait, mostly unridden, until next year at this time. The nervousness of the horses is increased by the sound of the buzzing motorcycles ridden by the Shriners from Spokane, who are riding in circles and figure eights slowly behind them. The sound of screeching tires is heard as a car driven by a car-club member from the county seat revs his engine, slips the clutch, spins his tires, and slams on his brakes in order to avoid crashing into the Shriners directly in front of him. A local politician running for county commissioner follows the race car in a 1939 Plymouth, waving at the crowd on one side while his wife waves at the crowd on the other side of the street.

Black smoke in the distance from loud diesels gives evidence that farm tractors, always an important part of the parade, are approaching down Main Street. The recently washed and waxed new tractors are driven by local workers from the hardware/implement dealer, and young children can be seen sitting inside the air-conditioned cabs waving to the crowd.

Traditional farming methods are not left out of the parade: large draft horses move slowly down Main Street; their well-groomed feet, the size of a dinner plate, lift, hesitate in the air, then slowly return to the pavement. The wooden wagons they pull are occupied by men playing fiddles and young local women seated on hay bales and waving to the crowd. As the wagons move by the crowd, applause erupts. The young women are the princesses of the parade, chosen by the community club for their community spirit. The year's fair queen follows, sitting on top of the back seat of a new red cadillac convertible donated for the parade by a Bremerite.

The parade continues down Main Street until it reaches one block east of the fairgrounds, where it takes a left and follows a back street around the center of town, where it will begin again. A slight delay often occurs as the parade makes its way to the starting point, but the crowd doesn't seem to mind. Many of the watchers use the time to buy a beer at the tavern, which is filled to overflowing with Bremer celebrants. The duplication of the spectacle gives the impression of a very large parade.

As the parade completes its second tour of Main Street the watchers move back toward the fairgrounds, where hundreds of pounds of hamburger are being grilled for the lunch break. The hamburger and hotdogs were made by a local grocer who has volunteered his labor for the last 15 years. Food is an important aspect of the Bremer Fair and Stock Show, yet the local inn is not open on this day. The owners are also at the fair eating at the cookshack.

Potluck Dinners

It is a tradition in Bremer for groups of six to eight families, including children, to dine together on fair day in the late afternoon. The meals have been prepared in advance and potluck style is the norm. Lawn chairs are scattered around yards throughout the town and countryside, as residents take this time to rest up for the dance to come that evening. After dinner a few of the early-morning risers use this time to sleep off any effects of the bourbon so that they can participate in the evening's celebration.

The meals served here often resemble the harvest noon meals. Fried chicken, coleslaw, home-baked beans, home-baked rolls, and desserts are customary. Even though microwave ovens are found in most of the kitchens in Bremer, today's ritual focuses on tradition and that means no microwave food, only "home-baked."

While the adults sit in lawn chairs, often with jackets on, the children talk about the parade and show off any prizes they may have won for best costume, best-decorated bicycle, most traditional costume, etc. The older children talk about the fairness of the judges and what animals they plan to show next year. This year there is also conversation of llamas. Where do they come from and what are they used for? This particular ritual, that of communal dining, illustrates the importance Bremer places on cohesion among the community residents. Those who are new to the community are invited to attend a dinner at someone's home and generally that same family or group of friends will continue to offer the invitation for years to come.

The Finale

Following dinner, the children are placed under the supervision of older relatives— grandparents or aunts and uncles who feel they "are just to old for all this activity"—or a young teenage girl who will be paid well for missing the teen dance at the local Grange. The teen dance is a nonalcoholic event chaperoned by several schoolteachers. The music is provided by a large record player and ends at midnight, at which time the chaperons will make their way to the adult fair dance already in progress. The role of chaperon is rotated among the local teachers every year so that no one misses the majority of the adult dance every year.

Although drinking is not approved of during the day, this celebration is an exception. Some of the men who have been working the cookshack and may have overindulged on alcohol have taken catnaps lying on their pickup seats; they are not sanctioned as they would be if this were any other day of the year. The tavern, which is generally quiet during the day, has been packed to overflowing, with some residents remaining there throughout the afternoon.

The fair dance is held in the same long and narrow cafe-by-day, tavern-by-night, and the music is provided by a country and western band. The celebrants range in age from 21 to 70, and young community club members are asked to watch for anyone underage attempting to come through the open doors. This task is voluntary and is simply another illustration of how Bremer socializes young men to become community leaders. By allowing volunteers to watch for underage youth, the tavern owner is placing his or her liquor license in the hands of a young male member of the community. This act is not overlooked by the volunteers, as they conscientiously watch everyone who walks in or out during the evening.

The large, dancing crowd, often ranging in the hundreds, creates a great deal of heat, making it mandatory that the doors at the front and back remain open. Country-swing dancing is the norm and couples in cowboy hats twirl and reel as the music grows in volume throughout the night. Conversation is limited, and on occasion when the band stops playing, someone is caught in midsentence yelling to be understood over the music, and suddenly everyone can hear what he or she is saying. The evening continues until about 2:00 a.m., almost 24 hours after the day began, when the "last call" for drinks is issued.

In one recent year, Bremerites at the dance were surprised at 2:00 a.m. to see five state police cars situated outside the tavern on Main Street waiting for those residents who had overindulged on alcohol during the evening. Following a Bremer custom of taking responsibility for local residents, those who lived outside the town limits and had had quite a bit to drink were invited to spend the night with in-town residents. As the lights were turned off at the cafe-by-day, tavern-by-night, residents could be seen walking and laughing down the dark streets of Bremer. The meaning of community had once more been celebrated.

Conclusion

The Bremer Fair and Stock Show exemplifies and reinforces the core community-control values of the community. The orientation toward the group is illustrated by the almost-mandatory obligation to attend and to participate in the event. The ascribed statuses in the community can nowhere be seen more clearly than in the continuity of the cooks in the cookshack, where positions are handed down from one generation to the next, and where even new members such as the school superintendent have an ascribed position.

The community orientation is also exemplified by the community's asking regional radio stations not to advertise the fair and stock show so as to maintain the community flavor and control. The volunteer labor to clean the grounds and prepare for the show is a reflection of the power of the community club and also of the respect the club holds among the community residents. The overlapping institutional structure of the community is also portrayed in the use of the new fair building as a fair building during the fair but otherwise as a storage building for golf carts.

A basic Bremer value is also embodied by the size and voluntary payment of fees at the golf course. The value of honesty is paramount in business, family, economic, and religious activity in the community. The particularistic values of the community are also illustrated by being allowed to play on the course, as long as you stay out of the way, even if a tournament is in process.

Socialization of future leaders can be seen as young community club members are given the responsibility of organizing the parade, emceeing the parade, and acting as bouncers for the evening dance. The high visibility of these positions is part of the process Bremer uses to train young men to take over the running of the community club, city council, church boards, and grain-growers co-op.

The orientation toward family is also evident in residents' commitment to participating in the fair and stock show and parade. The constant attention given to young people in the community for how well they attended to their animals throughout the year is also illustrated by signs found in the local businesses following the sale at the end of the fair. This short letter, signed by Bill Hollister, was attached to the bulletin board at the local bank: "Thank you for buying my pig at the sale. I didn't mind selling him because he was getting a bit ornery anyway." This note was matched with about 20 other notes and letters thanking the local bank for purchasing local animals raised by local adolescents.

The fair and stock show is a ritual that has had a long history and adds to the continuity of what it means to be a Bremerite. This expression of community represents what the basic expectations are to be a Bremerite and how those expectations are passed on from one generation to the next.

13

Community in Bremer . . .
and the United States

In this book we have portrayed the reality of life in Bremer as we have come to understand it. Throughout our investigation we have been impressed with the persistence of mutual ties, the taking into account of others, and strong identities that can be explained only by invoking the concept of community. Among the many indicators of belonging to and being committed to this geographic place are the following:

- A swimming pool, golf course, and fairgrounds, all built and maintained by volunteer labor

- Competing businesses that help one another and avoid selling certain products because another business does that

- The city council's buying from the highest bidder because it's that business's turn

- The community calendar with the birthdays, wedding anniversaries, and other important dates

- The defense of community boundaries by not advertising the annual fair

- The community club with subcommittees that oversee community activities, even public ones such as school affairs

- The bank, which pays below-market interest yet maintains customers and whose loans are publicly made

- The retaining of medical care by purchasing the retiring doctor's house and financing a new one, through volunteer subscription

- Invitations to social events, announcements of school board meetings, and anything else important being spread quickly by word of mouth

- Rejection of state and federal help, in favor of solving their own problems

We have showed that much of what happens in Bremer can be accounted for by invoking concepts of community control derived from a legacy of sociological thinking fostered by Tonnies, Durkheim, and others, and applied to U.S. communities in the 1940s by Loomis (1962). Leadership in the community is often ascribed rather than achieved and people are sanctioned for not adhering to community norms. Decisions, even those on governmental matters, often take into account the whole person and his or her situation rather than being simply the application of formal rules. Bremer is a social system that people identify with and that they defend from outsiders, sometimes forcefully.

Yet Bremer is not an isolated entity that has severed its relationships with the larger society. Farmers adhere to the dictates of the USDA crop-production programs, relying on monocultural production of soft white wheat for economic success. Federal conservation programs are utilized on most farms. Individuals watch TV signals brought in by satellite dishes, are eager to adopt new technologies, and consume the same mass-produced products available elsewhere in the United States.

However, Bremer has done what many communities have not been able to do. It has deflected the penetration of mass society and held some parts of it at arm's length. The power of mass society in this century has been its ability to mitigate intermediary allegiances—tying people to jobs, products, and organizations that at first ignored, and ultimately weakened, community boundaries. The tendency for horizontal ties of locality to weaken and be replaced with stronger vertical ties between individual organizations and regional and national organizations outside of the community, as described by Warren (1978), has simply not occurred. Evidence of vertical ties exist in the arenas of agriculture and some Main Street businesses, but not in other businesses, politics, or many social activities.

An umbrella of community identity and commitment remains strong, with the result that people take one another into account, as do the businesses and institutions that serve them. In Bremer, community has survived, against all odds.

Reasons for Persistence of the Bremer Community

It is far easier to provide convincing evidence for the existence of community than it is to explain its persistence. We have taken a snapshot of Bremer at a particular time in its history and can only speculate about some of the factors that have led to the activities and events described in this book. There is no community that serves as an experimental "control" against which we can compare Bremer in a scientifically rigorous way. Any insights into the reasons for persistence are by necessity somewhat speculative. Yet, we believe such speculation is important in understanding the likely future of Bremer and the potential applicability of lessons learned here to other communities.

In 1938 Louis Wirth, in an attempt to explain community, noted that small size, low density, and homogeneity contributed to the maintenance of such ties and set rural places apart from urban ones. Bremer, throughout the years, has maintained smallness and a low overall density of population, the latter now being somewhat lower than in the past. Most important, perhaps, homogeneity has been maintained. There has never been an influx of new residents who make their living in new ways. Soft white wheat and related crops remain the basis of the local economy, the growing of which is protected by USDA subsidies.

Most new residents come into the countryside through marriage and appear to be assimilated into the value structure of the community. The countryside has not become chopped up into small ranchettes or residences with large numbers of people who live there but commute to larger towns and cities to work. Agriculture remains the primary business of the community and the reason for living there.

Certainly, Bremer's isolation from larger urban places is a reason for the maintenance of its small size, low density, and homogeneity. The mountains of Idaho to the east and the drylands of Washington's Columbia Basin to the west result in there being no larger towns or cities within a reasonable commuting distance in these directions. Larger places that would serve as magnets for employment are 50 miles or more to either the north or south. Geographic separation may be a very important consideration in explaining the nature of the Bremer community.

Bremer has maintained its institutional base—it is possible to go about the rounds of daily life and have most of one's essential needs met without leaving the community. Although few, if any, residents do in fact restrict their activities to Bremer, it can satisfy the vast majority of people's needs for recreation, social activities, food, medical care, prescription drugs, education (through twelfth grade) and employment. Virtually all residents of the community get at least some of their basic institutional needs met there. Yet to suggest that the maintenance of these community services is a reason for the persistence of community raises the more fundamental question of why the services continue to exist, whereas in many nearby communities they have not.

The geographic isolation may be a reason; or it may be that in competition among communities Bremer merchants were simply more successful, something about which we can offer little insight.

At the same time, we believe the role of the community club has been crucial. Its involvement in both the traditionally public and private activities has encouraged the schools, businesses, city council, and individuals to take one another into account. The community club was the organizational device that worked successfully to keep a local doctor, to build recreational facilities that far exceed those of most small towns, and to help foster a norm of community involvement.

The Bremer Fair and Stock Show is noteworthy as an event fostered by the community club that both expresses and maintains community. It is an expression of the uniqueness of being a Bremerite and it is also a means of securing individual community involvement and offering recognition.

In the end, we believe community is maintained by a constellation of factors, from agricultural subsidies to the community club, from the existence of grocery stores to its distance from larger communities. These elements are interconnected in chains of causation. Community is the result of no less than the intertwining of the many structures and conditions described, and perhaps much more, including factors we have not been able to touch upon in this book, and others that remain unknown to us.

Still, if our detailed analysis of Bremer has revealed a Gordian knot that ties the community together, surely it is the community club. Its main significance is not, however, that a group of concerned male citizens gets together on Friday evenings with a will to solve community problems. Its importance is that it has successfully solved one of the problems most responsible for the demise of rural communities, i.e., the separation of town and countryside resources.

This separation of interest and commitment was first documented in sociological terms by Galpin in southern Wisconsin (1915). He noted the differences in interests and domain of control that produced conflict rather than cooperation between town residents and residents of the surrounding rural countryside. Legal jurisdictions produced boundaries between who was destined to pay for services and who, in the wider community, would likely benefit from them.

This tendency was exacerbated during the development of the mass society, when local organizations, both rural and town, bypassed local communities and thus tied people's interests directly to national interests. These tendencies were accurately described by Roland Warren in his discussion of how the forces of bureaucratization and suburbanization pulled people's interests out of local communities to the national scene (1978).

Rural residents of Bremer pay taxes to county government and receive, in return, a wide range of potential services, from law enforcement and recreational services to road maintenance, over which they have virtually no control. Any pretense of ballot box control is diluted through having only a fraction of the county's voters and only with luck being able to elect someone with a particular commitment to the Bremer area of the county.

The community club is a mechanism that allows the resources of town and rural residents to jointly support, through volunteerism, community-wide facilities that otherwise would simply not exist, from a swimming pool to the fairgrounds. People are not taxed, but the social obligations of being part of the Bremer community provide a type of social enforcement that goes well beyond what can be done publicly to help Bremer, the community, solve its important problems.

Community at What Price?

We would find it surprising if many readers of this book did not find certain attributes of Bremer somewhat distasteful, if not objectionable. At the same time, the attributes objectionable to some may not be deemed undesirable by others. The overall sense of community might be viewed as either oppressive or serenely protective. The obligation of speaking to whoever passes on the streets of Bremer may seem a tremendous burden or simply a joy of expression. Having to negotiate a loan at the bank in front of everyone else who happens to be there may seem an invasion of privacy, or it may seem okay since other people's deposits make it possible to acquire the loan. The exclusion of women from key community leadership roles and, in particular, the community club activities may be interpreted as a denial of basic rights or as acceptable because no one seems to object.

Rural community life is sometimes visualized as simple, with few interpersonal demands creating stress, as do the often conflicting roles of urban society. Readers with such a perspective may be disappointed to learn that stress can also come from needing to master the details demanded by rural life—remembering not only customers' names, but those of their family, and even the year and model of their tractor. One must keep up on details of what is happening in Bremer's schools and the lives of community members, with the only source of information being conversations with others. A perceptive newcomer well on the way to acceptance in the community noted, after receiving well over a hundred gifts at a community baby shower, that they were now obligated, so long as they lived there, to buy gifts for everyone else's new baby. Whether community expectations like these are interpreted as burdensome, as just a routine part of life, or as a reason for feelings of satisfaction depends on the outlook of individual Bremerites, as it would undoubtedly depend on the differing perspectives of outside observers.

There are many perspectives from which aspects of life in Bremer might be evaluated, and as outsiders we did not find ourselves reacting neutrally to many of them. Yet, as outside observers of a system of social organization overlaid with a distinctive culture, we found little to be gained by our attempting to pass judgment on what we considered desirable and undesirable. Suffice it to say that maintaining community exacts a price, just as does commitment to other social systems, from family to work organizations. It is one which to date Bremer residents seem willing to pay.

Lessons for Other Places

It is presumptuous, at best, to interpret the results of a case study of one community as having implications for others. No community anywhere else can be expected to be just like Bremer; surely each and every community in the United States is unique. Such is the inherent limitation of focusing on the whole of one community rather than focusing on characteristics of many communities and sampling large enough numbers of them from a total population of communities so that scientific generalization can be undertaken.

Still, our reason for choosing to study Bremer was in part to learn things that might help us understand processes and situations existing or not existing in other communities. Community studies went out of fashion in the 1960s, a result of the effort required to study individual communities at a time when the application of powerful statistical techniques to population samples was beginning to dominate social research. We chose Bremer because superficially it gave evidence that a strong sense of community existed, an impression that later proved correct. By examining the processes at work here we hoped to learn something about what processes we might examine to understand other communities. It is in hopes of assisting others with the results of our research that we offer this commentary on lessons learned.

How to Make Things Happen: Getting a Doctor

A fundamental premise of much community-development work is that people who care about a place will work to improve or maintain it. A problem that sometimes besets communities is that people do not care enough to work for its improvement, often expressing the lament, "I'm just too busy to help out." In modern communities, loyalties often seem directed toward specific causes—Boy Scouts, the park commission, the PTA, the fire department, etc. Instead of these entities being viewed as subparts of a larger community, they become competitive elements, so the efforts of one to recruit volunteers competes with the efforts of others, and the limit of each organization's interests becomes more restricted than the general community.

The community club and its omnipresence throughout the Bremer community, with its activities controlling both public- and private-sector issues, are critical in gaining the expression of community-wide concerns so that it is impossible for Bremerites to dismiss finding a new doctor, cleaning up after the volcanic eruption, or even buying locally, as someone else's problem. Forces of the mass society that emphasized vertical ties between local organizations and structures outside the community have undoubtedly weakened organizational structures that tie the elements of community together. Finding ways to develop and strengthen organizations "equivalent to" the Bremer Community Club may be of benefit to other communities.

But to do so is no simple matter. The community club works because it is legitimate within the community. It also sponsors a community-wide event (community fair) in which virtually all of the community's suborganizations play a role. A "community club" in name only is not a solution—rather the identification of and persistent playing out of a special community role are what make the difference—and in Bremer's case were what solved the problem of how to find and keep a doctor.

How Not to Make Things Happen:
A Case of Poor Judgment

In recent years the need for many geographical localities to come to grips with community-wide challenges has led to the creation of community-development process-action teams. The aim of these professional-development agents and their activities is to help community members identify problems and organize to resolve them. Sometimes this has led to the development of standardized methods that are then applied in one community after another. Often such methods include brainstorming techniques, preparation and prioritization of lists, and even games to help people learn how to work together toward common objectives. Applying mass-society methods to communities that retain community-control characteristics may be disastrous. The fate of one such team in Flemington, near Bremer, and its consequences for Bremer are perhaps instructive.

More than a hundred people showed up for a community potluck followed by a meeting with three announced purposes: (1) to meet the need of getting together as a community (commented on as "something we should do more often"); (2) to hear results of a community-wide survey that all community residents had been asked to fill out; and (3) to listen to a leadership trainer help them identify and prioritize Flemington's problems. After a brief discussion of the survey results, which had previously been distributed in local stores and which had been read by most people who were present, the community leadership "trainer," as she identified herself, walked to the front of the room and began. She mentioned that Flemington was "a pretty little town" and that this was her first visit. She then said that a grant had been received by the county to provide leadership-training skills for small towns like this one and that she hoped some community members would participate.

She then went on to explain the structure of "tonight's" meeting. The problems would be identified by all of the audience, after which the top problems would be written on the poster paper sitting on an easel. After the problems were identified the audience would line up and each person would walk by the easel and place a dot where they thought the problem was the greatest. "Remember," the trainer stated, "we will be selecting one 'hard' problem and one 'easy' problem."

An elderly gentleman raised his hand and said that the dogs running loose in the community were the biggest problem. The trainer wrote the problem on the paper, mentioning in passing that there had to be more important problems. Another problem mentioned was the old buildings in town and the need to clean them up even if the stores were empty. The loss of the high school to consolidation with Bremer was also mentioned.

After further discussion the audience was asked to proceed to the easel and place their red dots by the most important problem, yellow dots by the second most important, and so on. At first no one moved. Then, some 20 of the audience followed the instructions. Others sat quietly, eyeing one another, with signs of discomfort on their faces.

Once the topics with the most dots had been identified, the leadership trainer separated the topics by tables and informed the crowd that they would have seven minutes at each table to discuss each problem and then move on to the next table. It was then that many community members, and particularly the older ones recognized as community leaders, quietly rose, paused to thank the conductor of the survey for his work (which had been carefully and personally legitimated with them before being done), and left, mostly unnoticed by the leadership trainer.

An hour later the remaining participants were brought back together as a single group, and 20 minutes were spent trying to decide when another meeting would be scheduled, a meeting that would never be held.

During the next week the author of the survey received over 30 telephone calls; many residents wondered if he was the reason for the leadership trainer. They pointed out that just because they had gone along with the survey did not mean that they needed someone from outside coming in and telling them how to be leaders. The words of one caller:

> How stupid can you be? You must be from a city. We've been a community for over a hundred years and have been able to survive. You didn't even have the courtesy to ask Harold Metzger [longtime farmer and community leader who doesn't hold a public office] to talk. Who do you think you are?

About the trainer and her sponsoring organization:

> This is just like something they would do. They can't find enough ways to spend money, so they send people like you out into our towns and try to tell us how to live. We don't want any part of it. We may be having some problems, but we solved them in the past and we'll solve them this time.

When residents of Bremer were approached about going through a similar leadership-development meeting, their answer was quick and decisive. (See Allen, 1993, for a detailed analysis.) The message was that there was no need for someone from the outside to come in; they were satisfied with their community processes for getting things done.

Our intent here is not to critique the methods used by the community trainer. We have observed situations in which such methods work fairly well, particularly situations where people do not know one another or have few common ties. The colored dots, rotation of small discussion groups, and other process techniques often seem to work well when a structure for group process and established leadership does not already exist. A product of mass-society thinking, this method's application to communities such as Flemington simply did not and could hardly be expected to work.

Effective community action within Flemington, Bremer, and other established communities could probably proceed better if organizers first understood how decisions tend to get made and then built on those processes rather than attempting to summarily supplant them, as happened in the community meeting in Flemington. No amount of poster paper, magic markers, dots, and other process paraphernalia can substitute for an understanding of ongoing community processes where they exist.

Building Intentional Community

When we have described many of the characteristics of Bremer to urbanites, discussion has often shifted to the frustration some experience over a lack of community—neighbors who neither know nor speak to one another, the lack of knowledge about coworkers' personal lives, and the inappropriateness of "getting too close." Bremer has seemed, momentarily at least, idyllic and something to be sought.

Our discussion of Bremer may help explain the difficulty of creating community in urban places. The sense of community that exists in Bremer is not something Bremerites set out to create; it is something that happened. The relationships that developed, the intimate knowledge of one another's lives, the norms for interaction, and the way things get done—all these were simply worked out over a period of years. People have not given it up because for the most part it still works. Just as Milgram (1964) points out the impossibility of a New Yorker's speaking to everyone he or she meets on the way to work, and not being able to talk to everyone about his or her personal life, a Bremerite cannot do otherwise. The conditions of existence are so different.

Yet, there are lessons here too. To the extent that urbanites determine to enhance a sense of community, forces such as the community club and local cultural events, which crosscut existing institutions, may help. Typically, building community identity and mutual concerns is not a complete impossibility; nor, however, is it ordinarily possible to build then to the degree they exist in Bremer.

Community scholars, professionals with economic-development interests, and community leaders are intently looking for ways to create stable communities in urban and rural areas. The lessons from Bremer may provide further insight into that process. It is our belief, from studying Bremer, that many of these processes and organizational structures may be replicated in some form in communities where homogeneity, geographic isolation, and low population density are not local conditions.

To begin with, as we illustrated with the school-consolidation example, the decision-making process in Bremer relies heavily upon informal communication, primarily face-to-face. To successfully resolve the highly emotional issue of the potential loss of a school, the local leaders utilized a community-control strategy. That is, they spent many hours educating local citizens one-on-one about the realistic options available to the community. Many informal, nonelected community leaders were recruited for this task. This strategy is not consistent with mass-control orientations, which are often to hold a public meeting, gain local input, take a vote by those who are elected to office, and then make a decision. The Bremer strategy for problem solving gained, if not total community support, at least community acceptance of the change to their community.

The norms of community cleanliness also play a role in facilitating community-wide interaction when dealing with problem solving. As we reflect back on the earlier discussion of the maintenance of vacant homes in the countryside and of the local recreation facilities, it may at first appear as if these residents have a fetish for cleanliness. Yet, on closer examination, it becomes evident that the high level of outdoor activity (in clear view of other residents) provides an excellent structure for increased face-to-face interaction facilitating the informal problem-solving techniques used in Bremer.

Local economic activities on Main Street also illustrate processes that may be replicated in some form or another in other communities. The clearly defined range of products to be sold by each merchant may at first seem a result of poor business practice. Further examination reveals that the practice of selling products not sold by other businesses has created an environment of stability for local businesses over the long run, even though in the short term their individual profits may be lower than if another business technique were used. Employment opportunities were provided for young and old residents alike as each of the businesses filled its niche within the sphere of community economics.

Agricultural production plays an important role in many communities across the nation. Bremer is no different from many of them because of its reliance on farm subsidies for income. Yet Bremer farmers utilize the system for their benefit while finding new ways to maintain local interaction. The use of information technologies, such as home computers and satellites, among and between local farmers has replaced some of the previous forms of interaction. This has allowed the farmers to maintain much of their traditional communication about how each is farming and marketing his product. The computer networks provide a structure for maintaining cohesion among local farmers, which otherwise would have deteriorated because of the change in farming practices. As an example, computer networks can be formed around a variety of economic groups, maintaining community interaction and community identity.

The leadership structure in Bremer is organized horizontally. This horizontal leadership structure allows individuals with specific expertise or interest to lead in specific instances. It also facilitates the inclusion of nontown members in decision-making processes, which increases community cohesion as well as community identity. Rather than relying upon elected officials to manage community activities, informal leaders are recruited and given public support for leading specific activities.

Maintaining health care in communities plays an important economic and social role in maintaining community. Through creative and community-oriented fund-raising, the community has been able to retain health care in the face of a severe shortage of rural physicians in the nation. Primarily through local ownership of the health facility, flexibility has developed in the process of enhancing the recruitment of new physicians.

Various lessons can be gained for other communities from this examination of one rural community in eastern Washington. First, informal communication with community residents by formal and informal leaders creates community-wide acceptance of changes in the community. Second, a horizontal leadership structure that enables nontown leaders to participate in activities, many of which may be seen as predominantly focused on the town proper, increases the interaction between town residents and residents living in the countryside. The available pool of leaders is increased (a need in many rural communities) with the size of the community, providing additional resources for activities such as recruiting a physician. Third, a community club that is informal yet provides continuity between organizations in the community has been developed. This organizational structure seems well fitted to urban or rural communities. And finally, the use of social activities, such as school athletics and the fair and stock show, reinforces community identity and encourages informal interaction in a social setting among local residents. Providing a forum, however informal, for the discussion of the community as a whole seems to have played a major role in maintaining community in Bremer.

The Role of Community in Building
Social and Cultural Identity

The 20th-century model of American social and cultural development during the building of the mass society was one based on assimilation. To succeed in the United States, it was expected that certain things were expendable, including identity with one's ethnic heritage and identity with locality.

In an earlier time, when community-control processes were stronger, Durkheim, one of the founders of sociology, noted that societal allegiances were built through subgroups, arranged hierarchically, that brought allegiances to the societal level (1947). Thus, group identifications were seen as a building block of society, and their connections provided a critical building block for societal allegiance.

Development of the mass society rearranged the connections of individuals to the larger society in two important ways. First, many influences were considered to have less importance than in the past, including extended family, ethnic identity, and community. And second, as Roland Warren so aptly reported, ties of the newly important groups—professional associations, employment affiliations, and voluntary interest groups of all sorts—developed vertically, so rather than groups connecting upward in an umbrella arrangement, with interests broadening at each higher level of connection, individual vertical ties went straight from individuals to national groups that represented them. He described this as the strengthening of vertical ties at the expense of horizontal within-community ties.

For this sort of connective arrangement to work, it was convenient, and perhaps necessary, for individuals to accept common societal norms of interaction and depress individual cultural identities that encouraged different norms. At the very least, cultural identities, including those with local communities, were seen as expendable.

In recent times, this general assimilation model has been questioned, most forcefully by racial and ethnic groups. They argue that learning and identifying with subcultures can link people's individual interests under an umbrella of cultural beliefs in a new societal mode that respects diversity while still achieving a consensus on and commitment to larger social goals and ways of doing things. In essence, a tolerant, multicultural society, now described as desirable, is one in which people can identify closely with ethnic and other groups of common interest, but cooperate nationally for the common good.

In this context, it is of interest to consider one of the predominant approaches now being encouraged for rural community-development efforts. Small rural communities are being encouraged to assimilate with one another, to bury past rivalries, ignore boundaries, and work together for development. This kind of encouragement is considered appropriate because small size is a major inhibitor of development efforts.

Is it possible that admonitions to communities to give up their local identities, which in the past have given purpose to the striving of many community members, may destroy what's left of the motivation to have pride in local concerns and to solve local problems without providing a substitute for that motivation? Our own view is that intercommunity collaboration is important in many rural regions, but the existence of individual community ties should not be dismissed as unimportant in such efforts. To do so would be to exercise judgment as bad as that which guided the well-intentioned community-process-action-team efforts in Flemington. It would also imply the ignoring of much of a community's true resource base, as described next.

Ignoring the True Potential Resource Base of Community

Finally, a most important implication for other communities is one that may be poorly understood by many community-development professionals and others concerned with helping communities. It is simply this: what the true potential resource base of community can be. Wilkinson, in his effort to account for the decline in community ties, described the problem:

> Without a sufficient base of resources in the local area to meet primary needs, rural residents must do without or they must look outside the local territory for the resources they need. . . . rural people often travel great distances and to multiple centers to meet their needs for work, trade, education, health services, recreation, and government services. (1991, p. 113)

The lack of resources to meet residents' needs has been shown repeatedly to be a major factor in a community's inability to maintain community identity and commitment. A significant part of this problem is the tendency to separate village and town centers from the surrounding countryside along mental, political, governmental, and other lines.

A simple but common example of this misunderstanding occurred in an outsider's attempt to complement Bremer for a significant accomplishment. The report started by noting, "This small community of a mere 500 people has once again proven that for it major accomplishments are routine." What was the reporter's error? Unknowingly he had "halved" the population of Bremer! As we have noted throughout the pages of this book, the Bremer "community" consists of not only the 500 residents within the incorporated limits but also another 500 who identify strongly with the community and act on its behalf. One reason that Bremer's accomplishments sometimes seem so remarkable is this misunderstanding by outsiders of who belongs to the Bremer community.

In many cases it is likely that the reporter's perception would be correct in such an assessment of a rural community. Sometimes the town center has little connection to, and even little in common with, residents of the surrounding countryside.

Bremer, through its community club, its annual fair and stock show, its efforts to maintain a doctor and a golf course, has brought together and blended the resources of village and countryside. The development implication for other communities is a simple one: a way to strengthen, even double, a community's resource base in order to solve local problems is to find mechanisms for linking together the village and countryside resources that government structures have typically set apart.

Before efforts to promote regionalism, with its likely threat to what remains of local cultural and social identity, are adopted wholesale as the primary means of development for small communities throughout the United States, this less obvious but potentially powerful means of development should be examined. The mechanism for achieving that may or may not suggest the need for a voluntary community club. In other rural communities it may involve the formation of foundations, a technique we have seen used successfully, or the creation of new understandings and organized activities by county and city governments that truly take one another into account.

In many respects Bremer has achieved the entrepreneurial social infrastructure described by the Floras as a necessary ingredient for successful development (Flora and Flora, 1993). They have maintained a social capacity to confront difficult problems (getting a doctor), an obvious willingness to commit individual resources for accomplishing their collective goals, and have demonstrated an ability to handle controversy. At the same time, they have done this in their own way, under conditions different than the conditions by the Floras as essential. In Bremer, it has been done without development of strong vertical networks and diversity within those networks.

Our observations of Bremer reaffirm perhaps the most fundamental of development principles. To artificially separate social, cultural, economic, and other resource issues, and to treat each in ways that ignore the others, is to reduce them to something less than is essential for effective rural development.

Conclusion

We began our study of Bremer guided by conceptions of three eras of social and economic organization. At a societal level, the community-control era, in which people's lives are focused on and constrained to their community of residence, is mostly past. The mass society, with its emphasis on national markets and the linkage of people's lives to corporations and of local organizations to national ones regardless of community consequences, has peaked. The information era, with its emphasis on substituting information for other resources and the formation of networks regardless of geography, was at the start of this study just beginning to emerge. Our interest in the impacts of information technologies on communities was encouraged by anecdotal evidence of their rapid introduction into Bremer businesses and on farms. We were also guided in our study by the theoretical possibilities that existed for reshaping organizational connections and human behaviors that could influence community relationships.

What we have found is the persistence and active encouragement of community-control processes to a degree that goes far beyond that which contemporary sociological literature led us to expect. In every sphere of life, from politics to earning a living, there exist ascribed behaviors, particularistic decisions, informal rules, concern with the whole person, concern with tradition, and other community-guided behaviors. Community, as an umbrella group that guides behavior, is alive and well in Bremer. The struggle in which Bremerites engage on a daily basis is one between maintaining those community-control processes and responding to the intrusions of mass society—government agricultural programs, state regulations for schools, business and other officials from elsewhere who are given assignments to work in the community, etc. It is the strength of the former that gives them the ability to hold at bay many of the latter.

However, to the extent that Bremer's strong economic base, the benefits of which are well distributed throughout the community, provides the ability to maintain its community-control processes, an irony also exists. Much of the stability enjoyed by the agricultural community stems from a mass-society farm program that permeates agricultural productive practices. Bremer's well-being is undoubtedly protected by this assurance against really bad years, which in turn could affect the ability of both town and country residents to contribute to a doctor's account and make the other voluntary efforts that sustain the Bremer community.

While the mass society has been held at bay, albeit selectively, the influences of the information age are mostly too weak to have had major impacts on Bremer. Its presence to date is mostly in the trial use of new technologies that do not require great modifications in how businesses or people relate to one another.

We can speculate that the advent of the information age may aid Bremerites in their efforts to maintain community. If the information age truly marks a shift toward optional behaviors and allows communities to break many of the vertical ties on which they have become so dependent at the expense of local processes, as suggested in Chapter 3, then Bremer may start from a position of advantage. Having outlasted many of the mass-society pressures to give up community in favor of external ties, they may be able to take the initiative that other communities lack the internal capability to take.

No one knows what the future holds for Bremer. What will happen when the druggist retires? When the current doctor decides to leave? If there is another round of school consolidation? If farm subsidies are eliminated and a few years of wide fluctuations in wheat prices result in drastic agricultural changes? There are many ifs in the future of Bremer, just as there are for all communities.

Our guess, however, is that whatever the challenge, some predictable things will happen. Attendance at the community club meetings will be up, and most people in the community will be aware of the issues being discussed there. Any public forums will involve substantial attendance. Emotions as intense as those registered at the school board meeting with which we began this discussion of Bremer may be expressed. Pickups will likely be seen driving up and down the roads, with occasional stops for neighbors to talk with neighbors. Telephone calls for whatever purpose and most business transactions will also involve airing the pros and cons of whatever issue is facing the community. For a period of time the controversy will be everyone's business.

Bremerites will be doing what being a Bremerite is all about, working for the good of the community and its citizens in a situation where it is difficult to know where the interests of one end and the interests of the other begin. And whatever the ultimate decision or outcome, it also seems likely that more phone calls, and more stops to talk along the road, will follow. Much as the challenges facing communities never seem to end, neither does the challenge of maintaining community, a fact with which few Bremerites are likely to disagree.

Perhaps a good indication of how Bremer might deal with an outside threat comes from how it recently responded to a threat not to the community but to one of its members. Just as the final paragraphs of this book were being written in early 1994, ten years after this project commenced, a pastor of one of the Bremer churches was told by doctors that without an organ transplant he would have less than a year to live. He and his wife had recently returned to Bremer and to the church he attended as a boy, after spending most of his adult life elsewhere. Although his salary was less than half his previous salary, and required supplementing through doing home-maintenance work for others, he and his wife wanted the slower pace of Bremer and its concern of people for other people.

When news of the pastor's plight became public, the community responded immediately. Sixty-eight people, themselves members of five different churches, met to stuff nearly 3,000 envelopes for a fund-raising appeal throughout the region. The Bremer Fire Department was challenged to a basketball game by the fire department of a neighboring community, with a "grudge" match also being scheduled so that a game would be held in each community. The community club decided to sponsor a community dance. A neighbors' club planned to donate proceeds from a quilt raffle. Another church's members sponsored a card party, and another one planned a meal and auction. A truck was donated to gather aluminum cans for sale, and Bremer businesses agreed to donate a percentage of the next month's sales. Within two weeks more than $22,000 was raised, even before any of the events had been held or the book on how to raise funds had arrived from a national transplant-assistance organization devoted to helping groups raise funds for such purposes.

The effort to raise funds had already reached far beyond the community. It seems likely to reach to unknown individuals via mass-society and information-era means, the influences of which Bremer has worked so hard to restrain. There seems little choice—costs of the needed transplant exceed even the significant resource base of this proud community. The outcome of the fund-raising effort and the fate of the individual are yet to be known. What is clear, though, is that if the funds are successfully raised, it will be because once again Bremer, where community has been maintained, has acted as a community.

Appendix

Origins of This Study and the Research Methods

We, the authors of this study, are sociologists, and it is from this disciplinal background that the intellectual approach, theoretical formulations, and specific research methods were developed. These considerations influence both the potential and the limitations of our study of Bremer, and for these reasons are outlined in this Appendix. Herewith is also an explanation of how this formal study of Bremer came to be done.

In 1984, one of us (Allen) had just completed a master's degree in urban sociology at Portland State University, moved to Bremer with plans to continue his graduate education at Washington State University. He and his wife had a general preference for living in the rural countryside and were willing to endure a significant commute in order to achieve that possibility. Locating in Bremer was a practical decision, the culmination of a brief search for inexpensive housing. Intellectually, he also had a vague desire to contrast his recently completed urban experience of living near the central part of Portland with rural living, and to include a "community" emphasis in his Ph.D. program.

Initial interactions in the Bremer community were practical ones. The couple visited with neighbors, started shopping in Bremer, were called on by a community member who wanted birthdays and anniversaries for the community calendar, and were pleasantly surprised when a neighbor came by to plow snow out of their driveway. For financial reasons, he delayed his start of graduate school, and drew on his earlier life experiences of being raised on a ranch in eastern Oregon to gain employment from a nearby farmer, working through two complete cycles of planting and harvesting. His wife obtained part-time employment as a substitute teacher from 1985 to 1989. For practical reasons of doing what was expected by local residents and "getting along," their interactions in the community expanded.

Dillman had moved to the Palouse 15 years earlier, in 1969. He moved there to accept a position at Washington State University as an assistant professor of sociology and rural sociology, having just completed a Ph.D. program at Iowa State University with emphasis on community and social organization. He was immediately intrigued with the many small community centers that dotted the Palouse landscape and the apparent strength of social boundaries that often made cooperation between them difficult, though by no means impossible. Informal observations of how these communities appeared to function began to accumulate, but remained unsystematic until after the authors met.

Collaboration on this study began in a 1986 graduate seminar on rural sociology taught by Dillman, when informal observations about Bremer were shared by Allen with the class. A baby shower, the one mentioned in the book, had been held, no invitations had been sent, and more than 100 guests had signed the guest book. Other observations about the community were shared, as were attempts to explain them, and their significance from a "community" perspective expanded.

Following that seminar, the possibility of a dissertation being done on Bremer emerged. The issues of methods, ethics, personal involvement versus detached observation, and the enormous magnitude of and likely time commitment for conducting the proposed study were discussed. Occasional but systematic observations were made in the Bremer community during 1986 and 1987, but mostly as laboratory work for supporting Allen's program of graduate study. It was not until late 1987 that it was decided to propose to the sociology faculty that a dissertation study of Bremer be undertaken; the proposal was approved.

During the summer of 1987, prior to the decision to write the dissertation on Bremer, all of the businesspeople in Bremer and two other small communities in the area were interviewed by Allen for a Department of Rural Sociology study of the use of information technologies. These semistructured interviews provided important background for later interviews on other aspects of life in Bremer.

It was concluded that a survey of community members, the research method most often used in research by Dillman, could establish percentages for important behaviors (e.g., how many people owned their farms) but was unlikely to capture the dynamics of community interaction, many of which individuals might not even be aware. The main unit of observation for the proposed study was necessarily the community itself. Ethnographic observation, participant observation, and in-depth interviews were deemed essential.

With support from both the departments of sociology and rural sociology, Allen began systematically to conduct observations, attending community events even more intensively than in the past; and semistructured interviews were planned and conducted. Although the dissertation was completed in 1989, data collection continued until 1991. Many of the formal interviews were tape-recorded, but when respondents expressed any discomfort with that procedure, detailed notes were taken. Approximately ten thousand pages of notes and transcripts were produced.

A systematic effort was undertaken to determine whether geographic boundaries to the Bremer community existed, and where they were. Allen traversed all of the roads leading away from Bremer, asking each resident who lived in the next house down the road and whether they were part of the Bremer community. This process continued until both the members of a specific household and the preceding neighbors identified that household as part of another community. The result was a self-identified geographic community that extends approximately 15 miles in all directions from the incorporated limits of Bremer.

Residents of Bremer were informed in 1988, through informal conversations, that a dissertation on the community was being written, and efforts were made to legitimize it with perceived community leaders. It became common knowledge that the dissertation was being written, and locally it became known as "John's book." He was frequently asked about progress, and it appeared that the activity had become accepted as something that he needed to do to get his degree finished, and was okay with the residents. In the tradition of Bremer's social community, he was frequently asked and kidded about what he must be finding out about the community.

In the spring of 1988, a self-administered questionnaire was designed and mailed to Bremer and Flemington residents. A deliberate effort was made to design a survey that would be helpful to the community while also fulfilling needs of the study. The survey began by contacting all major organizations in the community and asking if they would like questions to be included in the planned community-wide survey. Representatives of the school district, city council, grain-growers' associations, local churches, soil conservation district, water district, and local businesses were systematically approached. The resulting questionnaire was 18 pages long and included 92 separate questions. It included questions from the organizations as well as many which community members understood to be relevant to the study.

Before being finalized it was pretested by 50 Bremer residents who were asked to fill out the survey form and comment on each question.

Ten of the residents were invited to Allen's home, where they went over each question to identify wording problems and any other concerns. The final questionnaire was printed in booklet form with a picture of Main Street on the cover. The construction and implementation procedures generally followed those of the Total Design Method (Dillman, 1978), except that a fourth contact of households was not made.

Five hundred forty-eight households within the community were each sent two questionnaires. One questionnaire, referred to above, contained questions pertaining to the household in addition to those for the individual. The companion questionnaire contained only individual questions. Both survey instruments contained Allen's local telephone number and the instruction for people to call if they had any questions. The survey was publicized by community leaders in meetings, and fliers about the survey were taped in windows of local businesses. Responses were received from 476 households, a response rate of 86 percent. A similar mailout procedure was utilized in Flemington, where Allen was not well known. The response rate for that community was 63 percent.

Results were compiled at Washington State University, printed in booklet form, and distributed to local businesses and libraries in both communities. Results were also presented and interpreted by Allen at public meetings in each of the communities.

In May of 1988, a survey instrument was designed for the high school students. With the cooperation of the school superintendent and high school principal, students in grades 8 through 12 were asked to complete the survey. Eighty-two students, or 91 percent of those who attended the Bremer school, completed the questionnaire.

Theoretical guidance for defining the questions that would comprise the focus of this study came from several sources. At first, attempts were made to formulate the directions for the study from recent community literature, none of which, as explained in Chapter 3, seemed capable of providing adequate guidance for framing the important questions that needed to be asked via each of the study methods. We found ourselves continually referring back to Vidich and Bensman's study of Springdale, for which the data were collected in the 1950s during the transformation of the United States toward a mass society (1958, 1968). Elsewhere, we were observing evidence of a societal transformation into an information age, and constantly found ourselves asking whether such evidence was emerging in rural communities, Bremer in particular (Dillman, 1985; Dillman, Beck, and Allen, 1989). The postulation of the three eras of community control, mass society, and information era, which was eventually accepted as a framework, provided a means of bringing together much of the past sociological literature while also anticipating new trends thought to be emerging in U.S. society as influences on community-oriented behaviors.

It also became clear to us that despite our desire to be comprehensive in our study of Bremer, and to include concepts from other disciplines, we lacked the resources and many of the skills that would have been necessary. Even in such a small community, focusing in detail on historical, psychological, and/or economic issues had to be ruled out, except as they manifested themselves in ways that could not be ignored in dealing with key sociological elements. The decision to constrain ourselves to concepts of human interaction, the central element of sociological analysis, in our effort to understand life in Bremer was reluctantly made, but essential.

Virtually all of the observational and ethnographic data were collected by Allen. This too was deliberate. Introducing an "outsider" as a collaborator would have, in our judgment, introduced a potential barrier to interaction that might well have prevented the entire study from being done. It was decided that the obvious rapport between Allen and community members should not be put at risk. Our collaboration evolved toward weekly and sometimes daily meetings to discuss the substance and methods of data-collection activities. Dillman provided the sounding board to facilitate interpretation of data and framing of additional issues to be explored. He also visited the community frequently, but as an observer of community activities and events, and not to conduct interviews.

Faced with a mountain of data and many potential ways of analyzing it, we decided to reduce it into only one of the ways that it might have been written up. The possibility of a more quantitatively oriented analysis was rejected when it became clear that the qualitative findings were primarily responsible for the communication of what we believed were the more revealing explanations of why community-control processes persisted and the ways in which community processes seemed threatened. We were also faced with the necessity of keeping discussions to a reasonable length and being able to explain factors that every Bremerite seemed to understand and be driven by implicitly but that seemed to leave our audiences at professional meetings puzzled. The sometimes lengthy descriptions of the act of farming, school board meetings, business practices such as getting a loan at the bank, buying breakfast at the stock show, and other events seemed to provide a solution for providing the background upon which more analytical observations could be developed in conceptual terms.

Methodologically, we attempted to triangulate our data from various sources—the interviews, survey responses, secondary data, newspaper articles, discussions with outside informants, and pages and pages of detailed notes. Practically, we attempted to reduce the enormous mountain of data before us to a representative and efficient amount that communicated the essence of community life in Bremer as we came to understand it.

Finally, it is impossible for us to complete an analysis of this nature without wondering whether we have understood and reported correctly. Further, we felt a strong moral obligation to protect identities by changing names and sources of information in ways that may be recognized as inaccurate by individuals familiar with the Bremer community. In addition, we have omitted entirely some data that in our view provided compelling illustrations of points we have otherwise made, because we could find no way to disguise them in ways that would have maintained the integrity of the analysis or prevented identities from being revealed with subsequent embarrassment and/or damage to individuals in their community relationships. These issues must be recognized as potential limitations of our descriptions of life in Bremer. Although we sought and utilized advice on these matters from individuals mentioned in the acknowledgments, we alone accept responsibility for these decisions and any errors of interpretation.

Interjecting ourselves into matters not generally intended by the participants to be communicated to outsiders in pursuit of scientific issues is at best a delicate matter. It is our hope that we have carried out the responsibility that goes with such intrusions morally as well as professionally, and we express once again our appreciation to the Bremerites who aided us in this endeavor.

Bibliography

Allen, John C. 1993. "Development in a Community Under Stress." *Community Development Journal* 3 28(2):154-166.

Bahrdt, Hans Paul. 1966. "Public Activity as Basic Forms of City Associations," in Roland L. Warren (ed.) *Perspectives on the American Community: A Book of Readings..* Pp. 78-85. Chicago: Rand McNally and Company.

Bender, Thomas. 1978. *Community and Social Change in America.* New Brunswick, NJ: Rutgers University Press.

Bryan, Enoch A. 1936. *Orient Meets Occident: The Advent of the Railways to the Pacific Northwest.* Pullman, WA: The Student Book Corporation.

Cleveland, Harlan. 1985. "The Twilight of Hierarchy: Speculation on the Global Information Society." *Public Policy Review* 45:185-195.

——. 1982. "Information as a Resource." *The Futurist* 12:34-39.

Cohen, A. P. 1985. *The Symbolic Construction of Community.* London and New York: Ellis Harwood Limited, Tavistock Publications.

Cordes, Sam M. 1988. "The Changing Rural Environment and the Relationship Between Health Services and Rural Development." Commissioned paper for Rural Health Services Research Agenda Conference, December 13-15, San Diego, CA.

Dillman, Don A. 1985. "The Social Impacts of Information Technologies in Rural North America." *Rural Sociology* 50(1):1-26.

——. 1990. "Information Technologies in Agriculture: The United States Experience," in M. Harkin, ed., *Information Technology in Agriculture, Food and Rural Development.* Commission of the European Communities, Luxembourg.

——. 1993. "Rural America Approaching the 21st Century," in *Proceedings of Joint Region Program Committee.* Pp. 76-83. Southern Rural Development Center, Corvallis, OR.

Dillman, Don A., and Donald M. Beck. 1986. "The Past is Not the Future: Urban Quality of Life as We Approach the 21st Century." *Urban Resources* 3(3):43-47.

Dillman, Don A., Donald M. Beck, and John C. Allen. 1989. "Rural Barriers to Job Creation Remain, Even in Today's Information Age." *Futures Research Quarterly* 5(4):43-55.

Durkheim, Emile. 1947. *The Division of Labor in Society.* Trans. George Simpson. Glencoe, IL: Free Press

Fitchen, Janet M. 1981. *Poverty in Rural America: A Case Study.* Boulder, CO: Westview Press.

———. 1991. *Endangered Spaces, Enduring Places.* Boulder, CO: Westview Press.

Flora, Cornelia Butler, and Jan L. Flora. 1993. "Entrepreneurial Social Infrastructure: A Necessary Ingredient." *The Annals of the American Academy of Political and Social Science* 529(September):48-58.

Friedland, William H. 1982. "The End of Rural Society and the Future of Rural Sociology." *Rural Sociology* 47(Winter):589-608.

Galpin, Charles J. 1915. "The Social Anatomy of an Agricultural Community." *Research Bulletin 34*, Madison: University of Wisconsin Agricultural Experiment Station.

Goe, Richard W., and Martin Kenney. 1986. "The Information Age: Implications for U.S. Agriculture." *Policy Studies Review.*

Hawley, Amos H. 1950. *Human Ecology: A Theory of Community Structure.* New York: The Ronald Press.

Hunter, Floyd. 1953. *Community Power Structure: A Study of Decision Makers.* Chapel Hill: University of North Carolina Press.

Jansen, Gary L. 1987. "The Effect of Community Size on Exchange Orientations in Marriage." *Rural Sociology* 52:501-509.

Kaufman, Harold F., and Kenneth P. Wilkinson. 1967. "Community Structure and Leadership: An Interactional Perspective in the Study of Community." State College: Mississippi State University *Social Science Research Bulletin 13.*

Loomis, Charles P. 1962. *Social Systems Essays on Their Persistence and Change.* Princeton, NJ: Prentice-Hall.

Loomis, Charles P., and J. Allan Beegle. 1950. *Rural Social Systems.* New York: Prentice-Hall, Inc.

Loomis, Charles P., and J. Allan Beegle. 1957. *Rural Social Systems.* Second Edition. New York: Prentice-Hall, Inc.

Lynd, Robert S., and Helen Merrel Lynd. 1929. *Middletown: A Study in Contemporary American Culture.* New York: Harcourt Brace Jovanovich.

Milgram, Stanley. 1970. "The Experience of Living in Cities: Adaptations to Urban Overload Create Characteristic Qualities of City Life That Can Be Measured." *Science* 167(13):1461-1468.

Milgram, Stanley, and P. Hollander. 1964. *Nation* 25:602.

Naisbitt, John. 1982. *Megatrends.* New York: Warner Books, Inc.

Newby, Howard. 1983. "The Sociology of Agriculture: Toward a New Rural Sociology." *The Annual Review of Sociology* 9:67-81.

Parsons, Talcott. 1950. *The Social System.* New York, NY: The Free Press.

Pomeranz, Y., G. Rubenthaler, and J. Sullivan. 1987. "Are We Ignoring Our Customers?" *Wheat Life,* June 11 and 12.

Pool, Ithiel de Sola. 1983. *Forecasting the Telephone: A Retrospective Technology Assessment of the Telephone.* Norwood, NJ: Ablex.

Reich, Robert. 1991. *The Work of Nations: Preparing Ourselves for 21st Century Capitalism.* New York: Alfred A. Knofp.

Rodefeld, Richard D. 1982. "Who Will Own and Operate America's Farms?," in Don A. Dillman and Daryl J. Hobbs, eds., *Rural Society in the U.S.: Issues for the 1980s.* Boulder, CO: Westview Press.

Salamon, Sonya. 1980. "Ethnic Differences in Farm Family Land Transfers." *Rural Sociology* 45(2):290-308.

Sanders, Irwin T. 1977. *Rural Society*. Englewood Cliffs, NJ: Prentice-Hall, Inc.

Scheurman, Richard D., and Clifford E. Trafzer. 1985. *The Volga Germans: Pioneers of the Northwest*. Moscow, ID: University of Idaho Press.

Seeley, John R., et al. 1957. *Community Chest: A Case Study in Philanthropy*. Toronto: University of Toronto Press.

Stein, Maurice R. 1960. *The Eclipse of Community: An Interpretation of American Studies*. Princeton: Princeton University Press.

Tonnies, Ferdinand. 1940. *Fundamental Concepts of Sociology (Gemeinschaft und Gesellschaft)*. Translated by Charles P. Loomis. New York: American Book Company.

United States Department of Agriculture, Economic Research Center. 1988. "Estimates." Washington, DC: USDA.

Vidich, Arthur J., and Joseph Bensman. 1958. *Small Town in Mass Society: Class, Power, and Religion in a Rural Community*. Princeton, NJ: Princeton University Press.

―――. 1968. *Small Town in Mass Society: Class, Power, and Religion in a Rural Community*. Princeton, NJ: Princeton University Press.

Warner, W. Lloyd, J. O. Low, Paul S. Lunt, and Leo Srole. 1963. *Yankee City*. Abridged from five volumes of *Yankee City Series*. New Haven, CT: Yale University Press.

Warren, Roland. 1978. *The Community in America*. Chicago: Rand McNally.

Washington Agricultural Statistics. 1986-87. Olympia, WA: Washington Department of Agriculture.

Weber, Max. 1925. *Wirtschaft and Gesellschaft*. Tubingen.

Wilkinson, Kenneth P. 1991. *The Community in Rural America*. New York: Greenwood Press.

Winser, Henry J. 1883. *Guide to the Northern Pacific Railroad and Its Allied Lines*. New York: Putman's Sons.

Wirth, Louis. 1938. "Urbanism as a Way of Life." *American Journal of Sociology* 44:1.

Index

About the Book and Authors

Can a meaningful sense of "community" exist within rural towns and villages of the United States as we approach the twenty-first century? The answer is a resounding yes for at least one rural community in the Pacific Northwest. Allen and Dillman explore a small town in the Northwestern United States, describing its inner workings—from businesses to schools, the town council to the churches, the resident doctor to the annual county fair—within the framework of a unique community organization model.

The authors' model orients this community in the vortex of contemporary forces, pointing up, for example, the need for face-to-face interaction among residents versus the larger society's demand for electronic communication. With increasing conflicts between the culture of rural communities and that of the "outside world" occurring, small towns all over the United States are losing their businesses, their doctors, and their sense of community. Yet the town described in this study is thriving.

Against All Odds identifies pride, determination, and a sense of belonging that must be nurtured—and the local organization that binds all of these factors together—in order to keep a small town alive in the face of powerful disruptive forces. Not since Vidich and Bensman's landmark *Small Town in Mass Society* has such a thoughtful examination of a contemporary rural community been available.

John C. Allen is assistant professor of rural sociology at the University of Nebraska. **Don A. Dillman** is professor of sociology, a rural sociologist, and director of the Social and Economic Sciences Research Center at Washington State University.